# CHOICE COOKING

## For those who care about their health and enjoy good food

### By the Canadian Diabetes Association

Canadian
Diabetes
Association

NC PRESS LIMITED
31 Portland Street
Toronto, Ontario
M5V 2V9

*Manuscript*: Judi Kingry, Cathy Patterson, Kay Spicer
*Editor*: Mark Eric Miller
*Designer*: First Image/Michael Gray
*Composition*: CompuScreen Typesetting Ltd.
*Photographer*: Doug Bradshaw
*Illustrator:* Mark Bulloch

| Canadian Cataloguing in Publication Data |
| --- |
| Main entry under title: Choice cooking |
| Includes index. ISBN 0-919601-69-3 |
| 1. Cookery.  2. Diabetes—Diet Therapy—Recipes. I. Canadian Diabetes Association. |
| TX715.C56          641.5          C82-094897-7 |

*Printed and bound in Canada*

# Contents

# Acknowledgements

The Canadian Diabetes Association gratefully acknowledges the contributions made by:

Members of the Canadian Diabetes Association, including diabetics, parents and spouses of diabetics, Division Nutrition Consultants, members of the National Nutrition Committee and the Cookbook Review Committee;

Dr. Gerald Wong, Dr. R.J. Gardiner and members of the Clinical and Scientific Section and the Professional Health Workers Section of the Canadian Diabetes Association.

Special thanks are given to Jan Eno, National Nutrition Consultant, Canadian Diabetes Association, who coordinated the project, to Larry Wright who assisted in the contract negotiations, to Deborah Slater who checked the recipe calculations, and to Carolyn Halsall who assisted in the preparation of the manuscript. Without the professional expertise of Spicer Kingry Associates, namely Kay Spicer, Judi Kingry and Cathy Patterson, who developed the recipes and wrote the manuscript, this cookbook would not have been possible.

# Foreword

Welcome to *Choice Cooking*, which is a unique combination of recipes that taste good and can help you and your family to better health.

The Canadian Diabetes Association has developed a cookbook which will be helpful to those of you with diabetes, as well as to everyone who cares about their health. Careful testing has been done to ensure that the recipes will work for you.

I am pleased that the guidelines "Canada's Food Guide" and "Nutrition Recommendations for Canadians" prepared by my Department have provided a framework for the nutrition notes and 200 recipes for you. As you read the cookbook and try the recipes, I encourage you to add variety to your food pattern along with a dash of moderation in fat, sugar and salt intakes. Then blend in a balance of the food you eat with the activity you do.

Congratulations to the Canadian Diabetes Association and good eating to you.

Monique Bégin
The Minister of
National Health and Welfare

# Introduction

Great food experiences are available to everyone these days. The wide variety of foods that can be made into delicious meals will provide the essential nutrients and energy required for good health. Foods need not be rich to be elegant. But they must be cooked to perfection, seasoned just right and attractively served.

*Choice Cooking* is a collection of recipes for tasty, nutritious foods that are suitable for the person with diabetes, yet can be enjoyed by the whole family. It is not necessary to prepare separate meals for the individual with diabetes, because use of the Food Choice System created by the Canadian Diabetes Association provides a wide selection of foods suitable and satisfying for everyone.

As we developed, tested and calculated these recipes, we took into consideration people who are weight conscious, people in different age groups, ethnic groups and geographic areas, to create recipes for everyday and gourmet dining. Also, fat, sugar and salt have been kept to a minimum, while herbs, spices and flavorings have been added to produce great tasting dishes.

The recipes are provided in both imperial and metric measures. They call for readily available ingredients, and use a broad range of cooking techniques. You'll find some old family favorites with a different twist, plus other food ideas which may be new to you. Emphasis has been placed on quick and easy-to-prepare dishes to suit today's busy lifestyle.

Each recipe has been kitchen-tested to meet our high standards of quality and appeal. The nutrient, energy and Food Choice values were calculated using the latest food composition tables.

Those who wish to control their weight will find *Choice Cooking* helpful, since the recipes include the energy (kilojoule [Calorie]) count for each serving. Even when daily food intake must be controlled or restricted for medical reasons, good food can still present one of life's greatest joys.

So read, cook, taste and enjoy. *Choice Cooking* is for you.

Judi Kingry                    Cathy Patterson                    Kay Spicer

# Meal Planning

Tasty, wholesome food provides great enjoyment. It also supplies energy and the essential nutrients for building and maintaining a healthy body. While people with diabetes have the same nutritional needs as anyone else, they must also balance the kind and amount of food they eat with their limited insulin supply. A qualified dietitian or nutritionist can help them achieve this balance by designing an individually tailored *Eating Plan*. Factors such as activity level, weight, age, medication and food preferences are considered by the dietitian as she prepares the plan and discusses it with the person with diabetes. An *Eating Plan* based on either the Food Group System or Exchange System can include meals prepared using this specially developed collection of recipes.

A comparison of the two systems is summarized below.

| Food Group System | Exchange System |
|---|---|
| 1 Protein Foods Choice* | 1 Meat Exchange |
| 1 Starchy Foods Choice | 1 Bread Exchange |
| 1 Milk Choice | 1 Milk Exchange |
| 1 Fruits & Vegetables Choice | 1 Fruit Exchange |
| 1 Fruits & Vegetables Choice | 1 Vegetable Exchange, Group A |
| 1 Fats & Oils Choice | 1 Fat Exchange |
| Extra Vegetables | Vegetable Exchange, Group B |
| Extras (unmeasured) | Calorie-Free Foods, List A |
| Extras (small measures) | Calorie Poor Foods, List B |

*Dietary calculations are based on protein foods low in fat. If protein foods high in fat are chosen frequently, the dietary calculations would be adjusted to account for the extra "hidden" fat.

The *Food Group System* is a revised form of the Exchange System of meal planning. It is based on *Canada's Food Guide*, with modifications to make it

7

suitable for people with diabetes. In the *Food Group System*, foods are classified into six groups according to their carbohydrate, protein and fat content. These groups are identified by different symbols.

The word *CHOICE* refers to a measured (or weighed) amount of food which can be replaced by another in that Food Choice Group. This system can be used to plan menus for the whole family, but the serving sizes will vary according to individual needs.

These recipes have been developed in both metric and imperial measures. Choose the system of measures that you prefer and use the tools designed for that system. Slight variations sometimes occur between the two systems, therefore it is most important to follow through the recipe using one system—metric *or* imperial—only.

*Nutrient Values* have been calculated for single servings of each recipe using current Food Composition tables. These figures should be regarded as approximate due to the variations between tables and the many factors which can alter the yield of a recipe.

*Wine is an ingredient* in a few of our recipes. A dry wine which contains little, if any, sugar is usually recommended. Most of the alcohol evaporates during cooking, leaving only the flavor behind. If a recipe specifies a sweeter wine such as port, the carbohydrate content is included in the calculations.

## The Food Groups

## PROTEIN FOODS ⬛

This group includes meat, fish, poultry, cheese and eggs. These are excellent sources of protein, which is essential for life. It is used for building, maintaining and repairing body tissues and also forms an important part of hormones and antibodies.

When shopping for meat, select cuts which look lean and have little visible fat distributed (marbled) throughout. Buy enough meat to allow for shrinkage during cooking—100 g (4 oz) raw, boneless meat will yield about 75 g (3 oz) cooked. When selecting chops or poultry, purchase double the weight required—500 g (1 lb) raw poultry or chops will yield about 250 g (½ lb) cooked.

Protein foods low in fat are listed first in the following chart. Choose them often, especially if you need to lose weight.

*One Choice* from the Protein Foods Group ⬛ contains approximately 7 g protein and 3 g fat and yields an energy value of about 230 kilojoules (55 Calories). All weights and measures are for cooked meats, fish and poultry unless otherwise stated.

| FOOD | MEASURE | MASS (WEIGHT) |
|---|---|---|
| **Cheese:** | | |
| All types, made from partly skim milk, e.g. Mozzarella, part-skim | 1 piece, 5 cm x 2 cm x 2 cm (2″ x ¾″ x ¾″) | 25 g |
| Cottage Cheese, all types | 50 mL (¼ cup) | 55 g |
| **Fish:** | | |
| Canned, drained, e.g. Chicken Haddie, Mackerel, Salmon, Tuna | 50 mL (¼ cup) | 30 g |
| Cod Tongues/Cheeks | 75 mL (⅓ cup) | 50 g |
| Fillet or Steak, e.g. Boston blue, Cod, Flounder, Haddock, Halibut, Perch, Pickerel, Pike, Salmon, Shad, Sole, Trout, Whitefish | 1 piece, 6 cm x 2 cm x 2 cm (2½″ x ¾″ x ¾″) | 30 g |
| Herring | ⅓ fish | 30 g |
| Sardines | 2 medium or 3 small | 30 g |
| Smelts | 2 medium | 30 g |
| **Shellfish:** | | |
| Clams, Mussels, Oysters, Scallops, Snails | 3 medium | 30 g |
| Crab, Lobster, flaked | 50 mL (¼ cup) | 30 g |
| Shrimp, fresh | 5 large | 30 g |
| frozen | 10 medium | 30 g |
| canned | 18 small | 30 g |
| **Meat and Poultry:** *e.g. Beef, Chicken, Ham, Lamb, Pork, Turkey, Veal, Wild Game:* | | |
| Back Bacon | 3 slices, thin | 25 g |
| Chop | ½ chop, with bone | 35 g |
| Minced or ground, lean | 30 mL (2 tbsp) | 25 g |
| Sliced, lean | 1 slice, 10 cm x 5 cm x 5 mm (4″ x 2″ x ¼″) | 25 g |
| Steak, lean | 1 piece, 4 cm x 3 cm x 2 cm (1½″ x 1¼″ x ¾″) | 25 g |

| FOOD | MEASURE | MASS (WEIGHT) |
|---|---|---|
| **Organ Meats:** | | |
| Heart, Liver | 1 slice, 5 cm x 5 cm x 1 cm (2″ x 2″ x ½″) | 25 g |
| Kidney, Sweet Breads, chopped | 50 mL (¼ cup) | 25 g |
| **Soybean:** | | |
| Bean Curd or Tofu, 1 block = 6 cm x 6 cm x 4 cm (2½″ x 2½″ x 1½″) | ½ block | 70 g |

### The following choices contain extra fat, so use them less often.

| FOOD | MEASURE | MASS (WEIGHT) |
|---|---|---|
| **Cheese:** | | |
| Cheese, all types made from whole milk, e.g. Brick, Brie, Camembert, Cheddar, Edam, Tilsit | 1 piece, 5 cm x 2 cm x 2 cm (2″ x ¾″ x ¾″) | 25 g |
| Cheese, coarsely grated, e.g. Cheddar | 75 mL (⅓ cup) | 25 g |
| Cheese, dry, finely grated, e.g. Parmesan | 45 mL (3 tbsp) | 15 g |
| Cheese, Ricotta | 50 mL (¼ cup) | 55 g |
| **Egg:** | | |
| Egg, in shell, raw or cooked | 1 medium | 50 g |
| Egg, scrambled | 50 mL (¼ cup) | 55 g |
| **Meat:** | | |
| Bologna, Summer Sausage or Salami | 1 slice, 5 mm, 10 cm diameter (¼″, 4″ diameter) | 40 g |
| Canned Luncheon Meat | 1 slice, 85 mm x 45 mm x 10 mm (3½″ x 1¾″ x ½″) | 40 g |
| Ground Beef, medium fat | 30 mL (2 tbsp) | 25 g |
| Sausage, Pork, Link | 1 link | 25 g |
| Spareribs or Shortribs, with bone | 10 cm x 6 cm (4″ x 2½″) | 65 g |

| The following choices contain extra fat, so use them less often. | | |
|---|---|---|
| FOOD | MEASURE | MASS (WEIGHT) |
| Stewing Beef | 1 cube, 25 mm (1″) | 25 g |
| Wiener | ½ medium | 25 g |
| **Miscellaneous:** | | |
| Peanut Butter, all kinds | 15 mL (1 tbsp) | 15 g |

## STARCHY FOODS ▪️

This group includes breads, cereals, grains, pasta, dried beans and peas, starchy vegetables and some prepared foods. Starch is a complex carbohydrate which gradually breaks down to sugar during digestion.

Some starchy foods are valuable sources of dietary fibers. These fibers are the portions of edible plants that are not digested by humans. Some of these fibers, such as those from dried peas and beans, delay carbohydrate absorption and thus slow the entry of sugar into the blood stream. Other fibers, such as cereal fibers, aid in elimination. A high-fiber diet also may help to promote weight loss by creating a feeling of fullness and satisfaction. To increase the fiber in your diet, try to choose more high-fiber foods such as dried beans, peas, lentils, whole grain breads and cereals.

*One Choice* from the Starchy Foods Group ▪️ contains approximately 15 g starch (carbohydrate) and 2 g of protein and yields an energy value of about 290 kilojoules (68 Calories).

| FOOD | MEASURE | MASS (WEIGHT) |
|---|---|---|
| **Breads** | | |
| Bagel, Kaiser Roll | ½ | 25 g |
| Bread Sticks, 11 cm x 1 cm (4½″ x ½″) | 2 | 20 g |
| Brewis, cooked | 50 mL (¼ cup) | 45 g |
| English Muffin, Crumpet | ½ | 25 g |
| Hamburger Bun, Hot Dog Bun | ½ | 30 g |
| Matzoh, 15 cm (6″ square) | 1 | 20 g |
| Melba Toast, rectangular | 4 | 15 g |
| Plain Roll | 1 small | 25 g |

| FOOD | MEASURE | MASS (WEIGHT) |
|---|---|---|
| Rusks | 2 | 20 g |
| Rye, coarse or Pumpernickel,<br>    10 cm x 10 cm x 8 mm (4″ x 4″ x ⅜″) | ½ slice | 25 g |
| Soda Crackers, | 8 small, 6 medium | 20 g |
| Whole Wheat, Cracked Wheat, Rye,<br>    White Enriched | 1 slice | 25 g |
| **Cereals** | | |
| Cooked Cereals, cooked<br>                     dry | 125 mL (½ cup)<br>30 mL (2 tbsp) | 125 g<br>20 g |
| Cornmeal, cooked<br>                 dry | 125 mL (½ cup)<br>30 mL (2 tbsp) | 125 g<br>20 g |
| *Ready-to-Eat Unsweetened Cereal | 125 mL (½ cup) | 20 g |
| Shredded Wheat Biscuit, rectangular<br>                               or round | 1 | 20 g |
| Wheat Germ | 75 mL (⅓ cup) | 30 g |
| **Cookies and Biscuits** | | |
| See "Prepared Foods," following. For more detail refer to Convenience Foods, Canadian Diabetes Association. | | |
| **Grains** | | |
| Barley, cooked<br>            dry | 125 mL (½ cup)<br>30 mL (2 tbsp) | 120 g<br>20 g |
| Bulgar, Kasha, cooked, moist<br>                    cooked, crumbly<br>                    dry | 125 mL (½ cup)<br>75 mL (⅓ cup)<br>30 mL (2 tbsp) | 70 g<br>40 g<br>20 g |
| Rice, cooked, loosely packed<br>         cooked, tightly packed | 125 mL (½ cup)<br>75 mL (⅓ cup) | 70 g<br>70 g |
| **Pastas** | | |
| Macaroni, cooked | 125 mL (½ cup) | 70 g |
| Noodles, cooked | 125 mL (½ cup) | 80 g |
| Spaghetti, cooked | 125 mL (½ cup) | 70 g |

*For more exact measures of various types of ready-to-eat cereals, see the cereals section of Convenience Foods which is available from the Canadian Diabetes Association.

| FOOD | MEASURE | MASS (WEIGHT) |
|---|---|---|
| **Starchy Vegetables** | | |
| Beans & Peas (dried), cooked | 125 mL (½ cup) | 80 g |
| Corn, canned, whole kernel | 125 mL (½ cup) | 85 g |
|    canned, creamed | 75 mL (⅓ cup) | 60 g |
| Corn, on the cob, 13 cm, 4 cm diameter (5", 1½" diameter) | 1 small cob | 140 g |
| Popcorn, unbuttered, large kernel | 750 mL (3 cups) | 20 g |
| Potatoes, whipped | 125 mL (½ cup) | 105 g |
| Potatoes, whole, 13 cm, 5 cm diameter (5", 2" diameter) | ½ | 95 g |
| Yam, Sweet Potatoes 13 cm, 5 cm diameter (5", 2" diameter) | ½ | 75 g |

**Food items found in this category contain an additional 5 g fat and consequently an extra 190 kilojoules (45 Calories) = 1 Fats & Oils Choice.**

| Prepared Foods | | |
|---|---|---|
| Baking Powder Biscuit, 5 cm diameter (2" diameter) | 1 | 30 g |
| *Cookies, plain, (e.g., Digestive, Oatmeal) | 2 | 20 g |
| Cup Cake, un-iced, 5 cm diameter (2" diameter) | 1 small | 35 g |
| Doughnut, cake type, plain, 7 cm diameter (2¾" diameter) | 1 | 30 g |
| Muffin, plain, 6 cm diameter (2½" diameter) | 1 small | 40 g |
| Pancake, homemade using 50 mL (¼ cup) batter | 1 small | 50 g |
| Potatoes, French Fried, 5 cm x 1 cm x 1 cm (2" x½" x ½") | 10 | 65 g |
| *Soup, canned (Prepared with equal volume of water) | 250 mL (1 cup) | 260 g |
| Waffle, homemade using 50 mL (¼ cup) batter | 1 small | 35 g |

*For more exact measures of various types of cookies and canned soups, see the appropriate section of Convenience Foods which is available from the Canadian Diabetes Association.

## MILK ◆

This group includes milk and yogurt. Your dietitian will indicate the type of milk you should use in your *Eating Plan*.

Plain yogurt may be substituted for milk, but avoid sweetened yogurts which have a "fruit bottom" or added syrup. They contain extra sugar. Try making your own fruit-flavored yogurt by combining one Milk Choice as plain yogurt with one Fruits & Vegetables Choice. For a completely new taste, add bits of cut-up cucumber, green pepper and tomato to plain yogurt. Plain yogurt plus dill and other herbs such as thyme and parsley may be used as a tasty dressing for salads. You may use 25 mL (2 tbsp) of this mixture as an Extra ++ in your meal plan.

The *Milk Food Choices* are a valuable source of many nutrients—protein, calcium and phosphorous (needed for strong bones and teeth), thiamine and riboflavin. Since milk and plain yogurt are a source of carbohydrate (lactose or milk sugar) they are included in measured amounts in meal planning.

*One Choice* from the Milk Group ◆ contains approximately:

| Type of Milk | Carbohydrate | Protein | Fat | Energy |
|---|---|---|---|---|
| Skim | 6 g | 4 g | 0 | 170 kilojoules (40 Calories) |
| 2% | 6 g | 4 g | 2 g | 240 kilojoules (58 Calories) |
| Whole | 6 g | 4 g | 4 g | 320 kilojoules (76 Calories) |

| FOOD | MEASURE | MASS (WEIGHT) |
|---|---|---|
| Milk, Buttermilk | 125 mL (½ cup) | 125 g |
| Evaporated Milk | 50 mL (¼ cup) | 50 g |
| Powdered milk, regular | 30 mL (2 tbsp) | 15 g |
| instant | 50 mL (¼ cup) | 15 g |
| Unflavored yogurt | 125 mL (½ cup) | 125 g |

## FRUITS & VEGETABLES ◢

This group includes fruits and many vegetables. Since certain vegetables such as corn and potatoes are high in starch, they are included in the Starchy Foods Group.

Fruits and vegetables are excellent sources of many vitamins and minerals as well as dietary fibers. Select a wide variety from this group for good health. Many fruits and vegetables (such as oranges, strawberries and turnips) are a valuable source of Vitamin C. Deep yellow fruits and dark green vegetables (such as peaches and winter squash) are usually high in Vitamin A.

Plan to have solid fruits and vegetables instead of juices. The natural sugar present in juice enters the blood rapidly, whereas the fiber content of solid fruits and vegetables slows the entry of sugar into the blood.

*One Choice* from the Fruits & Vegetables Group ◪ contains approximately 10 g of simple sugar (carbohydrate) and 1 g of protein, and yields an energy value of about 190 kilojoules (44 Calories).

| FOOD | MEASURE | MASS (WEIGHT) |
|---|---|---|
| **Fruits** *(fresh, frozen without sugar, canned in water)* | | |
| Apple, raw | ½ medium | 75 g |
| sauce | 125 mL (½ cup) | 120 g |
| Apricot, raw | 2 medium | 115 g |
| canned, in water | 4 halves, plus 30 mL (2 tbsp) liquid | 110 g |
| Banana, 15 cm (6″), with peel | ½ small | 75 g |
| Blackberries, raw | 125 mL (½ cup) | 70 g |
| canned, in water | 125 mL (½ cup), includes 30 mL (2 tbsp) liquid | 100 g |
| Blueberries, raw | 125 mL (½ cup) | 70 g |
| Cantaloupe, wedge with rind, 13 cm diameter (5″ diameter) | ¼ | 240 g |
| cubed or diced | 250 mL (1 cup) | 160 g |
| Cherries, raw, with pits | 10 | 75 g |
| canned, in water, with pits | 75 mL (⅓ cup), includes 30 mL (2 tbsp) liquid | 90 g |
| Fruit Cocktail, canned, in water | 125 mL (½ cup), includes 30 mL (2 tbsp) liquid | 120 g |
| Fruit, mixed, cut-up | 125 mL (½ cup) | 120 g |
| Grapefruit, raw, with rind | ½ small | 185 g |
| raw, sectioned | 125 mL (½ cup) | 100 g |
| canned, in water | 125 mL (½ cup), includes 30 mL (2 tbsp) liquid | 120 g |

| FOOD | MEASURE | MASS (WEIGHT) |
|---|---|---|
| Grapes, raw, | 125 mL (½ cup) | 75 g |
| canned, in water | 75 mL (⅓ cup), includes 30 mL (2 tbsp) liquid | 115 g |
| Honeydew Melon, raw, with rind | ¹⁄₁₀ | 225 g |
| cubed or diced | 250 mL (1 cup) | 170 g |
| Mandarin Oranges, canned, in water | 125 mL (½ cup), includes 30 mL (2 tbsp) liquid | 100 g |
| Nectarine | ½ medium | 75 g |
| Orange, raw, with rind | 1 small | 130 g |
| raw, sectioned | 125 mL (½ cup) | 95 g |
| Peaches, raw, with seed and skin, 6 cm (2½") diameter | 1 large | 130 g |
| raw, sliced, diced | 125 mL (½ cup) | 100 g |
| canned, in water, halves or slices | 125 mL (½ cup), includes 30 mL (2 tbsp) liquid | 120 g |
| Pear, raw, with skin and core | ½ | 90 g |
| canned, in water, halves | 2 halves, plus 30 mL (2 tbsp) liquid | 90 g |
| Pineapple, raw | 1 slice, 8 cm diameter, 2 cm thick (3¼" diameter, ¾" thick) | 75 g |
| raw, diced | 125 mL (½ cup) | 75 g |
| canned, in juice, sliced | 1 slice, plus 15 mL (1 tbsp) liquid | 55 g |
| canned, in juice, diced | 75 mL (⅓ cup), includes 15 mL (1 tbsp) liquid | 55 g |
| Plums, raw, prune type | 2 | 60 g |
| canned, in water | 3, plus 30 mL (2 tbsp) liquid | 100 g |
| canned, in apple juice | 2, plus 30 mL (2 tbsp) liquid | 70 g |
| Raspberries, raw, black or red | 125 mL (½ cup) | 65 g |
| Strawberries, raw | 250 mL (1 cup) | 150 g |
| Tangerine, raw | 1 | 115 g |
| raw, sectioned | 125 mL (½ cup) | 100 g |

| FOOD | MEASURE | MASS (WEIGHT) |
|------|---------|---------------|
| Watermelon, raw with rind | 1 wedge,<br>125 mm triangle,<br>22 mm thick<br>(5" triangle, 1" thick) | 310 g |
| cubed or diced | 250 mL (1 cup) | 160 g |
| **Dried Fruit** | | |
| Dates, without pits | 2 | 15 g |
| Prunes, raw, with pits | 2 | 15 g |
| Raisins, Currants | 30 mL (2 tbsp) | 15 g |
| **Juices** *(no sugar added or unsweetened):* | | |
| Apricot, Grape, Guava, Mango, Prune | 50 mL (¼ cup) | 55 g |
| Apple, Carrot, Pineapple | 75 mL (⅓ cup) | 80 g |
| Grapefruit, Orange | 125 mL (½ cup) | 130 g |
| Tomato, Tomato based mixed vegetables | 250 mL (1 cup) | 255 g |
| **Vegetables** *(fresh, frozen or canned):* | | |
| Beets, diced or sliced | 125 mL (½ cup) | 85 g |
| Carrots, diced | 125 mL (½ cup) | 75 g |
| Parsnips, mashed | 125 mL (½ cup) | 80 g |
| Peas, fresh or frozen | 125 mL (½ cup) | 80 g |
| canned | 75 mL (⅓ cup) | 55 g |
| Sauerkraut | 250 mL (1 cup) | 235 g |
| Snowpeas | 10 pods | 100 g |
| Squash, yellow or winter, mashed | 125 mL (½ cup) | 115 g |
| Tomatoes, canned | 250 mL (1 cup) | 240 g |
| Turnip, mashed | 125 mL (½ cup) | 115 g |
| Vegetables, mixed | 125 mL (½ cup) | 90 g |
| Water Chestnuts | 8 medium | 50 g |

## EXTRA VEGETABLES ++

The vegetables in this group are low in natural sugar and energy value. However, they are high in dietary fibers, vitamins and minerals. Use them when you feel like nibbling. Moderate amounts of these vegetables do not have to be measured or calculated in your meal plan. Usually 125 mL (½ cup) cooked vegetables from this group contains less than 3.5 g of carbohydrate and yields an energy value of 60 kilojoules (14 Calories) or less. For some vegetables, 250 mL (1 cup) would be counted as one Fruits & Vegetables Choice 🔲   . These are indicated with an asterisk (*) in the following list.

Artichokes, Globe or French
Asparagus
Bamboo shoots
Beans, String, green or yellow
Bean Sprouts, Mung or Soy
Broccoli
*Brussels Sprouts
Cabbage
Cauliflower
Celery
Chard
Cucumber
*Eggplant
Endive
Kale
*Kohlrabi

*Leeks
 Lettuce
 Mushrooms
*Okra
 Onions, green
*Onions, mature
 Parsley
 Pepper, green or red
 Radish
*Rhubarb
 Spinach
 Sprouts: Alfalfa, Radish, etc.
*Tomato, raw
 Vegetable Marrow
 Watercress
 Zucchini

## FATS & OILS ▲

This group includes a variety of high-fat foods such as vegetable oil, salad dressings, nuts, margarine and butter. All fats are a concentrated source of energy. Be especially careful to measure fats and oils if weight loss is necessary. If you have been advised to use polyunsaturated fats, choose oils such as safflower, sunflower, corn and soybean. Soft margarines in a tub with a label statement of "Polyunsaturated Fat 35%-55%, Saturated Fat 18%-25%" are recommended in preference to solid fats.

*One Choice* from the Fats and Oils Group ▲ contains approximately 5 g of fat and yields an energy value of about 190 kilojoules (45 Calories).

| FOOD | MEASURE | MASS (WEIGHT) |
|---|---|---|
| Bacon, side, crisp | 1 slice | 5 g |
| Butter, Margarine | 5 mL (1 tsp) | 5 g |
| Cream, Half and Half (cereal) 10% | 30 mL (2 tbsp) | 30 g |
| Sour 12-14% | 45 mL (3 tbsp) | 35 g |
| Cream Cheese, Cheese Spread | 15 mL (1 tbsp) | 15 g |
| Lard, Salt Pork, raw or cooked | 5 mL (1 tsp) | 5 g |
| Nuts, shelled: | | |
| Almonds ......................... | 8 nuts | 20 g |
| Brazil Nuts....................... | 2 nuts | 5 g |
| Cashews, Filberts, Hazelnuts ......... | 5 nuts | 10 g |
| Peanuts .......................... | 10 nuts | 10 g |
| Pecans ........................... | 5 halves | 5 g |
| Walnuts .......................... | 4 halves | 10 g |
| Oil, cooking and salad | 5 mL | 5 g |
| Pâté, Liverwurst, Meat Spreads | 15 mL (1 tbsp) | 15 g |
| Salad Dressing: Blue, French, Italian | 10 mL (2 tsp) | 10 g |
| Mayonnaise, Thousand Island | 5 mL (1 tsp) | 5 g |

The **complete** Good Health Eating Guide Food Groups in color, and other information about diabetes, is available from the Canadian Diabetes Association. For a price list, contact your local Branch or Division, or the National Office, Canadian Diabetes Association, 123 Edward Street, Suite 601, Toronto, Ontario M5G 1E2.

## Table of Abbreviations

h—hour
min—minute
mL—milliliter
L—liter
g—gram

kg—kilogram
mm—millimeter
cm—centimeter
tsp—teaspoon
tbsp—tablespoon

in—inch
lb—pound
pkg—package

# Menus

The following menus are examples of the variety of meals that can be prepared by using recipes from *Choice Cooking* to fit the meal plans of people with diabetes.

The portion sizes are not given, as they will be determined by each individual meal plan.

**Supper for Seniors**
*Gouda Wafers*
*Salmon Broccoli Loaf*
*German Rye Bread*
*Peppy Dill Wedges*
*Blueberry Cupcake with Lemon Pudding Sauce*

**Festive Fare**
*Tomato Basil Soup*
*Gourmet Lamb with Pork*
*Cranberry-Orange Relish*
*Asparagus Spears with Lemon Wedge*
*Parslied Potato*
*Mix'n' Mash Vegetables*
*Chocolate Almond Cream Puffs*

**Family Favorites**
*Rhubarb Refresher*
*Creamy Macaroni and Cheese*
*Cucumber and Fruit Salad*
*Orange Custard Cloud with Berry Sauce*
*Chocolate Chip Cookie*

**Soup Supper**
*Minestrone Soup*
OR
*Pea Soup—Newfoundland Style*
*Harvest Roll*
*Cheddar Cheese Cubes*
*Carrot Sticks*
*Strawberry Angel Mousse*

### Time for Tea
Choice of: –*Scotch Scone* with *Fruit*
*Spread* or Jelly
–*Orange Nut Bread*
–*Peanut Butter Nugget*
–*Shortbread*
Assorted Flavors Hot Tea
with
Lemon or Fresh Mint

### Sunday Brunch Lunch
*Cranberry Refresher*
*Pacific Salmon Pie*
OR
*Ham and Asparagus Roll-ups*
*Orange Sprout Salad*
*Cream Bread or Roll*
*Pina Colada Squares*

### Portable Lunch
*Savory Luncheon Bun*
Swiss Cheese Triangles
*Bread and Butter Pickles*
Crisp Celery and Zucchini Sticks
*Chocolate Chip Cookies*
OR
*Crispy Oatmeal Cookies*
OR
Fresh Fruit

### Dinner Party Buffet
*Baked Chicken with Wine Sauce*
OR
*Stuffed Baked Fillets* (fish)
*Marinated Vegetable Medley*
Steamed Snow Peas
Hot *Popovers*
*Strawberry Angel Pie*

### Chili Hot Pot
*Chili con Carne*
Tossed Greens with *Italian Dressing*
*Chocolate Mousse*
*Rice Krispie Square*

### Patio Party
*Sparkling Fruit Punch*
*Spicy Luncheon Roll*
OR
Sliced Assorted Cold Meats
*Four Bean Salad*
*Potato Salad*
*Celery Victor*
Fresh Strawberries with
*Soft Custard*

### Simple and Satisfying
*Crispy Baked Fish*
*Zucchini with Tomato Sauce*
Mixed Greens with *Herb Dressing*
*Baked Cinnamon Custard*
*Peanut Butter Cookies*

### Dinner at Home
Creole Fish Bake
Assorted Raw Vegetables
Whole Wheat Biscuit
Nova Scotia Gingerbread with
Whipped Topping

### Tempting for Teens
Peach Nectar
Pizza Lover's Pizza
Fresh Vegetable Sticks
Double Chocolate Roll

### Vegetarian
Creamy Celery Soup
Tofu Chop Suey
Steamed Brown Rice
Cantaloupe Wedge
with Cottage Cheese

### Saturday Supper
Iced Cucumber Soup
Tacos
Light and Lemony Cheesecake

### Après Ski Supper
Beef Burgundy
Whole Wheat Noodles
Broccoli with Lemon
Tossed Greens with Thousand
Island Dressing
Pear Half with
Chocolate Sauce

### Candlelight and Wine
Cream of Cauliflower Soup
Stuffed Butterfly Chop
Broiled Tomato with Herbs
Spinach Salad
Peachy Blueberry Pie

### Birthday Party
Cheeseburger Deluxe with
Toasted Roll
Hamburger Relish and Pickled
Onion Rings
Sunburst Salad
Ribbon Cream Torte
Chocolate Milk

### Meal in a Hurry
Chicken and Snow Pea Oriental
OR
Tuna Impromptu
with Fluffy Rice
Fresh Sliced Mushrooms
with Italian Dressing
Melon Wedge

### Holiday Celebration
Cranberry Refresher
Turkey Tetrazzini
Steamed Brussels Sprouts
Salad Royale
Marinated Cucumbers
Crêpes Elégantes

# Appetizers

The most appealing feature of appetizers is that they are small, interesting tidbits meant to titillate the appetite but not spoil it. Served piping hot from the oven or icy cold from the refrigerator, they are designed to be the perfect prelude to a meal or a stimulating first course.

Appetizers run the gamut from canapés and hors d'oeuvres to dips, relishes, spreads and nibbles.

Canapés are made by piling tasty foods on small round or square, thin slices of toast or bread, Melba toast or crackers. (The French word canapé means a couch.) We've taken the liberty of adding fresh ideas like cucumber and zucchini slices and mushroom caps to the list of appropriate bases.

Hors d'oeuvres are tantalizing dishes served "outside the main work." They are served on their own, independent of bread or crackers, and are usually eaten with a fork and knife as a small prelude to a meal.

Appetizers can be economical to expensive, delicate to sharp, but they are always gay and festive, perked up for their presentation with colorful garnishes to please the eye and tempt the palate.

On some occasions, the more substantial appetizers, or larger servings of smaller appetizers, can become a small meal like a supper, served with dessert and salad.

## STUFFED MUSHROOMS

*Select firm, white or creamy beige mushrooms for these hot hors d'oeuvres. Prepare them ahead if you wish. Cover and store them in the refrigerator up to 24 hours before baking. Do NOT substitute other cheeses; Gruyère works best and provides good flavor.*

| | | |
|---|---|---|
| 12 | medium mushrooms | 12 |
| 125 mL | shredded process Gruyère cheese | ½ cup |
| 50 mL | Seasoned Bread Crumbs (recipe, p.53) | ¼ cup |
| 5 mL | water | 1 tsp |

Clean mushrooms, remove stems. Reserve mushroom caps. Chop stems and measure 75 mL (1/3 cup). Cream cheese with fork until soft. Blend in bread crumbs, chopped stems and water. Work mixture with hands into 12 balls. Place one in each mushroom cap. Place on a lightly greased baking sheet. Bake in a 200°C (400°F) oven 10 min. Serve hot.

Makes 6 servings.

**Each serving: 2 mushrooms**

½ 🖉 Protein Choice

2 g carbohydrate
3 g protein
2 g fat

160 kilojoules
(38 Calories)

## PARTY MIX

*This toasted, crunchy combination is a real hit with the young crowd who can take some extra energy at snack time.*

| | | |
|---|---|---|
| 1 L | Shreddies | 4 cups |
| 500 mL | puffed wheat | 2 cups |
| 500 mL | Cheerios | 2 cups |
| 500 mL | small thin pretzels | 2 cups |
| 250 mL | unsalted peanuts or mixed nuts | 1 cup |
| 75 mL | vegetable oil | 1/3 cup |
| 15 mL | Worcestershire sauce | 1 tbsp |
| 5 mL | garlic salt | 1 tsp |

Combine Shreddies, puffed wheat, Cheerios, pretzels and nuts in a large bowl. Mix together oil, Worcestershire sauce and garlic salt. Sprinkle over cereal mixture and toss to lightly coat. Spread out in a large shallow cake pan or roaster. Toast in a 120°C (250°F) oven stirring every 15 min, for 1h.

Makes 30 servings, 2.5 L (10 cups).

**Each serving: 75 mL (1/3 cup)**

| | | |
|---|---|---|
| ½ ▢ | Starchy Choice | 8 g carbohydrate |
| 1 ▲ | Fats & Oils Choice | 2 g protein |
| | | 6 g fat |
| | | 390 kilojoules |
| | | (94 Calories) |

## CREAMY VEGETABLE DIP

*To use for dipping, prepare crisp carrot, celery, cucumber and zucchini sticks. Plush button mushrooms and plump red radishes are also perfect with this dip. It is a breeze to make.*

| 250 mL | creamed cottage cheese | 1 cup |
|---|---|---|
| 25 mL | ketchup | 2 tbsp |
| 45 mL | commercial sour cream | 3 tbsp |
| 8 drops | hot pepper sauce | 8 drops |
| 25 mL | chopped green onion | 2 tbsp |

Combine cottage cheese, ketchup, sour cream and hot pepper sauce in container of blender or food processor. Process 2 min or until very smooth. Add onion, blend just until mixed. Pour into container, cover tightly and refrigerate 1 to 2h to blend flavors.

Makes 300 mL (1¼ cups).

**Each serving: 45 mL (3 tbsp)**

| | | |
|---|---|---|
| 1 ∅ | Protein Choice | 2 g carbohydrate |
| | | 5 g protein |
| | | 3 g fat |
| | | 230 kilojoules |
| | | (55 Calories) |

## DILLY DIP

*This, like most dips, is versatile. A small dollop on a baked potato or a small bowl of salad greens is very tasty.*

| | | |
|---|---|---|
| 500 mL | 2% cottage cheese | 2 cups |
| 125 mL | commercial sour cream | ½ cup |
| 25 mL | chopped dill pickle | 2 tbsp |
| 15 mL | chopped fresh dill or 5 mL (1 tsp) dried dillweed | 1 tbsp |
| 1 mL | freshly ground pepper | ¼ tsp |

Place cottage cheese, sour cream, dill pickle, dill and pepper in container of blender or food processor. Purée until smooth. Makes 10 servings, 500 mL (2 cups) dip.

**Each serving: 45 mL (3 tbsp)**

1 🖉  Protein Choice

3 g carbohydrate
7 g protein
3 g fat

280 kilojoules
(67 Calories)

## EGGPLANT DIP

*Eggplant dip is popular in many Mediterranean countries. In the West it is often called poor man's caviar. It's good with raw vegetable dippers or on crisp Melba toast.*

| | | |
|---|---|---|
| 1 | medium eggplant | 1 |
| 3 | medium green onions, finely chopped | 3 |
| 1 | large tomato, peeled and chopped | 1 |
| 1 | small clove garlic, finely chopped | 1 |
| ½ | stalk celery, finely chopped | ½ |
| 15 mL | fresh lemon juice or vinegar | 1 tbsp |
| 15 mL | vegetable oil | 1 tbsp |
| 2 mL | salt | ½ tsp |
| 1 mL | freshly ground pepper | ¼ tsp |

Prick whole eggplant in several places with a fork. Place in a baking pan and bake in a 200°C (400°F) oven 30 min. Cool, peel and chop finely. (A blender or food processor can be used but avoid overprocessing. Dip is best when it has some crunch.) Combine eggplant, onions, tomato, garlic and celery. Add lemon juice, vegetable oil, salt and freshly ground pepper. Cover tightly and refrigerate for several hours to blend flavors.

Makes 16 servings.

**Each serving: 25 mL (2 tbsp)**

1 **++** Extra

2 g carbohydrate
1 g fat

70 kilojoules
(17 Calories)

## SALMON CREAM CHEESE SPREAD

*Use this smooth spread on crackers, Melba toast, cucumber and zucchini slices, in celery sticks or as a sandwich filling.*

| | | |
|---|---|---|
| **1 can** | 106 g (3¾ oz) salmon, drained | **1 can** |
| **50 mL** | cream cheese | **¼ cup** |
| **50 mL** | commercial sour cream | **¼ cup** |
| **25 mL** | chopped green onion or chives | **2 tbsp** |
| **15 mL** | chopped fresh dill or 5 mL (1 tsp) dried dillweed | **1 tbsp** |
| **5 mL** | vinegar | **1 tsp** |
| **2 mL** | salt | **½ tsp** |
| **pinch** | freshly ground pepper | **pinch** |

Blend salmon and cream cheese together in a small bowl. Stir in sour cream, green onion, dill, vinegar, salt and pepper. Mix thoroughly.

Makes 6 servings, 200 mL (¾ cup).

**Each serving: 25 mL (2 tbsp)**

½ **⊘** Protein Choice
1 **▲** Fats & Oils Choice

1 g carbohydrate
4 g protein
6 g fat

310 kilojoules
(74 Calories)

(**Note:** If crackers are served with the spread, remember to count them as **☐** Starchy Choice(s).)

## CHEESE 'N' CHUTNEY SPREAD

*Mix and fix this spread a few days ahead. It keeps beautifully, wrapped, in the refrigerator. Warm it to room temperature at serving time to bring out the full flavor of the Edam cheese highlighted by the sweet, spicey chutney. This spread is great on zucchini or cucumber slices.*

| | | |
|---|---|---|
| 500 mL | shredded Edam cheese | 2 cups |
| 20 mL | chutney | 4 tsp |
| 2 mL | curry powder | ½ tsp |
| 10 to 15 mL | 2% milk | 2 to 3 tsp |
| 4 | small green onions, finely chopped | 4 |

Combine cheese, chutney and curry powder in a mixing bowl; beat together adding milk, 5 mL (1 tsp) at a time until mixture holds together in a fairly smooth ball. Roll in chopped green onions. Wrap and store in refrigerator until serving time.

Makes 10 servings.

**Each serving: 25 mL (5 tsp)**

| | | |
|---|---|---|
| 1 ⬛ Protein Choice | | 3 g carbohydrate |
| ½ ▲ Fats & Oils Choice | | 7 g protein |
| | | 6 g fat |
| | | 390 kilojoules |
| | | (94 Calories) |

**VARIATION: CHEESE 'N' CHUTNEY BOATS**

| | | |
|---|---|---|
| 2 | medium zucchini | 2 |
| 1 batch | *Cheese 'n' Chutney Spread* (see above) | 1 batch |

Cut zucchini in half lengthwise; scoop out seedy pulp. Pack spread into hollow. Chill and serve sliced.

Makes 10 servings.                                       Nutrient value as above.

---

**Cheese is a protein food but may also be high in hidden fat. Cream cheese is included in the Fats and Oils ▲ Group.**

## CRABMEAT SPREAD

*Crabmeat and cottage cheese combine in this elegant-but-easy party starter. Serve it with celery, carrot or green pepper spears or on cucumber and zucchini slices or crisp crackers.*

| | | |
|---|---|---|
| 125 mL | 2% cottage cheese | ½ cup |
| 15 mL | fresh lemon juice | 1 tbsp |
| 15 mL | dry sherry | 1 tbsp |
| 15 mL | ketchup | 1 tbsp |
| 1 can | 142 g (5 oz) crabmeat | 1 can |
| 25 mL | *Tangy Boiled Dressing* (recipe, p.89) | 2 tbsp |
| 2 | medium green onions, finely chopped | 2 |
| | Salt and freshly ground pepper | |

Drain or press liquid from cottage cheese; place in blender or food processor container with lemon juice, sherry and ketchup. Process 2 to 3 min until very smooth. Rinse crabmeat and pat dry. Remove any pieces of shell. Add crabmeat and dressing to cheese mixture. Process with on-off motion 3 to 4 times, just until mixture is well blended. Stir in onions and salt and pepper to taste. Chill at least 1 h before serving to allow flavors to mingle.

Makes 5 servings, 300 mL (1¼ cups).

**Each serving: 50 mL (¼ cup)**

1 ▨  Protein Choice

2 g carbohydrate
8 g protein
1 g fat

210 kilojoules
(49 Calories)

(**Note:** If crackers are served with the spread, remember to count them as ▢ Starchy Choice(s).)

**To ensure success with any recipe, please read it through carefully before you begin to prepare it.**

## NIPPY CHEESE LOG

*Highlight this log at a snack party. A piece on a crisp cracker, fresh mushroom cap, zucchini or cucumber slice makes a tasty tidbit.*

| | | |
|---|---|---|
| 250 mL | shredded Edam cheese | 1 cup |
| 125 mL | 2% cottage cheese, well mashed | ½ cup |
| 50 mL | shredded aged Cheddar cheese | ¼ cup |
| 50 mL | grated Parmesan cheese | ¼ cup |
| 75 mL | finely chopped parsley | 1/3 cup |
| 1 mL | each of garlic powder and paprika | ¼ tsp |
| pinch | chili powder | pinch |
| 2 drops | hot pepper sauce | 2 drops |

Combine Edam, cottage, Cheddar and Parmesan cheeses, 15 mL (1 tbsp) parsley, garlic powder, paprika, chili powder and hot pepper sauce in a mixing bowl. Mix well. (A food processor works well.) Form into a log; roll in remaining chopped parsley. Wrap and refrigerate for several hours. Remove from refrigerator 20 min before serving time.

Makes 8 servings.

**Each serving: 25 mL (2 tbsp)**

1 🗹 Protein Choice
½ ▲ Fats & Oils Choice

1 g carbohydrate
8 g protein
6 g fat

380 kilojoules
(90 Calories)

## CHEESE PUFFS

*These mini cream puffs are surprisingly easy to make. Light-as-a-feather and crisp, they are best served piping hot. The batter can be made into 12 larger puffs to use as cases for tuna or chicken salad.*

| | | |
|---|---|---|
| 250 mL | water | 1 cup |
| 50 mL | margarine or butter | ¼ cup |
| 2 mL | salt | ½ tsp |
| pinch | freshly ground pepper | pinch |
| 250 mL | all purpose flour | 1 cup |
| 4 | eggs | 4 |
| 250 mL | grated Swiss cheese | 1 cup |
| 2 mL | dry mustard | ½ tsp |
| 5 mL | Dijon mustard | 1 tsp |
| 25 mL | mayonnaise | 2 tbsp |
| 45 mL | grated Parmesan cheese | 3 tbsp |
| pinch | paprika | pinch |

Combine water and margarine in a saucepan; add salt and pepper. Bring to a rapid boil. Add flour all at once, beating vigorously with a wooden spoon until mixture forms a ball and comes away from sides of pan. Remove from heat; cool 5 min. Add eggs one at a time, beating vigorously by hand or in a food processor for 10 seconds after each addition. Continue beating 1 to 2 min or process 20 seconds until smooth and glossy. Blend in Swiss cheese and mustards. Using 2 small spoons drop onto lightly oiled cookie sheets. Bake in a 200°C (400°F) oven for 20 min or until puffed and lightly browned. Prepare ahead to this point. Just before serving brush tops with a little mayonnaise and sprinkle with Parmesan cheese and paprika. Return to a 200°C (400°F) oven. Heat about 5 min.

Makes 36 puffs, 12 snack servings.

**Each serving: 3 puffs**

| | | |
|---|---|---|
| 1 | 🟢 Protein Choice | 7 g carbohydrate |
| ½ | ◻ Starchy Choice | 6 g protein |
| 1 | 🔺 Fats & Oils Choice | 10 g fat |
| | | 590 kilojoules |
| | | (142 Calories) |

## GOUDA WAFERS

*Homemade crunchy crackers like Gouda Wafers are snappy on their own as nibblers, or they provide the perfect contrast for creamy soups or chunky chowders.*

| | | |
|---|---|---|
| 125 mL | whole wheat flour | ½ cup |
| 50 mL | rice flour | ¼ cup |
| 2 mL | baking powder | ½ tsp |
| 1 mL | celery salt or salt | ¼ tsp |
| 125 mL | shredded medium or aged Gouda cheese | ½ cup |
| 15 mL | margarine | 1 tbsp |
| 25 mL | sesame seeds | 2 tbsp |
| 45 to 60 mL | ice water | 3 to 4 tbsp |

Combine whole wheat and rice flours, baking powder and celery salt in mixing bowl. Cut in cheese and margarine with a pastry blender or 2 knives until mixture resembles fine crumbs. Stir in sesame seeds. Add water slowly, mixing with fork to form a stiff dough. Form into ball. Roll out dough on a lightly floured board to a thickness of 3 mm (1/8 in). Cut into 5-cm (2-in) squares. Place on a lightly greased baking sheet. Bake in a 200°C (400°F) oven 8 to 10 min until very lightly browned. Remove immediately from baking sheet. Cool at room temperature 2 h. Store in a tightly covered container.

Makes 36 wafers, 12 servings.

**Each serving: 3 wafers**

| | | | |
|---|---|---|---|
| ½ | ☐ | Starchy Choice | 7 g carbohydrate |
| ½ | ▲ | Fats & Oils Choice | 2 g protein |
| | | | 3 g fat |
| | | | 260 kilojoules |
| | | | (63 Calories) |

# Beverages

Beverages can be prepared to suit any occasion. Frosty sparkling fruit drinks cool and comfort on a hot, sultry day. Dark, rich hot chocolate warms a blustery winter day. Foamy shakes cheer sulky children. A cup of coffee or tea ends an elegant dinner appropriately. Fruity punch sparkles at a party. And drinks can add variety to meals and even provide breakfasts in a hurry.

Not only are our beverages thirst-quenching and satisfying, they are nourishing and tasty. An endless variety can be made with fruit juices and nectars as the base. Milk-based drinks are good foods, providing protein, carbohydrate, fat, vitamins and minerals.

## CRANBERRY REFRESHER

*This bright red cooler is perfect for both summer picnics and Christmas cocktail parties. If a clearer beverage is desired, pour* Refresher *through a fine sieve or cheesecloth.*

| | | |
|---|---|---|
| **50 mL** | Cranberry Concentrate (see below) | ¼ **cup** |
| **200 mL** | water, sugar-free ginger ale or soda water | ¾ **cup** |

Dilute concentrate with water. Serve chilled, over ice cubes if desired.

Makes 1 serving.

**Each serving: 250 mL (1 cup)**

1 **++** Extra                                                3 g carbohydrate

50 kilojoules
(12 Calories)

## CRANBERRY CONCENTRATE

Cranberry Concentrate *can be frozen in a shallow square pan. Cut it into 8 equal blocks, then wrap and store them in the freezer. They will be ready to make 250 mL (1 cup) portions of* Cranberry Refresher.

| | | |
|---|---|---|
| **500 mL** | cranberries | **2 cups** |
| **625 mL** | water | **2½ cups** |
| **2** | slices lemon | **2** |
| | Artificial sweetener equivalent to 60 mL (12 tsp) sugar (12 aspartame tablets) | |

Combine cranberries, water and lemon slices in stainless steel or enamel saucepan. Bring to a boil; reduce heat and simmer uncovered 30 min. Add sweetener, stir until dissolved. Strain, stirring and mashing berries until a fairly dry pulp remains in strainer. Store concentrate in refrigerator.

Makes 8 servings, 500 mL (2 cups) *Cranberry Concentrate.*

**Each serving: 50 mL (¼ cup) concentrate**

1 **++** Extra                                                3 g carbohydrate

50 kilojoules
(12 Calories)

## RHUBARB REFRESHER

*More artificial sweetener may be added if a sweeter tasting beverage is desired.*

| | | |
|---|---|---|
| **125 mL** | Rhubarb Concentrate (see below) | ½ **cup** |
| **125 mL** | water, sugar-free ginger ale or soda water | ½ **cup** |

Dilute concentrate with water. Serve chilled, over ice cubes if desired.

Makes 1 serving.

**Each serving: 250 mL (1 cup)**

1 **++** Extra

2 g carbohydrate

30 kilojoules
(8 Calories)

## RHUBARB CONCENTRATE

*Make a good supply of* Rhubarb Concentrate *early in the summer when garden rhubarb is plentiful. It freezes well so plan to have some on hand for refreshing drinks all year.*

| | | |
|---|---|---|
| **500 g** | fresh or frozen rhubarb, cut into pieces | **1 lb** |
| **750 mL** | water | **3 cups** |
| **7** | whole cloves | **7** |
| | Artificial sweetener equivalent to 60 mL (12 tsp) sugar (12 aspartame tablets) | |

Combine rhubarb, water and cloves in stainless steel or enamel saucepan. Bring to a boil; reduce heat and simmer uncovered 30 min. Add sweetener, stir until dissolved. Strain; discard pulp. Pour into container and refrigerate, or store in the freezer in small covered containers for up to 9 months.

Makes 750 mL (3 cups) *Rhubarb Concentrate.*

**Each serving: 125 mL (½ cup) concentrate**

1 **++** Extra

2 g carbohydrate

30 kilojoules
(8 Calories)

## PEACH NECTAR

Peach Nectar *is great to have on hand for days when you feel like a change from the usual breakfast juice.*

| | | |
|---|---|---|
| **25 mL** | Peach Nectar Concentrate (see below) | **2 tbsp** |
| **125 mL** | water, sugar-free ginger ale or soda water | **½ cup** |

Dilute concentrate with cold water. Serve chilled, over ice cubes.

Makes 1 serving.

**Each serving: about 175 mL (2/3 cup)**

1 ◨ Fruits & Vegetables Choice

10 g carbohydrate
1 g protein
190 kilojoules
(44 Calories)

## PEACH NECTAR CONCENTRATE

*Prepare* Peach Nectar Concentrate *when the fruit is plentiful and at its peak. Freeze it in 25 mL (2 tbsp) amounts in ice cube trays, then pack the cubes in freezer bags. They can be stored in the freezer for up to 9 months.*

| | | |
|---|---|---|
| **12** | fully ripe peaches | **12** |
| **10 mL** | ascorbic acid color keeper | **2 tsp** |

Blanch, peel and pit peaches. Cut into chunks, sprinkle with ascorbic acid color keeper and place in a blender or food processor. Purée until very smooth and liquefied. Pour into a heavy saucepan. Boil, stirring occasionally, for about 15 min until mixture reduces by half. Cool. Store in covered container in refrigerator for up to 8 weeks, or freeze as suggested above.

Makes 375 mL (1½ cups) concentrate.

**Each serving: 25 mL (2 tbsp)**

1 ◨ Fruits & Vegetables Choice

10 g carbohydrate
1 g protein
190 kilojoules
(44 Calories)

## CHOCOLATE INSTANT BREAKFAST

*Here's a quick meal in a glass that can be made with or without the chocolate sauce.*

| 250 mL | skim milk | 1 cup |
|---|---|---|
| 1 | egg | 1 |
| ½ | small banana or very ripe, peeled pear | ½ |
| 10 mL | *Chocolate Sauce* (recipe, p. 200) | 2 tsp |
| 2 mL | vanilla | ½ tsp |

Combine milk, egg, banana, *Chocolate Sauce* and vanilla in a blender. Blend at high speed 1 min or until frothy.

Makes 1 serving.

**Each serving: about 375 mL (1½ cups)**

1 ⬚ Protein Choice
2 ◆ Milk Choices (2%)
1 ⬚ Fruits & Vegetables Choice

23 g carbohydrate
14 g protein
6 g fat

850 kilojoules
(202 Calories)

**Each half serving: 200 mL (¾ cup)**

2 ◆ Milk Choices (2%)

12 g carbohydrate
7 g protein
3 g fat

430 kilojoules
(103 Calories)

Skipping breakfast is not a recommended way to lose weight. Plan to have something nourishing in the morning. It can be simple and take only a few minutes, but it provides you with the energy and stamina to last until lunch time.

## TEA PUNCH

*This punch is quite concentrated, so don't be afraid to use plenty of ice. Aspartame acts as a flavor enhancer in this drink as well as a sweetener.*

| 250 mL | boiling water | 1 cup |
|---|---|---|
| 2 | 2-cup tea bags or 20 mL (4 tsp) tea leaves | 2 |
| | Artificial sweetener equivalent to 20 mL (4 tsp) sugar (4 aspartame tablets) | |
| 1 | lemon, thinly sliced | 1 |
| 175 mL | *Cranberry Concentrate* (recipe, p.34) | 2/3 cup |
| 125 mL | white grape juice | ½ cup |
| 75 mL | unsweetened apple juice | 1/3 cup |
| 500 mL | cold water | 2 cups |
| | Ice cubes | |

Pour boiling water over tea; let steep 5 min. Remove tea bags. Add sweetener, lemon slices, *Cranberry Concentrate*, grape juice, apple juice and water; stir until well mixed. Pour over ice cubes in 4 tall glasses.

Makes 4 servings.

**Each serving: 250 mL (1 cup)**

1 ◪ Fruits & Vegetables Choice

11 g carbohydrate
190 kilojoules
(44 Calories)

## SPARKLING FRUIT PUNCH

*Make this punch with a dry sparkling wine or a dry champagne in place of the ginger ale, if you wish. When wine or champagne is used the Food Choice remains the same, but the energy value increases to 310 kilojoules (73 Calories) per serving.*

| 375 mL | *Rhubarb Concentrate* (recipe, p.35) | 1½ cups |
|---|---|---|
| 125 mL | unsweetened orange juice | ½ cup |
| 75 mL | unsweetened apple juice | 1/3 cup |
| 5 mL | vanilla | 1 tsp |
| 3 drops | red food coloring, optional | 3 drops |
| 500 mL | sugar-free ginger ale, chilled | 2 cups |
| 250 mL | strawberries, halved | 1 cup |
| | Artificial sweetener | |
| | Ice cubes | |

Combine *Rhubarb Concentrate*, orange and apple juices, vanilla and food coloring, if desired. Chill thoroughly. Stir in ginger ale and strawberries. Sweeten to taste with artificial sweetener. Pour 175 mL (2/3 cup) over ice cubes in a glass or punch cup.

Makes 8 servings, 1.25 L (5 cups) punch.

**Each serving: 175 mL (2/3 cup)**

½ ▨ Fruits & Vegetables Choice

5 g carbohydrate

90 kilojoules
(20 Calories)

## HOT MULLED TODDY

*A hot toddy is an old-fashioned, warmer-upper, perfect for chilly days. Take it along in a thermos for a special treat outdoors.*

| 300 | mL | water | 1¼ | cups |
|---|---|---|---|---|
| 175 | mL | unsweetened apple juice | 2/3 | cup |
| 25 | mL | *Cranberry Concentrate* (recipe, p.34) | 2 | tbsp |
| 5 | cm | cinnamon stick | 2 | in |
| 2 | | whole allspice berries | 2 | |
| 1 | | whole clove | 1 | |
| 2 | | thin lemon slices | 2 | |

Combine water, apple juice, *Cranberry Concentrate*, cinnamon stick, allspice and clove. Heat to a boil; reduce heat, cover and simmer gently 20 min. Pour into mugs, garnish with lemon slices.

Makes 2 servings.

**Each serving: 250 mL (1 cup)**

1 ▨ Fruits & Vegetables Choice

11 g carbohydrate

190 kilojoules
(44 Calories)

Did you know that grapefruit does not contain any special ingredient to "melt" body fat? There is, in fact, no food that has a "fat melting" ability. However, grapefruit is a valuable source of Vitamin C and other nutrients.

## STRAWBERRY INSTANT BREAKFAST

*This fruit nog is quick, easy and nourishing, ideal for busy mornings when a sit-down breakfast is just too time consuming.*

| 250 mL | skim milk | 1 cup |
|---|---|---|
| 1 | egg | 1 |
| 125 mL | fresh or frozen unsweetened strawberries | ½ cup |
| 5 mL | vanilla | 1 tsp |
| | Artificial sweetener, optional | |

Combine milk, egg, strawberries and vanilla in a blender. Blend at high speed 1 min or until frothy. Sweeten to taste with artificial sweetener, if desired.

Makes 1 serving.

**Each serving: about 375 mL (1½ cups)**

1 ▨ Protein Choice
2 ◆ Milk Choices (2%)
½ ▨ Fruits & Vegetables Choice

18 g carbohydrate
14 g protein
6 g fat

770 kilojoules
(182 Calories)

## MILKY WAY COOLER

*A cooler like this stretches your Milk Choices. Serve it in tall glasses with colorful straws and perhaps a sprig of mint or a sprinkle of nutmeg as a garnish.*

| 250 mL | chilled, sugar-free carbonated beverage, any flavor | 1 cup |
|---|---|---|
| 125 mL | 2% milk | ½ cup |
| 3 | ice cubes | 3 |

Combine carbonated beverage and milk in a blender. Blend until frothy. Continue blending, adding ice cubes one at a time until mixture is slightly thickened.

Makes 1 serving.

**Each serving: about 400 mL (1-2/3 cups)**

1 ◆ Milk Choice (2%)

6 g carbohydrate
4 g protein
2 g fat

240 kilojoules
(58 Calories)

## FROSTY BOG

*This thick, frosty and tangy beverage is refreshing and can even be served as a light dessert.*

| 125 mL | crushed ice | ½ cup |
|---|---|---|
| 50 mL | plain yogurt | ¼ cup |
| 25 mL | *Cranberry Concentrate* (recipe, p.34) | 2 tbsp |
| | Artificial sweetener equivalent to 5 mL (1 tsp) sugar | |
| pinch | cinnamon | pinch |

Combine ice, yogurt, *Cranberry Concentrate* and sweetener in a blender. Blend at high speed 2 min or until frosty and thickened. Pour into glass. Sprinkle with cinnamon.

Makes 1 serving.

**Each serving: about 200 mL (¾ cup)**

1 ◆ Milk Choice (skim)

6 g carbohydrate
2 g protein
1 g fat

170 kilojoules
(41 Calories)

## SWISS MOCHA

*Swiss Mocha is a delicious after-dinner treat when you feel like a change from regular tea or coffee.*

| 25 mL | *Instant Swiss Mocha Mix* (recipe, p.42) | 2 tbsp |
|---|---|---|
| 250 mL | boiling water | 1 cup |
| | Artificial sweetener, optional | |

Place mix in a coffee mug. Stir in boiling water slowly until mix dissolves.

**VARIATION:**

**CAFÉ BAVARIAN**—To each mug of *Swiss Mocha* add a pinch of cinnamon and/or a few drops peppermint extract.

**Each serving: 250 mL (1 cup)**

1 ◆ Milk Choice (skim)

5 g carbohydrate
3 g protein

140 kilojoules
(32 Calories)

### INSTANT SWISS MOCHA MIX

*When you keep this homemade mix on hand it only takes seconds to make a good hot drink. It is an easy, economical way to include milk in meals.*

| 125 mL | instant skim milk powder | ½ cup |
|---|---|---|
| 25 mL | cocoa | 2 tbsp |
| 25 mL | instant coffee | 2 tbsp |

Combine skim milk powder, cocoa and instant coffee in container of blender. Blend at high speed until well mixed. (Or place dry ingredients in a jar; seal and shake until very well mixed.)

Makes 125 mL (½ cup) mix.

**Each serving: 25 mL (2 tbsp)**

1 ◆ Milk Choice (skim)

5 g carbohydrate
3 g protein

140 kilojoules
(32 Calories)

### SLIMMER'S SHAKE

*Try this shake when you need a change from everyday cereal breakfasts.*

| 125 mL | 2% milk | ½ cup |
|---|---|---|
| 75 mL | cornflakes or bran flakes | 1/3 cup |
| 125 mL | fresh or frozen unsweetened strawberries, or ¼ banana or peeled pear, or ½ peach | ½ cup |
| 50 mL | water | ¼ cup |
| | Artificial sweetener equivalent to 5 mL (1 tsp) sugar | |

Combine milk, cereal, fruit, water and sweetener in a blender. Blend at high speed until thick and frothy.

Makes 1 serving.

**Each serving: about 250 mL (1 cup).**   (Measure will vary slightly depending on fruit used.)

1 ☐ Starchy Choice
1 ◆ Milk Choice (2%)

22 g carbohydrate
5 g protein
2 g fat

530 kilojoules
(126 Calories)

## CHOCOLATE MILK

*Chocolate lovers of all ages will be delighted with the rich flavor that develops when our Chocolate Sauce is stirred into milk.*

| | | |
|---|---|---|
| **15 mL** | *Chocolate Sauce*<br>(recipe, p.200) | **1 tbsp** |
| **250 mL** | 2% or skim milk | **1 cup** |

Stir chocolate sauce into cold milk.

Makes 1 serving.

**Each serving: 250 mL (1 cup)**

2 ◆ Milk Choices

12 g carbohydrate
8 g protein
4 g fat

490 kilojoules
(116 Calories)

## HOT CHOCOLATE

*A pinch of cinnamon adds pizzazz to Hot Chocolate or cocoa.*

| | | |
|---|---|---|
| **15 mL** | *Chocolate Sauce*<br>(recipe, p.200) | **1 tbsp** |
| **250 mL** | hot 2% or skim milk<br>Cinnamon, optional | **1 cup** |

Stir *Chocolate Sauce* into hot milk. Dust lightly with cinnamon, if desired.

Makes 1 serving.

**Each serving: 250 mL (1 cup)**

2 ◆ Milk Choices

12 g carbohydrate
8 g protein
4 g fat

490 kilojoules
(116 Calories)

**Milk is an almost perfect food, but no single food contains all the nutrients that humans need. Although milk contains most of the essential nutrients, it is low in iron and Vitamin C.**

# Sauces and Basics

For built-in convenience, it is a good idea to spend spare moments in the kitchen while the stew simmers or the buns bake to prepare a few basics. It is a practice that saves both time and money.

Basics are dishes you can build on. For instance, there is no limit to the use of a good sauce. It enhances and bolsters the food with which it is served, binds ingredients together and keeps foods from drying out. A basic white sauce can be flavored with an unlimited variety of seasonings, while barbecue and spaghetti sauces have endless uses. Our basic sauces can be made ahead and stored for later use.

Crêpes, noodles and tortillas become staples for interesting dishes which can be prepared quickly if the fuss and muss of putting the bases together has been done in advance.

In the appropriate chapters you will discover recipes for other basics like broths, cream puffs, pie shells and biscuits that also make wonderful foundations for other meals.

## "SLIM SAUCES"

*You'll find dozens of uses for these sauces that are trimmed of fat and starch. They keep in the refrigerator for up to a week, so when preparing them, you might want to make extra to have on hand.*

### BASIC WHITE SAUCE

| 250 mL | 2% milk | 1 cup |
|---|---|---|
| 15 mL | all purpose flour | 1 tbsp |
| 5 mL | cornstarch | 1 tsp |
| 2 mL | salt | ½ tsp |
| 5 mL | vegetable oil | 1 tsp |
| pinch | white pepper, optional | pinch |

Combine milk, flour, cornstarch and salt in a saucepan or screw-top jar. Whisk or shake until there are no dry bits of cornstarch or flour. Stir-cook about 2 min, until mixture boils and thickens. Stir in oil. Season with white pepper, if desired.

### VARIATIONS:

**HERB SAUCE:** Stir 2 mL (½ tsp) each of dried thyme, sweet basil, oregano and parsley into thickened *Basic White Sauce.*

Serve on cooked vegetables, meat or fish and use as a base for crêpe fillings.

**BECHAMEL SAUCE:** Sauté 15 mL (1 tbsp) finely chopped onion in the 5 mL oil when preparing *Basic White Sauce,* then stir into thickened sauce.

Serve on cooked vegetables, meat or fish. Use as a base for crêpe fillings.

Makes 4 servings, 250 mL (1 cup).

**Each serving: 50 mL (¼ cup)**

1 ◆ Milk Choice (2%)

5 g carbohydrate
2 g protein
2 g fat

190 kilojoules
(46 Calories)

## SPAGHETTI SAUCE

*Serve this as a meatless sauce over our* Whole Wheat Noodles. *Crumbled, cooked meat or meatballs can be simmered along with the sauce if a more substantial meal is preferred.*

| | | | |
|---|---|---|---|
| 5 mL | vegetable oil | 1 | tsp |
| 2 | cloves garlic, chopped | 2 | |
| 1 | medium onion, chopped | 1 | |
| 1 can | 796 mL (28 oz) plum (Italian) tomatoes, mashed or puréed | 1 | can |
| 250 mL | water or broth | 1 | cup |
| 50 mL | tomato paste | ¼ | cup |
| 15 mL | dried parsley | 1 | tbsp |
| 5 mL | salt | 1 | tsp |
| 2 mL | each oregano, thyme and basil | ½ | tsp |
| 1 mL | ground cloves | ¼ | tsp |
| 1 mL | freshly ground pepper | ¼ | tsp |

Heat oil in a heavy saucepan. Sauté garlic and onion 3 min or until limp. Stir in tomatoes, water and tomato paste. Add parsley, salt, oregano, thyme, basil, cloves and pepper; stir well. Bring to a boil, reduce heat and simmer, stirring occasionally, 1 h until sauce is reduced by a quarter.

Makes 6 servings, 750 mL (3 cups).

**Each serving: 125 mL (½ cup)**

1 ◪ Fruits & Vegetables Choice

9 g carbohydrate
2 g protein
1 g fat

220 kilojoules
(53 Calories)

## SPEEDY BARBECUE SAUCE

*Brush this spicy, easy-to-prepare sauce on chops, steaks or chicken pieces for barbecuing on an outside grill or in the oven. Use sparingly because it contains some sugar.*

| | | | |
|---|---|---|---|
| 125 mL | undiluted tomato soup | ½ | cup |
| 45 mL | red wine or cider vinegar | 3 | tbsp |
| 15 mL | molasses | 1 | tbsp |
| 5 mL | celery seed | 1 | tsp |
| 2 mL | chili powder | ½ | tsp |

Combine tomato soup, vinegar, molasses, celery seed and chili powder in a jar. Seal; shake until mixed. Store, tightly covered, in the refrigerator.

Makes 175 mL (2/3 cup).

**Each serving: 15 mL (1 tbsp)**

1 **++** Extra

3 g carbohydrate
50 kilojoules
(12 Calories)

### MUSHROOM SAUCE

*Fresh mushrooms make the best sauce, but drained canned mushrooms can be used if fresh are unavailable.*

|        |                                         |        |
|--------|-----------------------------------------|--------|
|        | Vegetable oil or butter                 |        |
| 250 mL | chopped mushrooms (stems and pieces)    | 1 cup  |
| 250 mL | beef broth                              | 1 cup  |
| pinch  | freshly ground pepper                   | pinch  |
| 10 mL  | all purpose flour                       | 2 tsp  |
| 5 mL   | cornstarch                              | 1 tsp  |
| 25 mL  | water                                   | 2 tbsp |

Coat a frypan lightly with oil or butter. Add mushrooms; stir-cook 2 to 3 min until mushrooms look a bit dry. Add broth and pepper. Bring to a boil, reduce heat and simmer 5 min. Stir flour and cornstarch into water to form a smooth paste or shake together in a small screw-top jar. Add to mushroom mixture and stir-cook about 2 min until sauce thickens.

Makes 4 servings, 250 mL (1 cup) sauce.

**Each serving: 50 mL (¼ cup)**

1 **++** Extra

3 g carbohydrate
2 g protein

90 kilojoules
(20 Calories)

> **To mix water and flour into a smooth paste, place water in a jar, add flour, cover and shake until smooth.**

## VELOUTÉ SAUCE

*Serve with chicken or fish, depending on the broth used. Velouté makes an ideal sauce for crêpe fillings.*

| | | | |
|---|---|---|---|
| 250 | mL | chicken or fish broth | 1 cup |
| 15 | mL | all purpose flour | 1 tbsp |
| 5 | mL | cornstarch | 1 tsp |
| 2 | mL | salt | ½ tsp |
| 5 | mL | vegetable oil | 1 tsp |
| | pinch | white pepper, optional | pinch |

Combine broth, flour, cornstarch and salt in a saucepan or screw-top jar. Whisk or shake until there are no dry bits of cornstarch or flour. Stir-cook about 2 min, until mixture boils and thickens. Stir in oil. Season with white pepper, if desired.

Makes 4 servings, 250 mL (1 cup).

**Each serving: 50 mL (¼ cup)**

1  **++**  Extra

2g carbohydrate
1g fat

70 kilojoules
(17 Calories)

## CHEESE SAUCE

*This is the perfect sauce for cooked cauliflower, broccoli and asparagus. It is sensational over hard-cooked eggs on toast.*

Stir 125 mL (½ cup) shredded Cheddar cheese into *Basic White Sauce* (recipe, p.45) when oil is added. Whisk or stir briskly until cheese melts. (Do not allow sauce to boil; if it does it may begin to curdle.)

Makes 6 servings, about 275 mL (1 cup plus 2 tbsp).

**Each serving: 45 mL (3 tbsp)**

½  **⊘**  Protein Choice
½  **◆**  Milk Choice (2%)

3g carbohydrate
4g protein
4g fat

270 kilojoules
(64 Calories)

## STROGANOFF SAUCE

*For a quick* Stroganoff, *heat cooked beef strips or cooked meatballs in this sauce. You'll have a succulent topping for cooked* Whole Wheat Noodles.

| 125 mL | 2% cottage cheese | ½ cup |
|--------|-------------------|-------|
| 50 mL | 2% yogurt | ¼ cup |
| 1 batch | Mushroom Sauce (recipe, p.47) | 1 batch |

Purée cottage cheese and yogurt in a blender or food processor. Stir in *Mushroom Sauce.* Heat to simmer but do not boil. Serve immediately.

Makes 6 servings, 375 mL (1½ cups).

**Each serving: 50 mL (¼ cup)**

½ **⊘** Protein Choice

3 g carbohydrate
4 g protein
1 g fat

160 kilojoules
(37 Calories)

## FAT-FREE GRAVY

*Call this a waist-watcher gravy. There are only 70 kilojoules (16 Calories) in one serving. Serve it over meat loaf, roast meat and mashed potatoes.*

| 250 mL | beef broth and defatted roast drippings combined | 1 cup |
|--------|--------------------------------------------------|-------|
| 10 mL | all purpose flour | 2 tsp |
| 5 mL | cornstarch | 1 tsp |
| 5 mL | ketchup | 1 tsp |
| pinch | each of salt, freshly ground pepper and basil | pinch |

Combine beef broth, flour and cornstarch in a screw-top jar, cover and shake until well combined. Pour into saucepan, stir in ketchup, salt, pepper and basil. Stir-cook over medium heat about 2 min until gravy thickens.

Makes 4 servings, 1 cup (250 mL).

**Each serving: 50 mL (¼ cup)**

1 **++** Extra

3 g carbohydrate
1 g protein

70 kilojoules
(16 Calories)

## CELERY SAUCE

*No starchy thickener like flour or cornstarch is required in our Celery Sauce. It is delicious over hard-cooked eggs, steamed salmon and other fish.*

| | | |
|---|---|---|
| **375 mL** | celery slices (4 stalks) | **1½ cups** |
| **1** | medium potato, peeled and cut into pieces | **1** |
| **500 mL** | chicken broth | **2 cups** |
| **2 mL** | salt | **½ tsp** |
| **1 mL** | oregano | **¼ tsp** |
| **pinch** | freshly ground pepper | **pinch** |
| **pinch** | nutmeg | **pinch** |

Combine celery, potato and chicken broth in a saucepan. Add salt, oregano, pepper and nutmeg. Bring to a boil, reduce heat and simmer 15 min. Remove about 50 mL (¼ cup) celery slices. Purée remainder by pushing mixture through sieve, or processing it in blender, food processor or food mill. Stir reserved celery slices into purée.

Makes 6 servings, 500 mL (2 cups).

**Each serving: 75 mL (1/3 cup)**

½  Fruits & Vegetables Choice

5 g carbohydrate
2 g protein
120 kilojoules
(28 Calories)

## WHOLE WHEAT NOODLES OR SPAGHETTI

*Whole wheat flour increases the fiber content of pasta and at the same time makes it a little more tender.*

| | | | |
|---|---|---|---|
| 375 mL | whole wheat flour | 1½ | cups |
| 125 mL | all purpose flour | ½ | cup |
| 1 | whole egg | 1 | |
| 2 | egg whites | 2 | |
| 5 mL | salt | 1 | tsp |
| 50 mL | water | ¼ | cup |

Combine flours in a large bowl. Whisk together whole egg, egg whites and salt until slightly foamy. Stir into flours. Add a few drops of water until dough forms a ball. Knead on a lightly floured board until smooth and elastic. Divide dough into handful portions; work with one at a time. Cover remaining portions with plastic wrap or an inverted bowl to prevent drying. Flour board and rolling pin. Roll dough, stretching it occasionally by hand, until very thin, 3 mm (1/8 in). Set aside for 3 to 4 min to dry slightly but do not allow it to become brittle. Roll up each sheet of pasta into a cylinder. Cut the roll crosswise with a serrated knife to make noodles of desired width. Shake noodles out to partially dry on a clean cloth. Cook immediately, or freeze, or dry for later use.

*To cook fresh noodles:* Bring 6 L (5½ qts) water to a boil, add 10 mL (2 tsp) salt, bring back to boil. Stir noodles into the rapidly boiling water. Cook 3 to 4 min until al dente or done to your taste. Pour in 500 mL (2 cups) cold water to stop the cooking. Drain or use tongs or a spaghetti lifter to remove the pasta from water. Place in a warm bowl to serve.

Makes about 12 servings, 1.5 L (6 cups) cooked.

**Each serving: 125 mL (½ cup)**

1 ☐ Starchy Choice

15 g carbohydrate
4 g protein
1 g fat

360 kilojoules
(85 Calories)

**If you plan to keep whole wheat flour longer than 2 months, store it in your refrigerator or freezer in a tightly sealed container or bag. This will ensure its freshness.**

## CRÊPES

*Freeze or refrigerate crêpes to have on hand for a variety of special main dishes and elegant desserts. If crêpes are cooked in a well-seasoned pan or one with a non-stick finish, very little oil is required to prevent sticking.*

| | | |
|---|---|---|
| **175 mL** | 2% milk | **2/3 cup** |
| **2** | eggs | **2** |
| **7 mL** | vegetable oil | **1½ tsp** |
| **125 mL** | all purpose flour | **½ cup** |

Combine milk, eggs and 5 mL (1 tsp) vegetable oil in mixing bowl. Beat with rotary beater or mixer until well blended. Add flour; continue to beat until mixed. Allow to stand about 1 h. Brush a crêpe pan with a little of the remaining oil. Heat pan over medium heat until water dropped on surface dances. Pour 50 mL (¼ cup) batter into pan all at once, lifting pan off heat and turning so batter coats all surfaces evenly. Hold over heat, continuing to rotate about 30 to 40 seconds until top is dry and bottom light brown. Loosen edges and flip crêpe over, cooking other side 15 seconds. Slide crêpe out of pan onto waxed paper. Repeat until all batter is cooked. Place each cooked crêpe between layers of waxed paper. Well-wrapped crêpes can be stored in the refrigerator 2 days or in the freezer up to 3 months.

Makes 8 crêpes, each 15 to 18 cm (6 to 7 in).

**Each serving: 1 crêpe**

½ ⊘ Protein Choice
½ ◻ Starchy Choice

6 g carbohydrate
3 g protein
3 g fat

260 kilojoules
(63 Calories)

## FLUFFY DUMPLINGS

*Flavor these dumplings with herbs like dill, caraway and basil for unique taste variations. These dumplings are not doughy at all, but become light and fluffy as they steam over simmering stew or soup.*

| | | |
|---|---|---|
| **250 mL** | all purpose flour | **1 cup** |
| **10 mL** | baking powder | **2 tsp** |
| **2 mL** | salt | **½ tsp** |
| **15 mL** | margarine or butter | **1 tbsp** |
| **75 mL** | 2% milk | **1/3 cup** |

Combine flour, baking powder and salt. Cut in butter until mixture resembles fine crumbs. Add milk; stir until just moistened. Divide into 6 portions and spoon onto bubbling stew. Cover tightly and simmer 15 min without lifting lid.

Makes 6 small dumplings.

**Each serving: 1 dumpling**

1 ☐ Starchy Choice

14 g carbohydrate
3 g protein
2 g fat

360 kilojoules
(86 Calories)

## SEASONED BREAD CRUMBS

*Keep Seasoned Bread Crumbs in a covered container in your freezer to use as a tasty topping for casseroles and baked vegetables. They are also handy for breading fish, chicken, pork or veal.*

| 500 mL | fine dry bread crumbs | 2 cups |
|---|---|---|
| 125 mL | finely chopped onion | ½ cup |
| 125 mL | finely chopped fresh parsley or 25 mL (2 tbsp) dried parsley | ½ cup |
| 1 | clove garlic, finely chopped | 1 |
| 5 mL | oregano | 1 tsp |
| 75 mL | grated Parmesan cheese | 1/3 cup |

Combine bread crumbs, onion, parsley, garlic, oregano and cheese; mix thoroughly. Store in a tightly covered container in the freezer for up to 6 months.

Makes 16 servings, 750 mL (3 cups).

**Each serving: 45 mL (3 tbsp)**

½ ☐ Starchy Choice

8 g carbohydrate
2 g protein
1 g fat

210 kilojoules
(49 Calories)

## WHOLE WHEAT FLOUR TORTILLAS

*Tortillas are eaten like bread in Mexico, and are definitely a staple in the Mexican diet. They are called tacos when they are folded, crisped and filled with beans and/or meat and vegetable garnishes. Enchiladas are tortillas rolled around a filling and baked in a sauce. Tostadas are small tortillas cut from larger ones. Totopos or chips are made by cutting tortillas into wedges and crisping them—they make super scoops for dips. When these chips are topped with melted cheese and chilies they are called nachos.*

| | | |
|---|---|---|
| 125 mL | all purpose flour | ½ **cup** |
| 125 mL | whole wheat flour | ½ **cup** |
| 1 mL | salt | ¼ **tsp** |
| 15 mL | vegetable oil | 1 **tbsp** |
| 90 mL | warm water | 6 **tbsp** |

Combine flours and salt. Mix water and 10 mL (2 tsp) oil; stir into flour mixture to make a soft dough. Divide dough into 12 even pieces. Shape each into a small ball. Coat palms with remaining oil. Roll each ball in oiled hands. Place in a bowl and cover with a cloth or plastic wrap. Let stand about 15 min. Preheat an ungreased frypan. Shape each ball into a very flat, 10 cm (4 in) round patty. Roll out on a lightly floured surface to a 15 cm (6 in) circle. Cook each round on preheated frypan until bubbles form on top, and underside is flecked with brown. Turn; press down bubbles with towel. Cook until underside is flecked with brown but not too crisp and still flexible. Stack cooked tortillas; cover with a dry cloth towel. Serve immediately or reheat in 180°C (350°F) oven before serving.

Makes 6 servings, twelve 15 cm (6 in) tortillas.

**Each serving: two 15 cm (6 in) tortillas or four 7.5 cm (3 in) tortillas**

1 ☐ Starchy Choice

½ ▲ Fats & Oils Choice

14 g carbohydrate

3 g protein

2 g fat

360 kilojoules
(86 Calories)

# Soups

Soups are good for the body and soul. They are nourishing and sustaining, satisfying and soothing, whether hot or cold, thick or thin.

Making soup from scratch is one of the most creative and easiest of the culinary arts. It is also one of the most economical ways of preparing food. Odds and ends, cheaper cuts and bones, small bits of vegetables and seasonings go into the soup pot to simmer and develop into new flavor combinations. Long simmering makes the best broth and soup. A bit of salt also helps draw out the flavor of the ingredients.

Piping hot *Beef Broth* may lead off a presentation of cold chicken breasts and salad; *Iced Cucumber Soup* may usher in the roast chicken. It's a good idea to have the texture and temperature contrast with the food that follows.

This chapter includes soups with clear broths and bouillon as a base, as well as heartier, robust soups and creamy chowders suitable for family one-dish meals. The menu may be completed with a sandwich or salad, and a pleasing dessert.

## FRENCH ONION SOUP

*This classic is always a favorite. Our version cuts down on the fat. Consider French Onion Soup for a weekend specialty when you are not so rushed.*

| | | | |
|---|---|---|---|
| 15 mL | butter | 1 | tbsp |
| 1 | large, mild onion, thinly sliced | 1 | |
| 10 mL | all purpose flour | 2 | tsp |
| 50 mL | dry white wine | ¼ | cup |
| 1.25 L | water | 5 | cups |
| 4 cubes | beef bouillon | 4 | cubes |
| | Salt and freshly ground pepper | | |
| 4 | slices French bread | 4 | |
| 250 mL | shredded Swiss cheese | 1 | cup |

Melt butter in a heavy frypan. Add sliced onion, cover, cook over low heat about 5 min, until onion is tender. Remove lid, increase heat to high. Cook and stir until onions are golden. Reduce heat, stir in flour and wine. Simmer 1 min. Add water; stir in bouillon cubes. Bring to a boil, reduce heat and simmer 5 min. Season to taste with salt and pepper. Place bread slices in a 160°C (325°F) oven 5 min, to dry. Pour soup into 4 heated ovenproof bowls. Place a slice of bread on top of each; allow bread to soak up soup, then cover with 50 mL (¼ cup) cheese per bowl. Bake in a 160°C (325°F) oven 25 to 30 min until cheese is lightly browned.

Makes 4 servings, 1 L (4 cups).

**Each serving: 250 mL (1 cup) soup**

| | | |
|---|---|---|
| 1 **⊘** Protein Choice | 20 g carbohydrate |
| 1½ **▢** Starchy Choices | 11 g protein |
| 1½ **▲** Fats & Oils Choices | 11 g fat |
| | 930 kilojoules |
| | (223 Calories) |

## CLEAR MUSHROOM SOUP

*Mushroom slices simmer in a marvelous-tasting base, creating a potion ideal for whetting the appetite at the start of a full meal.*

| | | | |
|---|---|---|---|
| 250 g | fresh mushrooms, sliced | ½ | lb |
| 750 mL | chicken or beef broth | 3 | cups |
| 5 mL | soy sauce | 1 | tsp |
| 2 mL | grated lemon peel | ½ | tsp |
| 1 mL | salt | ¼ | tsp |

|        |                       |       |
|--------|-----------------------|-------|
| **pinch** | freshly ground pepper | **pinch** |
| 10 mL  | dry sherry            | 2 tsp |

Place mushrooms, broth and soy sauce in a saucepan. Bring to a boil, reduce heat and simmer 20 min. Stir in lemon peel, salt and pepper; simmer 2 min longer. Stir in sherry. Ladle into warm soup cups.

Makes 4 servings, 750 mL (3 cups).

**Each serving: 200 mL (¾ cup)**

½ ◨ Fruits & Vegetables Choice

4 g carbohydrate
4 g protein

140 kilojoules
(32 Calories)

## ICED CUCUMBER SOUP

*Cold soups generally need more salt than hot soups, so taste the soup after it has chilled. Be prudent, however, and do not overdo the salt.*

|        |                      |          |
|--------|----------------------|----------|
| 1      | medium cucumber      | 1        |
| 250 mL | chicken broth        | 1 cup    |
| 1      | green onion          | 1        |
| 2 mL   | dried mint           | ½ tsp    |
| 5 mL   | salt                 | 1 tsp    |
| pinch  | garlic powder        | pinch    |
| 5 mL   | fresh lemon juice    | 1 tsp    |
| 125 mL | commercial sour cream | ½ cup    |
| 375 mL | plain yogurt         | 1½ cups  |

Peel cucumber, remove seeds and slice. Reserve 4 slices. Put remainder in blender or food processor with broth, onion, mint, salt, garlic powder and lemon juice. Process until finely chopped but not liquefied. Combine sour cream and yogurt in a bowl; stir in cucumber mixture. Mix well and cover tightly. Refrigerate several hours to blend flavors before serving. Spoon into chilled bowls. Garnish with reserved thin cucumber slices.

Makes 4 servings, 1 L (4 cups).

**Each serving: 250 mL (1 cup)**

1 ◆ Milk Choice (2%)
½ ▲ Fats & Oils Choice

8 g carbohydrate
4 g protein
5 g fat

390 kilojoules
(93 Calories)

## MINESTRONE SOUP

Minestrone *is a substantial, tasty, inexpensive country soup that comes from the cuisine of Italy. One serving is hearty enough to be the foundation of a meal.*

| | | | |
|---|---|---|---|
| 5 mL | vegetable oil | 1 tsp |
| 500 g | lean ground beef | 1 lb |
| 250 mL | chopped onion | 1 cup |
| 250 mL | chopped celery | 1 cup |
| 250 mL | chopped green pepper or zucchini | 1 cup |
| 250 mL | shredded cabbage | 1 cup |
| 250 mL | diced potatoes | 1 cup |
| 250 mL | sliced carrots | 1 cup |
| 1 can | 796 mL (28 oz) tomatoes | 1 can |
| 1.5 L | water | 6 cups |
| 10 mL | salt | 2 tsp |
| 5 mL | Worcestershire sauce | 1 tsp |
| 1 mL | freshly ground pepper | ¼ tsp |
| 2 | bay leaves | 2 |
| 1 can | 398 mL (14 oz) red kidney beans | 1 can |
| 125 mL | elbow macaroni | ½ cup |
| | Grated Parmesan cheese, optional | |

Wipe deep heavy pot with oil. Add meat, stir to break apart and cook until brown. Drain off fat. Add onion, celery, green pepper, cabbage, potatoes, carrots, tomatoes, water, salt, Worcestershire sauce, pepper and bay leaves. Stir until well combined. Bring to a boil; reduce heat and simmer, covered, 1 h. Add kidney beans and macaroni and cook 30 min longer. Ladle into warm soup bowls and sprinkle each with 5 mL (1 tsp) grated Parmesan cheese, if desired.

Makes 14 servings, 3.5 L (14 cups).

**Each serving: 250 mL (1 cup)**

1 🖉 Protein Choice
1 ☐ Starchy Choice

16 g carbohydrate
10 g protein
3 g fat

550 kilojoules
(131 Calories)

## BORSCHT

*This quick and easy version of Borscht can be prepared without the cabbage, but the vegetable does add more body, character and flavor to the soup.*

| | | |
|---|---|---|
| 1 can | 540 mL (19 oz) sliced beets | 1 can |
| | Water | |
| 2 cans | each 284 mL (10 oz) beef broth or consommé | 2 cans |
| 500 mL | finely shredded cabbage | 2 cups |
| 250 mL | chopped celery | 1 cup |
| 125 mL | chopped onion | ½ cup |
| 1 | large bay leaf | 1 |
| 5 mL | salt | 1 tsp |
| 1 mL | freshly ground pepper | ¼ tsp |
| 25 mL | fresh lemon juice | 2 tbsp |
| 125 mL | commercial sour cream, optional | ½ cup |
| | Chopped dill or dried dillweed | |

Drain beets, reserving juice. Add water to beet juice to make 1 L (4 cups); mix with beef broth in large saucepan. Cut beet slices into julienne strips; add to liquid. Stir in cabbage, celery, onion, bay leaf, salt and pepper. Simmer, uncovered, about 30 min. Remove bay leaf. Stir in lemon juice. Ladle into warm soup bowls. Top each with 15 mL (1 tbsp) sour cream, if desired. Sprinkle with dill.

Makes 8 servings, 2.5 L (10 cups).

**Each serving: 300 mL (1¼ cups)**

1 🍎 Fruits & Vegetables Choice

9 g carbohydrate
4 g protein

220 kilojoules
(52 Calories)

(**Note:** Add ½ ▲ Fats & Oils Choice (2 g fat) per serving if sour cream is included.)

**Some of the best sources of potassium include apricots, bananas, cantaloupe, grapefruit, nectarines, oranges, broccoli, Brussels sprouts, mushrooms, parsnips, potatoes and tomatoes.**

## CREAMY VEGETABLE SOUP

*A new vegetable flavor is created from this blend of seven vegetables. The combination becomes a thick, creamy soup by mashing or puréeing the potatoes and vegetables in the broth.*

| | | |
|---|---|---|
| **3** | stalks celery | **3** |
| **1** | leek, washed and trimmed | **1** |
| **1** | small carrot | **1** |
| **1** | small white turnip | **1** |
| **1** | kohlrabi or ¼ small cabbage | **1** |
| **1** | medium potato | **1** |
| **125 mL** | green peas | **½ cup** |
| **1.25 L** | chicken broth | **5 cups** |
| **15 mL** | chopped fresh cilantro or fresh parsley or 5 mL (1 tsp) dried parsley | **1 tbsp** |

Wash and slice celery and leek (use only white and light green part). Place in a large saucepan. Wash, peel and chop carrot, turnip, kohlrabi and potato. Add to saucepan. Stir in peas and chicken broth. Bring to a boil, then boil gently 20 min until vegetables are tender. Add cilantro. Cook 1 min longer. Place about 500 mL (2 cups) at a time in a blender or food processor. Process until puréed and smooth. May be refrigerated at this point. Serve hot or chilled, garnished with chopped cilantro.

Makes 8 servings, 1.25 L (5 cups).

**Each serving: 175 mL (2/3 cup)**

| | | |
|---|---|---|
| ½ 🖉 | Protein Choice | 12 g carbohydrate |
| 1 🖉 | Fruits & Vegetables Choice | 4 g protein |
| | | 270 kilojoules (64 Calories) |

## CREAMY CELERY SOUP

*If Celery Sauce is made ahead and stored in the refrigerator, it only takes minutes to transform it into soup.*

| | | |
|---|---|---|
| **500 mL** | Celery Sauce (recipe, p.50) | **2 cups** |
| **250 mL** | 2% milk | **1 cup** |
| **250 mL** | chicken broth | **1 cup** |

Combine sauce, milk and broth in a saucepan; stir well. Heat to simmer but *do not boil.* Ladle into hot soup cups or bowls.

Makes 6 servings, 1 L (4 cups).

**Each serving: 175 mL (2/3 cup)**

1 ◆ Milk Choice (2%)

8 g carbohydrate
4 g protein
1 g fat

240 kilojoules
(57 Calories)

### CREAM OF CAULIFLOWER SOUP

*Broccoli, asparagus, bean, and even tomato soup can be made like* Cream of Cauliflower Soup. *First the chosen vegetable is simmered in chicken broth until tender, then the soup is puréed.*

| 500 mL | cauliflower flowerettes | 2 cups |
|--------|------------------------|--------|
| 125 mL | chopped celery | ½ cup |
| 375 mL | chicken broth | 1½ cups |
| 250 mL | evaporated 2% milk | 1 cup |
| 2 mL | salt | ½ tsp |
| pinch | white pepper | pinch |
| 1 | green onion, thinly sliced | 1 |

Combine cauliflower, celery and chicken broth in a saucepan. Bring to a boil; reduce heat and simmer 10 min until vegetables are tender. Place about 500 mL (2 cups) at a time in a blender or food processor and purée. Return to saucepan. Stir in milk, salt and pepper. Heat over medium heat, stirring occasionally, until hot but *do not boil.* Ladle into warm bowls, garnish with green onion slices.

Makes 4 servings, 800 mL (3¼ cups).

**Each serving: 200 mL (¾ cup)**

2 ◆ Milk Choices (skim)

9 g carbohydrate
7 g protein
2 g fat

350 kilojoules
(82 Calories)

> **Heat milk-based soups just to simmering. If they are allowed to boil, they may curdle.**

## LENTIL SOUP

*Split lentils require a surprisingly short simmering period for this flavorful, all-vegetable soup.*

| | | | | |
|---|---|---|---|---|
| 250 | mL | split red lentils | 1 | cup |
| 3 | | stalks celery, coarsely chopped | 3 | |
| 2 | | medium carrots, sliced | 2 | |
| 1 | | small green pepper, chopped | 1 | |
| 1 | | small onion, chopped | 1 | |
| 75 | mL | chopped fresh parsley | 1/3 | cup |
| 1.5 | L | water | 6 | cups |
| 10 | mL | salt | 2 | tsp |
| 1 | mL | freshly ground pepper | ¼ | tsp |

Wash lentils and combine with celery, carrots, green pepper, onion, parsley, water, salt and pepper in large saucepan. Bring to a boil. Reduce heat; simmer 25 min or until vegetables are tender.

Makes 10 servings, 1.8 L (7½ cups).

**Each serving: 175 mL (2/3 cup)**

1 ☐ Starchy Choice

15 g carbohydrate
5 g protein

340 kilojoules
(80 Calories)

## TORTILLA SOUP

*The crunch from the bite-sized pieces of crisp tortillas are a surprise in this Mexican-style soup. Use 250 mL (1 cup) drained, canned tomatoes when fresh ones are not in season.*

| | | | | |
|---|---|---|---|---|
| 10 | mL | vegetable oil | 2 | tsp |
| 1 | | small onion, thinly sliced | 1 | |
| 1 | | clove garlic, finely chopped | 1 | |
| 2 | | tomatoes, chopped | 2 | |
| 1 | mL | freshly ground pepper | ¼ | tsp |
| 1 | L | chicken broth | 4 | cups |
| | | Salt | | |
| 125 | mL | finely chopped celery | ½ | cup |
| 125 | mL | finely chopped carrot | ½ | cup |
| 2 | | crisp 15 cm (6 in) *Whole Wheat Flour Tortillas* (recipe, p.54), broken | 2 | |

| 25 mL | crushed, dried chilies (seeds and veins removed) | 2 tbsp |
| 125 mL | crumbled, crisp bacon (4 slices side bacon) | ½ cup |
| 125 mL | shredded farmers cheese | ½ cup |

Heat oil in medium saucepan. Sauté onion and garlic about 5 min until onion is limp but not browned. Stir in tomatoes and pepper. Cook 10 to 15 min. Stir in broth and salt to taste. Simmer 15 min. Add celery and carrot. Simmer 10 min longer. Place 1/3 of a broken tortilla in each soup bowl. Ladle soup over chips. Sprinkle each serving with chilies, bacon and cheese.

Makes 6 servings, about 1.25 L (5 cups).

**Each serving: 200 mL (¾ cup)**

| 1 | ⊘ | Protein Choice | 7 g carbohydrate |
| ½ | ◪ | Fruits & Vegetables Choice | 7 g protein |
| 1 | ▲ | Fats & Oils Choice | 8 g fat |
| | | | 530 kilojoules (128 Calories) |

## VARIATION: CHICKEN TORTILLA SOUP

*Add 150 g (6 oz) cubed, cooked chicken (or lean meat) with celery and carrots.*

**Each serving: 225 mL (7/8 cup)**

| 2 | ⊘ | Protein Choices | 7 g carbohydrate |
| ½ | ◪ | Fruits & Vegetables Choice | 14 g protein |
| 1 | ▲ | Fats & Oils Choice | 11 g fat |
| | | | 760 kilojoules (183 Calories) |

### TOMATO BASIL SOUP

*Hot, herb-flavored tomato soup is an excellent starter for a meal featuring a substantial entrée like roast or steak. It will be superb if made in the late summer when fresh tomatoes are at their prime—juicy and plentiful.*

| | | |
|---|---|---|
| 5 mL | vegetable oil or butter | 1 tsp |
| 125 mL | chopped carrots | ½ cup |
| 75 mL | chopped leek (white part only) | 1/3 cup |
| 1 | large green onion, chopped | 1 |
| 1 | clove garlic, finely chopped | 1 |
| 1 can | 796 mL (28 oz) tomatoes or 6 medium, fresh tomatoes | 1 can |
| 1 L | chicken broth or water | 4 cups |
| 5 mL | salt | 1 tsp |
| 5 mL | ground basil | 1 tsp |
| 1 | bay leaf | 1 |
| pinch | each of thyme and freshly ground pepper | pinch |
| | Fresh parsley, chopped | |

Heat oil in large, heavy saucepan; add carrots, leek, onion and garlic. Sauté, stirring often, for 2 to 3 min. Add tomatoes, chicken broth, salt, basil, bay leaf, thyme and pepper; cover and simmer 30 min. Remove bay leaf. Purée soup in a blender or food processor, then strain it through a sieve. Ladle into soup bowls. Garnish with a sprinkling of chopped fresh parsley.

Makes 6 servings, 1.5 L (6 cups).

**Each serving: 250 mL (1 cup)**

1 ▰ Fruits & Vegetables Choice

8 g carbohydrate
2 g protein
1 g fat

210 kilojoules
(49 Calories)

---

*On facing page, from lower right*: Party Mix, Rhubarb Refresher, Crabmeat Spread with fresh vegetables, Slimmer's Shake, Cheese Puffs, Gouda Wafers with Cheese 'n' Chutney Spread.

## CHICKEN SOUP

*The flavors from the chicken, vegetables and herbs blend to make an excellent broth. Barley is added to make this a satisfying soup, perfect for a wintery day.*

| | | | | |
|---|---|---|---|---|
| 1.5 | kg | chicken, cut in pieces | 3 | lb |
| 2.25 | L | water | 9 | cups |
| 3 | | large stalks celery with leaves | 3 | |
| 1 | | small onion | 1 | |
| 125 | mL | chopped onion | ½ | cup |
| 125 | mL | finely chopped carrot | ½ | cup |
| 125 | mL | chopped fresh parsley | ½ | cup |
| 125 | mL | uncooked barley | ½ | cup |
| 25 | mL | fresh lemon juice | 2 | tbsp |
| 15 | mL | salt | 1 | tbsp |
| 2 | mL | freshly ground pepper | ½ | tsp |
| 1 | mL | celery seed | ¼ | tsp |
| 375 | mL | cut fresh green beans, 2.5 cm (1 in) pieces | 1½ | cups |

Place chicken, water, leaves from celery stalks and small onion in a large saucepan. (Reserve celery stalks.) Cover saucepan and bring to a boil; reduce heat and simmer 1.5 h until chicken is tender. Remove chicken. Strain broth into bowl; chill until fat sets on top, remove fat; return broth to saucepan. Remove skin and bones from chicken, discard. Cut chicken into bite-sized pieces, set aside. Chop reserved celery stalks, add to broth with chopped onion, carrot, parsley, barley, lemon juice, salt, pepper and celery seed. Cover and simmer 20 min. Add green beans and chicken; continue cooking 15 min or until beans are tender.

Makes 8 servings, 3 L (12 cups).

**Each serving: 375 mL (1½ cups)**

| | | |
|---|---|---|
| 2 | ⊘ | Protein Choices |
| 1 | ⊘ | Fruits & Vegetables Choice |

11 g carbohydrate
14 g protein
5 g fat

610 kilojoules
(145 Calories)

---

*On facing page, from lower right*: Sunburst Salad, Marinated Vegetable Medley, Orange and Sprout Salad, Variety Coleslaw.

## BEEF BROTH

*Basic broth is derived from the gentle simmering of good meat bones, vegetables and herbs. It is simple to make, but plenty of time must be allowed for the cooking. When you make your own broth you can control its saltiness. Actually, it is best to wait and add salt, if required, to the sauce, soup or stew being made with the broth.*

| | | |
|---|---|---|
| 1 kg | beef neck bones with meat | 2 lbs |
| 4 L | cold water | 16 cups |
| 2 | medium carrots, cut into 2 cm (¾ in) pieces | 2 |
| 1 | medium onion stuck with 3 cloves | 1 |
| 1 | leek, washed and chopped | 1 |
| 1 | stalk celery, chopped | 1 |
| 1 | clove garlic, chopped | 1 |
| 6 | sprigs fresh parsley or 15 mL (1 tbsp) dried parsley | 6 |
| 1 | large bay leaf | 1 |
| 1 mL | thyme | ¼ tsp |
| 750 mL | hot water | 3 cups |

Put neck bones in a deep, heavy saucepan. Cover with cold water. Bring to a boil. Reduce heat and simmer, skimming occasionally, about 1 h. Do not stir or the broth will cloud. Add carrots, onion, leek, celery, garlic, parsley, bay leaf, thyme and hot water. Bring to a boil, reduce heat and simmer 4 h. Strain into a clean container; discard bones, meat, vegetables and herbs. Chill broth until fat sets on the top; remove fat and discard. Cover and store in refrigerator up to 5 days or in freezer up to 3 months.

Makes 8 servings, 2 L (8 cups).

**Each serving: 250 mL (1 cup)**

1 **++** Extra                                          negligible food value

### VARIATION: BROWN BEEF BROTH

Place the bones in a roasting pan and allow them to roast uncovered in a 180°C (350°F) oven 20 min. Add the vegetables; allow them to brown 10 min. Place bones and vegetables in saucepan. Add about 125 mL (½ cup) cold water to roasting pan and scrape down any brown bits, then add to saucepan with the herbs and add 4 L (16 cups) water. Proceed to simmer for 4 h.

## FISH CHOWDER

*When we think of chowder, fish and seafood versions come to mind. It originates from the French word chaudière, meaning pot, and that is what chowder is—a one-pot stew that can also be made from meat and vegetables.*

| | | |
|---|---|---|
| 15 mL | butter | 1 tbsp |
| 250 mL | chopped onion | 1 cup |
| 125 mL | chopped celery | ½ cup |
| 375 mL | cubed raw potatoes | 1½ cups |
| 125 mL | coarsely chopped carrot | ½ cup |
| 500 mL | boiling water | 2 cups |
| 2 mL | summer savory or thyme | ½ tsp |
| 2 mL | salt | ½ tsp |
| 1 mL | freshly ground pepper | ¼ tsp |
| 500 g | fish fillets, fresh, smoked or frozen, partially thawed | 1 lb |
| 500 mL | 2% milk | 2 cups |

Melt butter in a heavy saucepan; add onion and celery; cook and stir 5 min or until tender-crisp. Add potatoes, carrot, water, savory, salt and pepper. Cover and simmer 20 min or until vegetables are tender. Cut fish into bite-sized pieces; add to vegetable mixture; simmer 10 min longer. Add milk. Heat just until mixture bubbles but *do not boil*. Ladle into hot soup bowls.

Makes 8 servings, 2 L (8 cups).

**Each serving: 250 mL (1 cup)**

2 🟢 Protein Choices
1 🟥 Fruits & Vegetables Choice

10 g carbohydrate
14 g protein
7 g fat

670 kilojoules
(159 Calories)

## CLAM CHOWDER

*Classic chowders are made with whole milk and cream. Not this one. It is a light and flavorful chowder made with 2% milk.*

| | | |
|---|---|---|
| 1 can | 142 g (5 oz) clams | 1 can |
| 250 mL | cubed potatoes (1 cm/½ in cubes) | 1 cup |
| 125 mL | chopped celery | ½ cup |
| 50 mL | chopped onion | ¼ cup |
| 2 mL | salt | ½ tsp |
| 1 mL | white pepper | ¼ tsp |
| 1 L | 2% milk | 4 cups |

| | | | |
|---|---|---|---|
| 15 mL | margarine or butter | 1 | tbsp |
| 25 mL | instant skim milk powder | 2 | tbsp |

Combine clams, clam liquid, potatoes, celery, onion, salt, pepper, milk, margarine and skim milk powder in a large, heavy saucepan. Stir until well mixed. Cook on low heat just until mixture bubbles. Then reduce heat and simmer but *do not boil* about 20 min, stirring occasionally, until potatoes are tender.

Makes 7 servings, 1.75 L (7 cups).

**Each serving: 250 mL (1 cup)**

2 ◆ Milk Choices (2%)

12 g carbohydrate
9 g protein
5 g fat

540 kilojoules
(129 Calories)

### CHICKEN BROTH

*Pale broths or stocks are made from chicken, veal, lamb or fish bones. They are all made exactly the same way as beef broth, and they are best if the bones are raw and not browned.*

| | | | |
|---|---|---|---|
| 1 kg | chicken backs and necks | 2 | lbs |
| 2.5 L | water | 10 | cups |
| 2 | stalks celery, chopped | 2 | |
| 1 | medium cooking onion, sliced | 1 | |
| 1 | carrot, sliced | 1 | |
| 1 | bay leaf | 1 | |
| 1 | whole clove garlic | 1 | |
| 8 | peppercorns | 8 | |
| 2 mL | salt | ½ | tsp |
| 2 mL | each of basil and thyme | ½ | tsp |

Rinse chicken parts under cold water. Place in a large saucepan and cover with water. Add celery, onion, carrot, bay leaf, garlic, peppercorns, salt, basil and thyme. Bring to a boil, reduce heat and simmer 2 to 2.5 h, skimming off foam occasionally. Strain into a clean container; discard seasonings. Chill broth until fat sets on the top; remove fat. Cover and store in refrigerator up to 5 days or in the freezer up to 3 months.

Makes 7 servings, 1.75 L (7 cups).

**Each serving: 250 mL (1 cup)**

1 ++ Extra                                           negligible food value

## PEA SOUP—NEWFOUNDLAND-STYLE

*Hearty Pea Soup offers an economical and satisfying way to round out a light meal or even to act as the meal itself. A ham bone with a little ham clinging to it can be substituted for the salt pork.*

| | | |
|---|---|---|
| 500 mL | dried split peas | **2 cups** |
| | Water | |
| 250 mL | lean salt pork, cut into small pieces | **1 cup** |
| 500 mL | chopped turnip | **2 cups** |
| 250 mL | chopped carrot | **1 cup** |
| 125 mL | chopped potato | **½ cup** |
| 125 mL | chopped onion | **½ cup** |
| 75 mL | chopped celery leaves | **1/3 cup** |
| 5 mL | salt | **1 tsp** |
| 1 mL | freshly ground pepper | **¼ tsp** |

Combine peas and 2.5 L (10 cups) water in a large saucepan. Bring to a rapid boil; boil 2 min; turn off heat and let stand 1 h. Place salt pork in sieve; rinse well under cold running water. Place in another saucepan with 500 mL (2 cups) water. Cover, bring to a boil; reduce heat and simmer 30 min. Strain off liquid into a bowl; chill until fat sets on top, remove fat; add liquid to peas. Trim off and discard fat from salt pork; add lean pieces to peas. Add turnip, carrot, potato, onion, celery leaves, salt and pepper. Bring to a boil, reduce heat and simmer 1.5 h until vegetables are tender. Purée soup if a smooth texture is desired.

Makes 10 servings, 2.5 L (10 cups).

**Each serving: 250 mL (1 cup)**

1 **⊘** Protein Choice
2 **☐** Starchy Choices

30 g carbohydrate
12 g protein
1 g fat

750 kilojoules
(177 Calories)

# Salads

Just what is a salad? It is usually a medley of raw vegetables, or fruits and vegetables, or vegetables and meat, fish or beans dressed with oil and vinegar and seasonings. A salad is lovely to look at and makes a nutritional contribution to any meal. It can be simply a leafy green side dish, an attractive course in a meal or a substantial meal in itself.

Crisp, tart salads served up in small portions make superb appetizers. Delicately dressed and crisply green, they make wonderful accompaniments to meats and main courses. They become the main course itself when made with meats, poultry, seafood or beans. A fruit salad can easily double as an appetizer or as a dessert.

Tossed, molded, hot, cold, tart or sweet, you will find them all in our collection. Choose salads that will add flavor and provide color and texture contrasts to your meal. Many include high protein foods to bolster diets.

We have also included a collection of classic salad dressing recipes that go easy on the sugar and oil. Low fat, 2% cottage cheese and yogurt are used for creaminess in some dressings because they are lower in energy than richer creams and dressings.

## ORANGE AND SPROUT SALAD

*Cool, crunchy bean sprouts combine with tangy orange for a scrumptious salad that could star as an appetizer.*

| | | |
|---|---|---|
| 500 mL | lettuce, torn into pieces | 2 cups |
| 250 mL | fresh bean sprouts, washed and patted dry | 1 cup |
| 2 | small oranges, peeled and sectioned | 2 |
| 2 | stalks celery, sliced | 2 |
| 25 mL | toasted slivered almonds | 2 tbsp |

**Dressing:**

| | | |
|---|---|---|
| 25 mL | orange juice | 2 tbsp |
| 15 mL | cider vinegar | 1 tbsp |
| 15 mL | vegetable oil | 1 tbsp |
| 2 mL | celery seed | ½ tsp |
| 1 mL | salt | ¼ tsp |
| | Liquid Artificial Sweetener equivalent to 15 mL (1 tbsp) sugar | |

Combine lettuce, bean sprouts, oranges, celery and almonds in a salad bowl. Make dressing by combining orange juice, vinegar, oil, celery seed, salt and artificial sweetener in a small jar. Cover and shake until well mixed. Pour over salad; toss well.

Makes 4 servings.

**Each serving: about 250 mL (1 cup)**

| | |
|---|---|
| 1 ◨ Fruits & Vegetables Choice | 10 g carbohydrate |
| 1 ▲ Fats & Oils Choice | 2 g protein |
| | 6 g fat |
| | 430 kilojoules (102 Calories) |

**Nuts are a source of protein, but they also contain a large amount of hidden fat.**

## MOLDED CRANBERRY SALAD

*Ruby red cranberries make this mold look like a salad jewel on the holiday table. It is a gem served not only with roast turkey but also with ham, pork and chicken.*

| | | | |
|---|---|---|---|
| 1 packet | unflavored gelatin | 1 packet | |
| 500 mL | sugar-free ginger ale | 2 cups | |
| 500 mL | cranberries, coarsely chopped | 2 cups | |
| 15 mL | fresh lemon juice | 1 tbsp | |
| 10 mL | grated orange peel | 2 tsp | |
| | Artificial sweetener equivalent to 25 mL (5 tsp) sugar (5 aspartame tablets) | | |
| 125 mL | finely chopped celery | ½ cup | |
| ½ | medium apple, chopped | ½ | |

Sprinkle gelatin over 50 mL (¼ cup) ginger ale; let stand 5 min to soften. Combine remaining ginger ale, cranberries, lemon juice and orange peel in a saucepan. Bring quickly to a boil. Remove from heat. Add softened gelatin and sweetener; stir until gelatin dissolves. Chill until partially set. Stir in celery and apple. Spoon into a rinsed 1.5-L (6-cup) mold. Refrigerate at least 4 h until set.

Makes 6 servings.

**Each serving: about 125 mL (½ cup)**

½ 🍎 Fruits & Vegetables Choice

6 g carbohydrate
1 g protein

120 kilojoules
(28 Calories)

## JELLIED BEET MOLD

*Beets add life to meals that might otherwise be colorless. They are refreshing as well in an icy-cold molded salad such as this one.*

| | | | |
|---|---|---|---|
| 1 can | 398 mL (14 oz) diced beets | 1 can | |
| 200 mL | unsweetened orange juice | ¾ cup | |
| 10 mL | vinegar | 2 tsp | |
| 1 packet | unflavored gelatin | 1 packet | |
| 250 mL | shredded zucchini | 1 cup | |
| 125 mL | finely chopped celery | ½ cup | |

Drain liquid from beets into a small saucepan; reserve beets for later. Stir in orange juice and vinegar. Sprinkle gelatin over top; let stand 5 min to soften. Stir over medium heat just until all granules are dissolved. Pour into bowl; cool. Refrigerate until partially set. Spread shredded zucchini and celery on paper towels and blot out excess moisture. Fold reserved beets, zucchini and celery into gelatin mixture. Rinse a 1 L (4 cup) mold with cold water. Spoon gelatin mixture into mold. Refrigerate at least 4 h until set.

Makes 6 servings.

**Each serving: about 125 mL (½ cup)**

1 ◨ Fruits & Vegetables Choice

8 g carbohydrate
2 g protein

170 kilojoules
(40 Calories)

## SALAD ROYALE

*What a colorful, tasty salad! It accents the true colors and best flavors of other foods. The combination of canned beets and pineapple makes a wonderful winter salad.*

| 1 | can | 398 mL (14 oz) diced beets | 1 | can |
| 200 | mL | unsweetened grape juice | ¾ | cup |
| 10 | mL | fresh lemon juice | 2 | tsp |
| 1 | packet | unflavored gelatin | 1 | packet |
| 1 | can | 398 mL (14 oz) unsweetened, crushed pineapple, drained | 1 | can |
| 5 | mL | horseradish | 1 | tsp |
| | pinch | cinnamon | | pinch |

Drain liquid from beets into a small saucepan, reserve beets for later. Add grape and lemon juice to beet juice. Sprinkle gelatin over top; let stand 5 min to soften. Stir over medium heat just until all granules dissolve. Refrigerate until partially set. Fold in reserved diced beets, crushed pineapple, horseradish and cinnamon. Rinse a 1 L (4 cup) jelly mold with cold water. Spoon gelatin mixture into mold. Refrigerate at least 4 h until set.

Makes 8 servings.

**Each serving: about 75 mL (1/3 cup)**

1 ◨ Fruits & Vegetables Choice

10 g carbohydrate
1 g protein

190 kilojoules
(44 Calories)

## FESTIVAL FRUIT SALAD

*Jellied fruit is sure to rate tops with the kids. Serve it as a salad or a dessert. It turns into an elegant-looking dessert treat for adults too by spooning it into six parfait glasses to set.*

| | | | |
|---|---|---|---|
| 625 | mL | sugar-free carbonated orange beverage | 2½ cups |
| 2 | packets | unflavored gelatin | 2 packets |
| 25 | mL | fresh lemon juice | 2 tbsp |
| 2 | mL | almond flavoring | ½ tsp |
| 125 | mL | plain yogurt | ½ cup |
| 1 | | small orange, peeled and sectioned | 1 |
| ½ | | banana, peeled and sliced | ½ |
| 125 | mL | red grapes, halved and seeded | ½ cup |
| 125 | mL | seedless green grapes, halved | ½ cup |
| 75 | mL | drained, unsweetened pineapple chunks | 1/3 cup |

Sprinkle gelatin over 50 mL (¼ cup) orange beverage; let stand 5 min to soften. Combine remaining orange beverage with lemon juice in saucepan. Bring to a boil. Remove from heat; add softened gelatin and almond flavoring; stir until gelatin dissolves. Chill until partially set. Stir in yogurt. Fold in orange, banana, grapes and pineapple. Rinse a 1.5 L (8 x 4 in) loaf pan with cold water. Spoon gelatin mixture into pan. Refrigerate at least 4 h until set. Unmold and cut into 4 cm (1½ in) slices to serve.

Makes 6 generous servings.

**Each serving: about 175 mL (2/3 cup)**

1 ▨ Fruits & Vegetables Choice

10 g carbohydrate
3 g protein

220 kilojoules
(52 Calories)

## SUNBURST SALAD

*Bright, cheery salads add color and texture to meals any time of the year. Vary the flavor of this colorful mold by adding chopped green pepper or chopped green onion.*

| | | | |
|---|---|---|---|
| 1 | packet | unflavored gelatin | 1 packet |
| 50 | mL | cold water | ¼ cup |
| 125 | mL | boiling water | ½ cup |

| 250 mL | sugar-free ginger ale | 1 cup |
| 50 mL | unsweetened orange juice | ¼ cup |
| 2 mL | ground ginger | ¼ tsp |
| 2 | small oranges, peeled and sectioned | 2 |
| 250 mL | finely shredded cabbage | 1 cup |
| 125 mL | grated carrot | ½ cup |
| 50 mL | chopped pecans or walnuts | ¼ cup |

Sprinkle gelatin over cold water; let stand 5 min to soften. Add boiling water and stir to dissolve. Stir in ginger ale, orange juice and ginger. Chill until partially set. Stir in orange sections, cabbage, carrot and nuts. Rinse a 1 L (4 cup) mold with cold water. Spoon gelatin mixture into mold. Refrigerate at least 4 h until set.

Makes 4 servings.

**Each serving: about 175 mL (2/3 cup)**

1 ◨ Fruits & Vegetables Choice
1 ▲ Fats & Oils Choice

10 g carbohydrate
3 g protein
5 g fat

410 kilojoules
(97 Calories)

## MARINATED CUCUMBERS

*Few salads are as easy to make as this low-energy relish salad. Remember to drain the cucumbers well before serving with fish, chicken or cold meats.*

| 1 | medium cucumber | 1 |
| 125 mL | *Herb Dressing* (recipe, p.88) | ½ cup |

Cut cucumber into thin slices. Layer in bowl with drizzles of *Herb Dressing*. Refrigerate overnight. Drain to serve.

Makes 4 servings.

**Each serving: ¼ recipe**

1 ++ Extra

2 g carbohydrate

30 kilojoules
(8 Calories)

## CUCUMBER LIME MOLD

*Cool as a cucumber describes this creamy mold spiked with a tang of lime. It is a great accompaniment for hot or cold fish, chicken, pork or ham.*

| | | | |
|---|---|---|---|
| 250 | mL | water | 1 **cup** |
| 15 | mL | fresh lime juice | 1 **tbsp** |
| 15 | mL | vinegar | 1 **tbsp** |
| 1 | **packet** | unflavored gelatin | 1 **packet** |
| 250 | mL | 2% cottage cheese | 1 **cup** |
| 2 | mL | salt | ½ **tsp** |
| 2 | mL | Worcestershire sauce | ½ **tsp** |
| 2 | **drops** | hot pepper sauce | 2 **drops** |
| 375 | mL | coarsely shredded, unpeeled, seeded cucumber (1 large) | 1½ **cups** |
| 10 | mL | finely grated onion | 2 **tsp** |

Combine water, lime juice and vinegar in saucepan. Sprinkle gelatin over top; let stand 5 min to soften. Stir over medium heat just until all granules dissolve. Pour into medium bowl. Combine cottage cheese, salt, Worcestershire sauce and hot pepper sauce in container of blender or food processor; process until smooth. Stir into gelatin mixture. Refrigerate until partially set. Press cucumber between paper towels to remove any excess moisture. Fold cucumber and onion into gelatin mixture. Rinse a 1 L (4 cup) mold with cold water. Spoon gelatin mixture into mold. Refrigerate at least 4 h until set.

Makes 6 servings.

**Each serving: about 75 mL (1/3 cup)**

1 **⊘** Protein Choice

3 g carbohydrate
7 g protein
1 g fat

210 kilojoules
(49 Calories)

## CUCUMBER AND FRUIT SALAD

*Cucumber, apples and cantaloupe team up in a super-slim, sprightly salad. It is refreshing as the starter for a meal or as a side salad with the main course.*

| | | |
|---|---|---|
| 1 | large English cucumber | 1 |
| 2 | medium red apples | 2 |
| 1 | small cantaloupe or honey dew | 1 |
| 50 mL | plain yogurt | ¼ **cup** |

| 25 mL | fresh lime or lemon juice | 2 tbsp |
| 2 mL | dried mint or 5 mL (1 tsp) chopped fresh mint | ½ tsp |
|  | Lettuce or spinach leaves |  |
| 15 mL | sunflower seeds | 1 tbsp |

Wash cucumber, core apples, peel and seed cantaloupe. Cut all into bite-sized pieces and place in salad bowl. Stir or whisk together yogurt, lime juice and mint. Pour over cucumber mixture; toss well. Serve on lettuce or spinach leaves. Sprinkle with sunflower seeds.

Makes 8 servings.

**Each serving: about 125 mL (½ cup)**

1 � Fruits & Vegetables Choice

10 g carbohydrate
1 g protein
1 g fat

220 kilojoules
(53 Calories)

## MUSHROOM SALAD

*Slices from fresh firm mushrooms add distinction to this tossed salad.*

| 1 | medium head romaine lettuce | 1 |
| 250 mL | fresh mushroom slices | 1 cup |
| ½ | medium English cucumber, chopped | ½ |
| 50 mL | *Thousand Island Dressing* (recipe, p.91) | ¼ cup |
| 50 mL | sunflower or pumpkin seeds | ¼ cup |

Wash lettuce leaves; pat dry with paper towels. Tear into bite-sized pieces; place in salad bowl. Add mushrooms, cucumber and dressing; toss to mix well. Sprinkle with sunflower seeds.

Makes 6 servings.

**Each serving: about 250 mL (1 cup)**

½ � Fruits & Vegetables Choice
½ ▲ Fats & Oils Choice

5 g carbohydrate
2 g protein
3 g fat

230 kilojoules
(55 Calories)

## CAESAR SALAD

*The amounts of garlic, mustard and Worcestershire sauce can be increased for those who like a more highly seasoned salad. We've kept ours on the mild side.*

| | | | |
|---|---|---|---|
| 1 | large bunch romaine lettuce | 1 | |
| 1 | clove garlic, finely chopped | 1 | |
| 2 mL | salt | ½ | tsp |
| 1 mL | dry mustard | ¼ | tsp |
| 25 mL | olive or vegetable oil | 2 | tbsp |
| 25 mL | fresh lemon juice | 2 | tbsp |
| 5 mL | Worcestershire sauce | 1 | tsp |
| 1 | egg yolk | 1 | |
| 3 | anchovy fillets, chopped, optional | 3 | |
| 250 mL | toasted bread cubes | 1 | cup |
| 4 | slices side bacon, crisply cooked and crumbled | 4 | |
| 15 mL | grated Parmesan cheese | 1 | tbsp |

Wash romaine lettuce, pat dry and chill. Combine garlic, salt, mustard, oil, lemon juice, Worcestershire sauce, egg yolk and anchovy fillets, if desired, in a large salad bowl. Mix well with a fork. Tear romaine into bite-sized pieces and place in bowl. Add bread cubes, bacon and Parmesan cheese; toss well.

Makes 6 servings.

**Each serving: about 250 mL (1 cup)**

½ ☐ Starchy Choice
2 ▲ Fats & Oils Choices

7 g carbohydrate
4 g protein
9 g fat

520 kilojoules
(125 Calories)

## SPINACH SALAD

*Most supermarkets have packages of spinach leaves available throughout the year. It is a nice change from lettuce. Make and refrigerate this salad 4 to 6 hours before serving. This allows flavors to mellow.*

| ½ **pkg** | fresh spinach, or small bunch | ½ **pkg** |
|---|---|---|
| 1 | large mild onion, cut into rings | 1 |
| 1 | large orange | 1 |
| | Orange juice | |
| 10 **mL** | vegetable oil | 2 **tsp** |
| 1 | clove garlic, finely chopped | 1 |
| 2 **mL** | salt | ½ **tsp** |
| 1 **mL** | freshly ground pepper | ¼ **tsp** |

Wash spinach, remove tough stems and discard; pat leaves dry; tear into pieces and place in salad bowl. Add onion rings. Peel orange and remove sections with knife. Cut each section in half; add to spinach. Squeeze juice from remaining orange membrane into a measure; pour in enough additional orange juice to make 50 mL (¼ cup). Add oil, garlic, salt and pepper to orange juice; stir well. Pour over spinach mixture; toss to mix well. Cover and refrigerate several hours.

Makes 4 servings.

**Each serving: about 375 mL (1½ cups)**

1 🟦 Fruits & Vegetables Choice
½ 🔺 Fats & Oils Choice

10 g carbohydrate
2 g protein
3 g fat

320 kilojoules
(75 Calories)

## CRUNCHY LAYERED SALAD

*A thin coating of dressing spread over this salad keeps the air out, allowing the lettuce and vegetables to remain crisp and fresh during the long chilling. So our layered salad is a great one to make when company is coming.*

| | | |
|---|---|---|
| **1.5 L** | coarsely shredded lettuce | **6 cups** |
| **1** | medium red onion, chopped | **1** |
| **250 mL** | chopped green or red sweet pepper | **1 cup** |
| **250 mL** | chopped celery | **1 cup** |
| **250 mL** | frozen peas, uncooked | **1 cup** |
| **250 mL** | *Tangy Boiled Dressing* (recipe, p.89) | **1 cup** |
| **3** | slices bacon, crisply cooked and crumbled | **3** |
| **250 mL** | shredded Cheddar cheese | **1 cup** |

Place lettuce in an even layer in a 23 cm (9 inch) square glass dish or salad bowl. Add layers of onion, green pepper, celery and peas. Spoon dressing over top layer; spread to all edges of dish. Sprinkle with bacon and cheese. Cover with plastic wrap. Refrigerate at least 6 h. (Will keep up to 3 days in refrigerator if not mixed.) To serve, cut into squares.

Makes 9 servings.

**Each serving: about 7.5 cm (3 in) square**

| | | |
|---|---|---|
| 1 | ⬛ Protein Choice | 6 g carbohydrate |
| ½ | ⬛ Fruits & Vegetables Choice | 7 g protein |
| ½ | ⬛ Fats & Oils Choice | 6 g fat |

440 kilojoules
(106 Calories)

## VARIETY COLESLAW

*For generations cabbage has been used for economical, crisp salads with a pleasing sweet taste. Shred it for best results. The addition of chopped red apple, pineapple chunks or a few raisins transforms a basic coleslaw into a special occasion salad.*

| 500 mL | shredded cabbage | 2 cups |
|---|---|---|
| 1 | medium carrot, finely chopped | 1 |
| 25 mL | chopped green pepper | 2 tbsp |
| 50 mL | *Tangy Boiled Dressing* (recipe, p.89) | ¼ cup |
| 25 mL | plain yogurt | 2 tbsp |

**Choice of One:**

| ½ | apple, chopped, or | ½ |
|---|---|---|
| 75 mL | drained, unsweetened pineapple chunks, or | 1/3 cup |
| 25 mL | raisins | 2 tbsp |

Combine cabbage, carrot and green pepper in a bowl. Combine *Tangy Boiled Dressing* with yogurt. Add apple, or pineapple, or raisins to cabbage mixture. Pour on dressing and mix gently.

Makes 4 servings.

**Each serving: about 125 mL (½ cup)**

1 ◼ Fruits & Vegetables Choice

8 g carbohydrate
2 g protein
1 g fat

210 kilojoules
(49 Calories)

> **Most jellied salads call for the gelatin mixture to be partially set before ingredients are mixed into it. Gelatin in this state is syrupy-thick, like the consistency of unbeaten egg white.**

## MARINATED VEGETABLE MEDLEY

*In this relish salad, the marinating gives the garden vegetables a lightly pickled taste. The longer the vegetables are left in the refrigerator the better the flavor will be.*

| | | | |
|---|---|---|---|
| 50 mL | vinegar | ¼ | cup |
| 15 mL | vegetable oil | 1 | tbsp |
| 5 mL | onion salt | 1 | tsp |
| 2 mL | freshly ground pepper | ½ | tsp |
| 250 mL | cauliflower flowerettes | 1 | cup |
| 250 mL | broccoli flowerettes | 1 | cup |
| 250 mL | celery slices | 1 | cup |
| 1 | medium carrot, sliced | 1 | |
| ½ | cucumber, sliced | ½ | |
| 1 | firm medium tomato, cut into 8 wedges | 1 | |

Combine vinegar, oil, onion salt and pepper in a screw-top container; cover and shake until well mixed. Combine cauliflower, broccoli, celery, carrot and cucumber in a large bowl. Pour oil mixture over vegetables; toss until well coated. Cover and refrigerate at least 3 h or up to 3 days to marinate. Add tomato wedges just before serving.

Makes 6 servings.

**Each serving: about 175 mL (2/3 cup)**

½ ◨ Fruits & Vegetables Choice
½ ▲ Fats & Oils Choice

5 g carbohydrate
2 g protein
2 g fat

190 kilojoules
(46 Calories)

## CELERY VICTOR

*Celery simmered in a broth redolent of lemon and herbs makes a distinctive salad after it is chilled. It makes the taste buds tingle when served either as an appetizer or a side salad.*

| 6 | celery hearts or 24, 10 cm (4 in) celery stalks | 6 |
|---|---|---|
| 125 mL | wine vinegar | ½ cup |
| 125 mL | water | ½ cup |
| 15 mL | fresh lemon juice | 1 tbsp |
| 10 mL | dried parsley | 2 tsp |
| 5 mL | oregano | 1 tsp |
| 2 mL | thyme | ½ tsp |
| 1 | bay leaf | 1 |
| 2 mL | salt | ½ tsp |
| 1 mL | freshly ground pepper | ¼ tsp |
| pinch | cayenne | pinch |
| | Lettuce leaves | |
| 25 mL | capers | 2 tbsp |
| 25 mL | chopped pimento | 2 tbsp |

Wash and cut celery hearts in half lengthwise. Cook in lightly salted water about 7 min until tender crisp. Add vinegar, water, lemon juice, parsley, oregano, thyme, bay leaf, salt, pepper and cayenne. Simmer 4 min longer. Allow to cool in liquid. Remove from liquid, drain well, place each piece on a lettuce leaf. Sprinkle each serving with capers and pimento.

Makes 6 servings.

**Each serving: ½ celery heart or 4 stalks**

1 **++** Extra

3 g carbohydrate

50 kilojoules
(12 Calories)

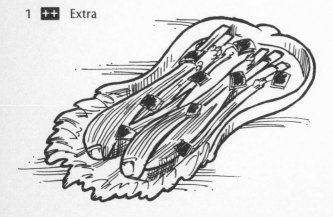

## POTATO SALAD

*Allow time for the flavors to blend and develop in this salad popular for picnics and other casual occasions. Garnish it with sliced red radishes when in season.*

| | | |
|---|---|---|
| 2 | medium potatoes | 2 |
| 1 | bay leaf | 1 |
| 50 mL | chopped onion | ¼ cup |
| 25 mL | chopped celery | 2 tbsp |
| 50 mL | *Tangy Boiled Dressing* (recipe, p.89) | ¼ cup |
| 2 mL | prepared mustard | ½ tsp |
| 1 mL | celery seed | ¼ tsp |
| | Salt and freshly ground pepper | |

Wash potatoes. Place in a saucepan with bay leaf; cover with water. Cook over medium heat until tender. Drain, cool 5 min. Peel potatoes and cut into small pieces. Combine potatoes, onion and celery in a bowl. Mix together dressing, mustard and celery seed. Pour over potato mixture; mix gently. Season to taste with salt and pepper. Refrigerate at least 2 h before serving.

Makes 500 mL (2 cups).

**Each serving: about 125 mL (½ cup)**

1 ☐ Starchy Choice

16 g carbohydrate
3 g protein
1 g fat

360 kilojoules
(85 Calories)

## GARBANZO GARDEN GREEN SALAD

*Garbanzo beans are often called chick peas. Actually they are creamy yellow beans with a nutlike taste that goes well with crisp vegetables. You will find them dried and in cans at the supermarket.*

| | | | |
|---|---|---|---|
| 500 | mL | shredded lettuce | 2 cups |
| 300 | mL | drained, canned or cooked garbanzo beans | 1¼ cups |
| 125 | mL | sliced celery | ½ cup |
| 50 | mL | chopped green pepper | ¼ cup |
| 50 | mL | mild onion, chopped | ¼ cup |
| 25 | mL | chopped parsley | 2 tbsp |
| 25 | mL | fresh lemon juice | 2 tbsp |
| 10 | mL | vegetable oil | 2 tsp |
| | pinch | garlic powder | pinch |
| | | Salt and freshly ground pepper | |

Combine lettuce, garbanzo beans, celery, green pepper and onion in a salad bowl. Mix together parsley, lemon juice, vegetable oil and garlic powder. Pour over salad; toss. Season to taste with salt and pepper.

Makes 4 servings.

**Each serving: about 200 mL (¾ cup)**

½ ⊘ Protein Choice

1 ☐ Starchy Choice

½ ▲ Fats & Oils Choice

15 g carbohydrate

5 g protein

4 g fat

490 kilojoules
(116 Calories)

> **Most dark green leafy and yellow fruits and vegetables are good sources of Vitamin A: apricots, broccoli, cantaloupe, carrots, nectarines, peaches, spinach and squash.**

## FOUR BEAN SALAD

*Men tend to like this hearty salad. It is best if made at least a day before serving to allow the flavors to blend.*

| | | | |
|---|---|---|---|
| 1 | can | 398 mL (14 oz) cut green beans | 1 can |
| 1 | can | 398 mL (14 oz) cut wax beans | 1 can |
| 1 | can | 398 mL (14 oz) red kidney beans | 1 can |
| 1 | can | 284 mL (10 oz) lima beans | 1 can |
| 125 | mL | thinly sliced mild onion | ½ cup |
| 250 | mL | chopped celery | 1 cup |
| 75 | mL | chopped green pepper | 1/3 cup |

**Dressing:**

| | | | |
|---|---|---|---|
| 125 | mL | vegetable oil | ½ cup |
| 50 | mL | white vinegar | ¼ cup |
| 10 | mL | sugar | 2 tsp |
| 5 | mL | each of salt, dry mustard and thyme | 1 tsp |
| 1 | mL | freshly ground pepper | ¼ tsp |
| | pinch | garlic powder | pinch |

Drain green, wax, kidney and lima beans; combine in a large bowl. Add onion, celery and green pepper; mix gently. Whisk or shake together vegetable oil, vinegar, sugar, salt, mustard, thyme, pepper and garlic powder. Pour over bean mixture. Toss to mix well. Cover and refrigerate (stirring occasionally) at least 1 day before serving. Drain off excess juice before serving.

Makes 8 servings.

**Each serving: about 125 mL (½ cup)**

½ ⊘ Protein Choice
1 ☐ Starchy Choice
½ ▲ Fats & Oils Choice

17 g carbohydrate
6 g protein
5 g fat

580 kilojoules
(137 Calories)

## CRUNCHY TUNA SALAD IN PEPPER CUPS

*Each serving of this main course salad sits in its own cup, so it is easy to serve on a luncheon or party plate. Waist-watchers will love it because it is a low fat and low energy dish.*

| | | |
|---|---|---|
| 1 packet | unflavored gelatin | 1 packet |
| 125 mL | water | ½ cup |
| 1 can | 284 mL (10 oz) condensed consommé, undiluted | 1 can |
| 2 | large, nicely shaped green peppers | 2 |
| 125 mL | coarsely chopped onion | ½ cup |
| 1 can | 198 g (7 oz) flaked tuna, drained | 1 can |
| 2 | medium tomatoes, peeled, seeded and chopped | 2 |
| 250 mL | coarsely chopped iceberg lettuce | 1 cup |
| 2 mL | grated lemon peel | ½ tsp |
| 15 mL | fresh lemon juice | 1 tbsp |
| 2 mL | salt | ½ tsp |
| pinch | freshly ground black pepper | pinch |
| 4 | crisp lettuce leaves | 4 |
| 50 mL | commercial sour cream | ¼ cup |

Sprinkle gelatin over water to soften; let stand 5 min. Pour consommé into medium saucepan. Cut peppers in half crosswise to form shells; remove core and seeds carefully. Bring consommé to boil; add pepper shells cut side up. Cover and boil 3 min. Remove shells; turn upside down to drain, then refrigerate. Bring consommé back to boiling; add onion and boil 30 seconds. Stir in gelatin until it dissolves. Pour into a bowl. Refrigerate until partially set. Fold in tuna, tomatoes, chopped lettuce, lemon peel, lemon juice, salt and pepper. Spoon into pepper shells, piling high. Refrigerate at least 4 h until set. Place each pepper on a lettuce leaf at serving time. Garnish with a dollop of sour cream.

Makes 4 servings.

**Each serving: ½ green pepper, filled**

2½ 🖊 Protein Choices
1 🖊 Fruits & Vegetables Choice

9 g carbohydrate
20 g protein
5 g fat

680 kilojoules
(161 Calories)

## TUNA OR SALMON SALAD

*Here is a salad that makes a great sandwich when teamed with whole wheat bread. Present it with fresh tomato wedges and cucumber rings and warm-from-the-oven whole wheat biscuits for a light luncheon or supper.*

| | | |
|---|---|---|
| 1 can | 198 g (7 oz) chunk tuna or 220 g (7¾ oz) salmon, drained | 1 can |
| 75 mL | 2% cottage cheese | 1/3 cup |
| 125 mL | finely chopped celery | ½ cup |
| 50 mL | finely chopped onion | ¼ cup |
| 25 mL | *Tangy Boiled Dressing* (recipe, p.89) | 2 tbsp |
| 25 mL | finely chopped fresh parsley | 2 tbsp |
| 2 mL | grated lemon peel | ½ tsp |
| 1 mL | tarragon, optional | ¼ tsp |

Mash together tuna and cottage cheese with a fork. Add celery, onion, dressing, parsley, lemon peel and tarragon, if desired. Mix until well blended.

Makes about 400 mL (1-2/3 cups).

**Each serving: 100 mL (6 tbsp)**

2 ⊘ Protein Choices

2 g carbohydrate
16 g protein
4 g fat

450 kilojoules
(108 Calories)

## HERB DRESSING

*You can shake up a jar of this dressing in 5 minutes from start to finish. It is one of the most versatile dressings to have on hand to toss with greens, or to drizzle over hot or cold asparagus spears and any chilled, crisply cooked vegetables.*

| | | |
|---|---|---|
| 375 mL | buttermilk | 1½ cups |
| 15 mL | chopped fresh parsley | 1 tbsp |
| 15 mL | finely chopped onion | 1 tbsp |
| 2 mL | each of garlic powder, thyme, tarragon and salt | ½ tsp |
| 1 mL | freshly ground pepper | ¼ tsp |
| 5 mL | vinegar | 1 tsp |
| 1 mL | Worcestershire sauce | ¼ tsp |

Pour buttermilk into a screw-top jar. Add parsley, onion, garlic powder, thyme, tarragon, salt and pepper. Close jar tightly and shake briskly. Add vinegar and Worcestershire sauce and shake again. Refrigerate for about 2 h to allow flavors to mingle. Shake well before serving. Store, covered, in the refrigerator up to 4 weeks.

Makes 12 servings, 375 mL (1½ cups).

**Each serving: 25 mL (2 tbsp)**

1 ++ Extra

2 g carbohydrate
1 g protein

50 kilojoules
(12 Calories)

### TANGY BOILED DRESSING

*Make this creamy smooth salad dressing to have on hand to add variety to your salad creations. It is a tasty as well as economical substitute for store-bought dressings.*

| 500 | mL | water | 2 | cups |
|---|---|---|---|---|
| 250 | mL | cider vinegar | 1 | cup |
| 3 | | eggs | 3 | |
| 50 | mL | all purpose flour | ¼ | cup |
| 15 | mL | dry mustard | 1 | tbsp |
| 5 | mL | salt | 1 | tsp |
| 1 | mL | freshly ground pepper | ¼ | tsp |
| 25 | mL | margarine or butter | 2 | tbsp |
| | | Artificial sweetener equivalent to 125 mL (½ cup) sugar | | |

Beat or whisk together water, vinegar, eggs, flour, mustard, salt and pepper in a heavy saucepan. Cook over medium heat, stirring constantly, about 6 min until smooth and thickened. Stir in margarine and artificial sweetener. Whisk until smooth. Pour into clean jars. Store, covered, in the refrigerator up to 3 months.

Makes 875 mL (3½ cups) boiled dressing.

**Each serving: 25 mL (2 tbsp)**

1 ++ Extra

1 g carbohydrate
1 g protein
1 g fat

70 kilojoules
(17 Calories)

## ITALIAN DRESSING—SLIM 'N' TRIM

*This dressing may gel in the refrigerator. If it does, add a few drops of boiling water and shake or whisk to liquefy. It is refreshing served on crisp greens.*

| | | | |
|---|---|---|---|
| 75 | mL | homemade or canned chicken broth | 1/3 cup |
| 15 | mL | vegetable oil | 1 tbsp |
| 15 | mL | hot water | 1 tbsp |
| 15 | mL | fresh lemon juice | 1 tbsp |
| 15 | mL | cider or wine vinegar | 1 tbsp |
| 1 | | small clove garlic, peeled | 1 |
| | pinch | each of salt, freshly ground pepper, curry, thyme, oregano and parsley | pinch |

Place broth, oil, water, lemon juice, vinegar, garlic, salt, pepper, curry, thyme, oregano and parsley in a screw-top jar or bowl. Shake or whisk to blend ingredients. Refrigerate at least 30 min. Remove garlic. Shake or whisk again before using.

Makes 8 servings, about 125 mL (½ cup).

**Each serving: 15 mL (1 tbsp)**

1 **++** Extra

2 g fat

70 kilojoules
(18 Calories)

---

Children prefer raw vegetables to cooked ones: for example, raw beans, broccoli, cauliflower, carrots, turnips and zucchini. Keep an assortment of washed raw vegetables in a covered container in the refrigerator. Children will reach for them in preference to sweet cookies and "junk" foods.

## THOUSAND ISLAND DRESSING

*Not only is this a tangy dressing for greens, it makes a succulent sauce for hot or cold vegetables, fish and meats. Try it also as a sandwich spread in place of butter or mayonnaise.*

| | | |
|---|---|---|
| **250 mL** | Tomato French Dressing (recipe, p.91) | **1 cup** |
| **25 mL** | chopped pickle relish | **2 tbsp** |
| **25 mL** | chopped capers | **2 tbsp** |
| **25 mL** | plain yogurt | **2 tbsp** |

Combine dressing, relish, capers and yogurt. Mix well. Store covered in the refrigerator up to 4 weeks.

Makes 20 servings, about 300 mL (1¼ cups).

**Each serving: 15 mL (1 tbsp)**

1 **++** Extra

3 g carbohydrate

50 kilojoules
(12 Calories)

## TOMATO FRENCH DRESSING

*Tomato soup makes a wonderfully convenient base for this delicious dressing. Vary the herb combinations to suit your own palate.*

| | | |
|---|---|---|
| **1 can** | 284 mL (10 oz) tomato soup | **1 can** |
| **25 mL** | vinegar | **2 tbsp** |
| **5 mL** | dried cilantro or dried parsley | **1 tsp** |
| **5 mL** | sweet basil | **1 tsp** |
| **2 mL** | dry mustard | **½ tsp** |
| **1 mL** | garlic powder | **¼ tsp** |
| **1 mL** | Worcestershire sauce | **¼ tsp** |
| **pinch** | freshly ground pepper | **pinch** |

Pour soup into a bowl or screw-top jar. Add vinegar, cilantro, sweet basil, mustard, garlic powder, Worcestershire sauce and pepper. Whisk or shake together until well blended. Refrigerate at least 2 h for flavors to blend. Store, covered, in the refrigerator up to 4 weeks.

Makes 16 servings, about 250 mL (1 cup).

**One serving: 15 mL (1 tbsp)**

1 **++** Extra

3 g carbohydrate

50 kilojoules
(12 Calories)

## TOFU MAYONNAISE

*Enjoy the richness of mayonnaise with only a fraction of the energy in our smooth mayonnaise-like dressing made with tofu (bean curd) as the base.*

| 250 | mL | drained, mashed tofu | 1 | cup |
|---|---|---|---|---|
| 25 | mL | vinegar | 2 | tbsp |
| 5 | mL | Dijon mustard | 1 | tsp |
| 5 | mL | soy sauce | 1 | tsp |
| 5 | mL | dried parsley | 1 | tsp |
| 2 | mL | garlic powder | ½ | tsp |
| 2 | mL | salt | ½ | tsp |

Combine tofu, vinegar, mustard, soy sauce, parsley, garlic powder and salt in container of blender or food processor. Process about 1 min until smooth (or beat ingredients together until smooth). Place in screw-top jar. Store, covered, in the refrigerator up to 4 weeks.

Makes 24 servings, 375 mL (1½ cups).

**Each serving: 15 mL (1 tbsp)**

1 **++** Extra

1 g protein

20 kilojoules
(4 Calories)

Food energy is measured in kilojoules (Calories) and is provided by the carbohydrate, protein and fat contained in our food. Vitamins and minerals are important for good health but do not in themselves provide energy (kilojoules or Calories).

## SUPREME SALAD SEASONING

*Just a pinch or two of this seasoning mix sprinkled on green salads gives them added zest. It can also be used for seasoning other dishes—stews, casseroles, soups, sauces.*

| | | |
|---|---|---|
| 75 mL | grated Parmesan cheese | 1/3 cup |
| 50 mL | sesame seeds | ¼ cup |
| 25 mL | paprika | 2 tbsp |
| 15 mL | poppy seeds | 1 tbsp |
| 5 mL | chicken bouillon (1 cube, crushed) | 1 tsp |
| 10 mL | dried parsley | 2 tsp |
| 5 mL | onion flakes | 1 tsp |
| 5 mL | garlic powder | 1 tsp |
| 5 mL | celery seed | 1 tsp |
| 2 mL | salt | ½ tsp |
| 2 mL | freshly ground pepper | ½ tsp |

Combine Parmesan cheese, sesame seeds, paprika, poppy seeds, chicken bouillon, parsley, onion flakes, garlic powder, celery seed, salt and pepper in a screw-top jar. Shake until well mixed. Store in the refrigerator up to 4 mon.

Makes 24 servings, 250 mL (1 cup).

**Each serving: 10 mL (2 tsp)**

1 ++ Extra

1 g protein
1 g fat

50 kilojoules
(13 Calories)

# Vegetables

The food we eat would be drab and monotonous without the magnificent colors, unique flavors and varied textures that vegetables bring to brighten and round out a meal. Just think how dull it would be if refreshing green peas, rich gold carrots or cheery red beets never appeared on dinner plates!

Nutritionally, vegetables make a significant contribution to a healthful, well-balanced diet by providing carbohydrate, vitamins and minerals, plus dietary fiber.

Enjoy vegetables at their best by mastering all the wonderful ways of cooking them. Indifferent treatment makes them lifeless. The most important and the trickiest thing is to avoid overcooking them. Garden fresh vegetables are best and should be cooked until just barely tender for the ultimate flavor, texture and nutrient content. Frozen vegetables are good, too, especially if they are steamed or cooked for a short time in broth or water.

Canned vegetables have been cooked in their processing, so they need just to be warmed for serving at their tastiest.

## MIX 'N' MASH VEGETABLES

*Here is a chance to create something different out of our traditional winter vegetables. Your guests will have quite a time guessing the ingredients.*

| | | |
|---|---|---|
| 375 mL | chopped turnip or rutabaga | 1½ **cups** |
| 375 mL | chopped carrot | 1½ **cups** |
| 250 mL | chopped sweet potato | 1 **cup** |
| 10 mL | margarine or butter | 2 **tsp** |
| | Salt and freshly ground pepper | |

Place turnip, carrot and sweet potato in a medium saucepan. Steam or cook in boiling water, about 20 min until tender. Drain well. Mash or whip until smooth. Stir in margarine; season to taste with salt and pepper.

Makes 4 servings.

**Each serving: 125 mL (½ cup)**

| | |
|---|---|
| 1 ▨ Fruits & Vegetables Choice | 11 g carbohydrate |
| ½ ▲ Fats & Oils Choice | 1 g protein |
| | 2 g fat |
| | 280 kilojoules |
| | (66 Calories) |

## SKINNY SCALLOPED POTATOES

*Potatoes have more charm when their skins are left on. They are easier to fix, have more flavor and provide more dietary fiber than when they are skinned.*

| | | |
|---|---|---|
| 500 mL | *Basic White Sauce* (recipe, p.45) | 2 **cups** |
| 4 | medium potatoes, unpeeled, scrubbed and sliced | 4 |
| 2 | medium onions, sliced | 2 |

Layer sauce, potatoes and onions in a lightly greased 1.5 L (6 cup) shallow casserole, ending with sauce. Cover and bake in a 180°C (350°F) oven 40 min. Uncover and bake about 20 min longer until potatoes are tender and top is browned.

Makes 6 servings.

**Each serving: 200 mL (¾ cup)**

| | |
|---|---|
| 2 ▢ Starchy Choices | 28 g carbohydrate |
| ½ ▲ Fats & Oils Choice | 6 g protein |
| | 3 g fat |
| | 690 kilojoules |
| | (163 Calories) |

## BAKED STUFFED POTATOES

*These potatoes can be baked, stuffed and refrigerated for a day in advance of final reheating before serving. If refrigerated, allow a slightly longer reheating time. Try different flavors; substitute equal amounts of chopped fresh chives or dill pickles for parsley. Skins will be softer if potatoes are wrapped before baking.*

| | | |
|---|---|---|
| **4** | small baking potatoes | **4** |
| **125 mL** | 2% cottage cheese | **½ cup** |
| **75 mL** | water | **1/3 cup** |
| **25 mL** | chopped fresh parsley | **2 tbsp** |
| **25 mL** | grated Parmesan cheese | **2 tbsp** |
| | Paprika, optional | |

Wash potatoes, prick with a fork. Wrap potatoes individually in aluminum foil, if desired. Bake in a 200°C (400°F) oven 35 min until cooked and soft. Remove from oven; unwrap. Cut a small slice off the top of each potato. Scoop out potato; reserve shells. Mash potato with cottage cheese, water, parsley and Parmesan cheese; beat until smooth. Spoon this mixture back into potato shells. Place on a baking sheet. Sprinkle with paprika, if desired. Reheat in a 200°C (400°F) oven 10 to 15 min until heated through.

Makes 4 servings.

**Each serving: 1 stuffed potato**

1 ⊘ Protein Choice
1 ☐ Starchy Choice

16 g carbohydrate
8 g protein
2 g fat

480 kilojoules
(114 Calories)

---

*On facing page, from lower right*: Mix 'n' Mash Vegetables, Orangey Harvard Beets, Asparagus Risotto, Confetti Peas, Zucchini with Tomato Sauce.

## ZUCCHINI WITH TOMATO SAUCE

*Zucchini cooks very quickly and tastes best when it still has some crunch, so do not overcook it. Serve this colorful dish as an accompaniment to roast meat or poultry.*

| | | |
|---|---|---|
| 10 mL | margarine or butter | 2 tsp |
| 25 mL | chopped green onion | 2 tbsp |
| 1 | small clove garlic, finely chopped | 1 |
| 15 mL | all purpose flour | 1 tbsp |
| 1 mL | salt | ¼ tsp |
| pinch | freshly ground pepper | pinch |
| 200 mL | tomato juice | ¾ cup |
| 4 | small zucchini | 4 |
| 250 mL | shredded Mozzarella cheese | 1 cup |

Heat margarine in a small saucepan. Sauté onion and garlic over low heat until limp but not brown. Stir in flour, salt and pepper until smooth. Add tomato juice. Stir-cook 3 to 4 min until sauce is thickened. Wash zucchini; trim off ends; cut in half lengthwise. Drop into boiling salted water and cook about 2 min. Zucchini should still be fairly crisp. Drain; place cut side up in a warm oven-proof dish. Drizzle tomato sauce over zucchini pieces then sprinkle with shredded Mozzarella cheese. Place under broiler just long enough to melt cheese.

Makes 4 servings.

**Each serving: 2 zucchini halves**

| | | |
|---|---|---|
| 1 ⊘ Protein Choice | | 8 g carbohydrate |
| 1 � Fruits & Vegetables Choice | | 9 g protein |
| 1 ▲ Fats & Oils Choice | | 8 g fat |

590 kilojoules
(140 Calories)

---

*On facing page, from lower right*: Stuffed Butterfly Chops, Stuffed Baked Fillets, Baked Chicken with Wine Sauce, Calgary Pot Roast.

## GREEN BEANS WITH WATER CHESTNUTS

*Slice the green beans and water chestnuts ahead of time, but cook just before meal time. Serve them tender-crisp and piping hot. Thin, fresh asparagus spears can be substituted for the green beans.*

| | | | |
|---|---|---|---|
| 375 g | fresh green beans | 12 oz | |
| 125 mL | chicken broth | ½ cup | |
| 5 mL | finely chopped ginger root | 1 tsp | |
| 1 | small clove garlic, finely chopped | 1 | |
| 75 mL | thinly sliced water chestnuts | 1/3 cup | |
| 5 mL | soy sauce | 1 tsp | |
| | Freshly ground pepper | | |

Wash and drain green beans. French-cut in half lengthwise; set aside. Combine chicken broth, ginger root and garlic in a frypan; bring to a boil. Add green beans and water chestnuts; sprinkle with soy sauce. Cover tightly and steam 7 to 8 min until tender-crisp. If moisture has not dried off, remove cover, raise heat briefly and shake pan to evaporate remaining liquid. Season to taste with pepper. Serve piping hot.

Makes 4 servings.

**Each serving: 200 mL (¾ cup)**

1 ▰ Fruits & Vegetables Choice

9 g carbohydrate
2 g protein

190 kilojoules
(44 Calories)

## LUBECK CABBAGE

*Cook this dish in the oven or on top of the range. The mild, mellow flavor will surprise and delight your taste buds. The dish originates in northern Germany. For variety use red cabbage.*

| | | | |
|---|---|---|---|
| 75 mL | chicken broth | 1/3 cup | |
| 75 mL | dry white wine | 1/3 cup | |
| 2 | whole allspice berries | 2 | |
| 2 mL | cumin or caraway seeds, optional | ½ tsp | |
| 1 L | shredded cabbage | 4 cups | |
| 1 | small mild onion, thinly sliced | 1 | |
| ½ | medium apple, peeled and thinly sliced | ½ | |

Combine broth, wine, allspice and cumin seeds, if desired, in a heavy saucepan or casserole with a tight fitting lid. Toss cabbage, onion and apple together; add to saucepan. Bring quickly to a boil. Reduce heat to very low, cover tightly; simmer slowly for 1.5 to 2 h or bake in a 160°C (325°F) oven for 1.5 to 2 h until cabbage is tender. If moisture has not evaporated, remove cover, raise heat briefly and shake pan to evaporate remaining liquid.

Makes 4 servings.

**Each serving: 175 mL (2/3 cup)**

1 ▰ Fruits & Vegetables Choice

9 g carbohydrate
1 g protein

170 kilojoules
(40 Calories)

## CONFETTI PEAS

*Prepare Confetti Peas for a colorful, flavorful change from plain, buttered peas. You'll be pleasantly surprised at the flavor since not even a speck of butter is added.*

| 125 mL | chopped, sweet red pepper | ½ cup |
|--------|---------------------------|-------|
| 125 mL | chopped celery | ½ cup |
| 75 mL | chopped onion | 1/3 cup |
| 125 mL | chicken broth | ½ cup |
| 375 mL | frozen peas | 1½ cups |
| | Salt and freshly ground pepper | |

Combine red pepper, celery, onion and 75 mL (1/3 cup) broth in a frypan. Stir-cook over medium heat 3 min. Add peas and remaining broth. Continue to stir-cook over medium heat 5 to 6 min, just until vegetables are tender and liquid evaporates. Season to taste with salt and pepper.

Makes 4 servings.

**Each serving: 125 mL (½ cup)**

1 ▰ Fruits & Vegetables Choice

10 g carbohydrate
4 g protein

240 kilojoules
(56 Calories)

## POPEYE PIE

*Even fussy eaters will decide they like spinach when you serve this pie. Popeye Pie also adds a little protein to a meal.*

| | | |
|---|---|---|
| **1 pkg** | 283 g (10 oz) fresh or 340 g (12 oz) frozen chopped spinach | **1 pkg** |
| **2** | eggs, well beaten | **2** |
| **250 mL** | 2% milk | **1 cup** |
| **75 mL** | finely chopped celery | **1/3 cup** |
| **50 mL** | finely chopped onion | **¼ cup** |
| **25 mL** | grated Parmesan cheese | **2 tbsp** |
| **2 mL** | each of salt and nutmeg | **½ tsp** |

Wash fresh spinach, discard stems. Shake off excess water and place leaves in a heavy saucepan; cover and steam over low heat 5 to 7 min, just until leaves are wilted. Drain spinach, chop and press out excess liquid. Or thaw frozen spinach and press out excess liquid. Combine eggs, milk, celery, onion, Parmesan cheese, salt and nutmeg. Fold in spinach. Pour mixture into a well greased 1 L (9 in) pie plate. Bake in a 190°C (375°F) oven 45 min or until a sharp knife inserted in center comes out clean. Cut into wedges and serve warm.

Makes 6 servings.

**Each serving: 1/6 pie**

| | | |
|---|---|---|
| 1 ▨ | Protein Choice | 5 g carbohydrate |
| ½ ▨ | Fruits & Vegetables Choice | 6 g protein |
| | | 3 g fat |
| | | 300 kilojoules |
| | | (71 Calories) |

## ORANGEY HARVARD BEETS

*Color is always important in meals. It affects how people react to food by contributing eye appeal. Beets always brighten dinner plates. Orangey Harvard Beets have an intriguing sweet-sour taste with a hint of orange.*

| | | |
|---|---|---|
| **1 can** | 398 mL (14 oz) diced or sliced beets | **1 can** |
| **10 mL** | white vinegar | **2 tsp** |
| **5 mL** | grated orange peel | **1 tsp** |
| **5 mL** | cornstarch | **1 tsp** |
| **15 mL** | orange juice | **1 tbsp** |

Pour beets and their juice into a saucepan. Stir in vinegar and orange peel. Bring to a boil. Combine cornstarch and orange juice to make a smooth paste; stir into beets. Continue to stir-cook until liquid thickens and coats beets with a smooth, thin sauce.

Makes 4 servings.

### Each serving: 125 mL (½ cup)

½ ▱ Fruits & Vegetables Choice

6 g carbohydrate
1 g protein

120 kilojoules
(28 Calories)

## ASPARAGUS RISOTTO

*Risotto is popular in northern Italy. In our version, the rice stretches the asparagus and makes a handsome escort for chicken, pork or beef.*

| 250 | g | fresh asparagus | ½ | lb |
|---|---|---|---|---|
| 15 | mL | margarine or butter | 1 | tbsp |
| 1 | | small onion, chopped | 1 | |
| 250 | mL | uncooked, long grain rice | 1 | cup |
| 625 | mL | hot chicken broth | 2½ | cups |
| 25 | mL | grated Parmesan cheese | 2 | tbsp |
| | | Salt and freshly ground pepper | | |

Wash and snap off butt ends of asparagus; cut stems into 1 cm (½ in) pieces. Set tips aside. Melt margarine in a saucepan or flame-proof casserole. Add asparagus pieces and onion; stir-cook 5 min until onion is transparent and soft. Stir in rice and chicken broth; bring to a boil. Cover, simmer 10 min. Add asparagus tips; simmer 5 min longer. Stir in 15 mL (1 tbsp) Parmesan cheese, and salt and pepper to taste. Let stand, covered, 5 min. Sprinkle with remaining Parmesan.

Makes 6 servings.

### Each serving: 200 mL (¾ cup)

2 ▢ Starchy Choices
½ ▲ Fats & Oils Choice

28 g carbohydrate
5 g protein
3 g fat

670 kilojoules
(159 Calories)

## CRISPY BAKED PARSNIPS

*Crispy on the outside, soft and flavorful inside, these parsnips present a change of pace from everyday vegetables.*

| | | |
|---|---|---|
| **500 g** | parsnips (4 medium) | **1 lb** |
| **25 mL** | 2% milk | **2 tbsp** |
| **5 mL** | vegetable oil | **1 tsp** |
| **50 mL** | dry bread crumbs | **¼ cup** |
| **1 mL** | salt | **¼ tsp** |
| **pinch** | freshly ground pepper | **pinch** |

Peel parsnips and cut into sticks of uniform thickness about 6 cm (2½ in) long. Steam or cook in a small amount of boiling water about 10 min, just until tender crisp. Cool slightly. Mix milk and oil. Dip parsnip pieces into mixture then coat with bread crumbs. Season with salt and pepper. Place on a lightly greased baking sheet. Bake in a 220°C (425°F) oven 20 min until crisp and light brown.

Makes 4 servings.

**Each serving: 125 mL (½ cup)**

1 ☐  Starchy Choice

14 g carbohydrate
2 g protein
2 g fat

350 kilojoules
(82 Calories)

## SCALLOPED TOMATOES

*Make up this easy vegetable side-dish when you need a change from routine vegetables. It takes just a few minutes to prepare.*

| | | |
|---|---|---|
| **1 can** | 540 mL (19 oz) tomatoes | **1 can** |
| **50 mL** | chopped onion | **¼ cup** |
| **50 mL** | chopped green or sweet red pepper | **¼ cup** |
| **25 mL** | chopped fresh parsley | **2 tbsp** |
| **125 mL** | *Seasoned Bread Crumbs* (recipe, p.53) | **½ cup** |
| | Salt and freshly ground pepper | |

Drain juice from tomatoes into a frypan; reserve tomatoes. Add onion, green pepper and parsley to frypan. Stir-cook over medium heat about 4 min, until vegetables are tender and liquid is nearly evaporated. Reserve 15 mL (1 tbsp)

*Seasoned Bread Crumbs*; stir in remaining crumb mixture and reserved tomatoes. Cover and cook over medium heat about 8 min until heated through. Season to taste with salt and pepper. Pour into a serving dish, sprinkle with reserved crumb mixture.

Makes 4 servings.

**Each serving: 125 mL (½ cup)**

1 ▰ Fruits & Vegetables Choice

12 g carbohydrate
2 g protein

240 kilojoules
(56 Calories)

### LENTIL STUFFED TOMATOES

*Use these tomatoes as a side-dish with oven-cooked meals. They may be stuffed up to 4 h in advance, refrigerated, then heated. In such cases, allow a longer heating time. Cooked, brown lentils can be found in the canned food section of your grocery store.*

| | | |
|---|---|---|
| 4 | firm, medium tomatoes | 4 |
| 50 mL | celery, finely chopped | ¼ cup |
| 15 mL | onion, finely chopped | 1 tbsp |
| 15 mL | green pepper, finely chopped | 1 tbsp |
| 2 mL | curry powder | ½ tsp |
| 1 mL | salt | ¼ tsp |
| 250 mL | cooked, brown lentils, drained | 1 cup |
| 15 mL | grated Parmesan cheese | 1 tbsp |

Core tomatoes; cut a thin slice from the top of each. Scoop out pulp and juice; place in a shallow frypan; mash. Place tomato shells cut-side-down on paper towel to drain. Add celery, onion, green pepper, curry and salt to tomato pulp and juice. Stir-cook over medium heat until vegetables are tender, about 5 min. Add lentils and continue stir-cooking until mixture is thick. Spoon into tomato shells. Sprinkle with Parmesan cheese. Place stuffed tomatoes in muffin cups, set on a baking sheet. Bake in a 200°C (400°F) oven 10 min or until heated through.

Makes 4 servings.

**Each serving: 1 stuffed tomato**

1 ▢ Starchy Choice

13 g carbohydrate
5 g protein
1 g fat

340 kilojoules
(81 Calories)

# Meat, Fish and Poultry

Meat, fish and poultry make a major contribution to our daily protein needs. Our menus are usually planned around one of them, complemented by cooked vegetables and salads.

It is best to choose lean cuts with little marbling which are trimmed of exterior fat. This will help cut down on fat consumption.

Most fish is generally low in fat. It cooks up quickly, even from the frozen state. There are many different types of fish available, so it can add variety to your menus.

Poultry is quite lean, except for the skin. If you want it to remain moist, it is best to roast or cook it with liquid.

These high protein foods are usually the costliest part of a meal, so they deserve careful cooking.

## VEGGY MEAT LOAF

*Not only do vegetables extend the meat, but they add fiber and flavor when mixed into a meat loaf. Lean ground pork may be used instead of the ground beef.*

| | | |
|---|---|---|
| 2 | medium carrots | 2 |
| 1 | stalk celery | 1 |
| 1 | small onion | 1 |
| 250 mL | beef broth or water | 1 cup |
| 50 mL | dry bread crumbs | ¼ cup |
| 15 mL | dried parsley | 1 tbsp |
| 1 | egg, beaten | 1 |
| 5 mL | salt | 1 tsp |
| 2 mL | freshly ground pepper | ½ tsp |
| 500 g | lean ground beef | 1 lb |

Place carrots, celery and onion in the container of a food processor or blender; process with on/off action until finely chopped (or shred by hand). Combine vegetables and 125 mL (½ cup) broth in a frypan. Stir-cook over medium heat 7 min until vegetables are tender-crisp. Combine in a mixing bowl the remaining broth with bread crumbs, parsley, egg, salt and pepper; add braised vegetables and ground beef; mix thoroughly. Form into a firm loaf 5 cm (2 in) thick. Place in a shallow baking dish large enough for juices to drain away from meat loaf. Bake in a 180°C (350°F) oven 50 min until meat is no longer pink. Remove from oven and immediately place meat loaf on a warm serving platter so fat will not be absorbed.

Makes 6 servings.

**Each serving: 1 slice, 4 cm (1½ in) thick**

2 🖸 Protein Choices
½ 🖸 Fruits & Vegetables Choice

5 g carbohydrate
16 g protein
7 g fat

620 kilojoules
(147 Calories)

### SALISBURY STEAK WITH MUSHROOM SAUCE

Salisbury Steak *elevates ground beef to a more elegant level. It is enjoyed by all ages.*

| | | |
|---|---|---|
| 625 **g** | lean ground beef | 1¼ **lbs** |
| 50 **mL** | cracker crumbs or dry bread crumbs | ¼ **cup** |
| 125 **mL** | finely chopped onion | ½ **cup** |
| 1 | clove garlic, finely chopped | 1 |
| 5 **mL** | prepared mustard | 1 **tsp** |
| 2 **mL** | salt | ½ **tsp** |
| **pinch** | freshly ground pepper | **pinch** |
| 1 | egg, beaten | 1 |
| 375 **mL** | *Mushroom Sauce* (recipe, p.47) | 1½ **cups** |

Combine ground beef, cracker crumbs, onion, garlic, mustard, salt and pepper in a mixing bowl; add egg, mix thoroughly. Divide into 6 portions; shape each into a patty. Lightly oil a frypan. Cook patties, turning often, 10 to 12 min, depending on thickness until evenly browned and meat is no longer pink. Remove meat to a warm serving platter. Heat *Mushroom Sauce* and spoon over meat.

Makes 6 servings.

**Each serving: 1 patty with** *Mushroom Sauce*

3 ⊘ Protein Choices
½ ☐ Starchy Choice

7 g carbohydrate
21 g protein
9 g fat

810 kilojoules
(193 Calories)

## BEEF BURGUNDY

Beef Burgundy *is best made a day ahead for all the flavors to blend. Refrigerate it, then reheat it at serving time.*

| | | |
|---|---|---|
| 2 | slices bacon, chopped | 2 |
| 500 mL | coarsely chopped onions | 2 cups |
| 1 kg | lean stewing beef | 2 lbs |
| 25 mL | all purpose flour | 2 tbsp |
| 5 mL | salt | 1 tsp |
| 2 mL | dried herbs (thyme or marjoram or mixture) | ½ tsp |
| 1 mL | each of freshly ground pepper and garlic powder | ¼ tsp |
| 375 mL | dry red wine | 1½ cups |
| 375 mL | beef broth | 1½ cups |
| 15 mL | tomato paste | 1 tbsp |
| 250 g | fresh mushrooms, cut into chunks | ½ lb |

Cook bacon in a heavy frypan until crisp; blot fat from bacon with paper towel; set aside. Cook onions in bacon fat until tender. Remove onions to another dish. Trim fat from beef and cut into 2.5 cm (1 in) cubes. Brown beef in frypan. Add flour, salt, herbs, freshly ground pepper and garlic powder; stir-cook 1 min. Stir in bacon, wine, beef broth and tomato paste. Simmer, loosely covered, 2 h. Add mushrooms and reserved onions; adjust seasoning to taste; simmer 20 min longer.

Makes 6 servings.

### Each serving: 250 mL (1 cup)

| | | |
|---|---|---|
| 4 ⊘ | Protein Choices | 8 g carbohydrate |
| 1 ⊘ | Fruits & Vegetables Choice | 29 g protein |
| | | 12 g fat |
| | | 1070 kilojoules (256 Calories) |

## CHEESEBURGERS DELUXE

*These burgers will become a favorite during barbecue season. They may be served as a main course with potato salad, or in a toasted bun. Vary the flavor by substituting blue or Cheddar cheese for the Swiss cheese.*

| | | | |
|---|---|---|---|
| 500 g | lean ground beef | 1 | lb |
| 1 | egg, beaten | 1 | |
| 50 mL | quick rolled oats | ¼ | cup |
| 2 mL | salt | ½ | tsp |
| pinch | freshly ground pepper | pinch | |
| 2 | green onions, finely chopped | 2 | |
| 125 mL | shredded Swiss or Mozzarella cheese | ½ | cup |

Combine meat, egg, rolled oats, salt and pepper; mix until well combined. Divide into 8 portions; shape each into a flat patty. Top each of 4 patties with ¼ of green onions and cheese. Cover each with a remaining patty; pinch edges together to form 4 firm burgers. Broil or barbecue until meat is no longer pink. *Do not overcook* or the cheese will leak out.

Makes 4 servings.

**Each serving: 1 burger**

4 ⊘ Protein Choices
½ ▲ Fats & Oils Choice

4 g carbohydrate
26 g protein
14 g fat

1030 kilojoules
(246 Calories)

## BEEF STEAK WITH HERB GARNISH

*Steak is flavorful, so the companions can be plain like a baked potato and a crisp green vegetable. Be sure to make the herb garnish ahead of time to allow flavors time to blend.*

| | | | |
|---|---|---|---|
| 25 mL | finely chopped green onion or scallion | 2 | tbsp |
| 25 mL | finely chopped fresh parsley | 2 | tbsp |
| 25 mL | fresh lemon juice | 2 | tbsp |
| 15 mL | vegetable oil | 1 | tbsp |
| 1 | small clove garlic, very finely chopped | 1 | |
| 1 mL | salt | ¼ | tsp |
| pinch | freshly ground pepper | pinch | |
| 625 g | boneless beef fillet, rib eye or sirloin steak | 1¼ | lbs |

Combine onion, parsley, lemon juice, oil, garlic, salt and pepper in a glass bowl; let stand at room temperature at least 2 h. At meal time, broil or sauté meat to desired doneness in a heavy frypan lightly brushed with oil. Spoon herb garnish over each serving.

Makes 4 servings.

**Each serving: about 100 g (4 oz)**

4  ⊘  Protein Choices
½  ▲  Fats & Oils Choice

1 g carbohydrate
26 g protein
15 g fat

1010 kilojoules
(243 Calories)

### MINUTE STEAK EXTRAORDINAIRE

*Minute steaks are always thin so they cook quickly. Here they become a superb dish for a last-minute meal when you wish to serve something fancy.*

| 500 g | minute steaks | 1 lb |
|---|---|---|
| 1 | clove garlic, cut in half | 1 |
| | Salt and freshly ground pepper | |
| 15 mL | butter | 1 tbsp |
| 15 mL | brandy | 1 tbsp |
| 50 mL | finely chopped fresh parsley | ¼ cup |
| 75 mL | dry white wine | 1/3 cup |
| 75 mL | evaporated 2% milk | 1/3 cup |

Rub steaks with cut surfaces of garlic clove. Season to taste with salt and pepper. Melt butter in a heavy frypan. Add steaks, cook over medium heat to desired doneness—about 2 min per side for medium. Remove steaks to platter; keep warm. Add brandy to frypan; stir over medium heat 1 min, scraping up pan juices; add parsley and wine; continue stir-cooking 2 min. Reduce heat; stir in milk and return steaks to sauce; spoon sauce over meat. Serve immediately.

Makes 4 servings.

**Each serving: about 75 g (3 oz) meat plus sauce**

3  ⊘  Protein Choices
1  ▲  Fats & Oils Choice

2 g carbohydrate
22 g protein
13 g fat

890 kilojoules
(213 Calories)

## CALGARY POT ROAST

Calgary Pot Roast *is always a hit and it is easy to prepare. Braising in tomato sauce guarantees tender, flavorful beef.*

| | | |
|---|---|---|
| **1.5 kg** | boneless, lean beef brisket, cross rib, chuck or blade roast | 3½ **lbs** |
| 5 **mL** | dry mustard | 1 **tsp** |
| 2 **mL** | salt | ½ **tsp** |
| 125 **mL** | chopped onion | ½ **cup** |
| 1 **can** | 213 mL (7½ oz) tomato sauce | 1 **can** |
| 25 **mL** | vinegar | 2 **tbsp** |
| 2 **mL** | thyme | ½ **tsp** |
| 1 **mL** | freshly ground pepper | ¼ **tsp** |

Trim all fat from roast. Rub dry mustard and salt into the surface of the meat. Place in a lightly greased, oven-proof dish. Top with onion. Combine tomato sauce, vinegar, thyme and pepper; pour over roast and cover tightly. Bake in a 160°C (325°F) oven 3 h until meat is tender.

Makes 10 servings.

**Each serving: about 75 g (3 oz)**

3 ⊘ Protein Choices

2 g carbohydrate
23 g protein
10 g fat

800 kilojoules
(190 Calories)

---

**Tips for trimming waistlines:**
(a) **Minimize fat when preparing foods by using cooking methods which help to remove fat, such as baking, barbecuing, broiling and roasting. If meat must be fried, use a non-stick frypan without adding fat.**
(b) **Trim excess visible fat from meats and remove fat from pan juices of cooked meats before serving.**
(c) **Limit the use of sausages, wieners and other processed meats.**
(d) **Use small amounts of dressings and oils. Spread butter or margarine thinly on breads.**
(e) **Drink skim or low fat milk. Choose cheeses that are low in fat.**
(f) **Control portion sizes.**

## BRAISED STEAK AND GREEN PEPPER

*The green pepper should still have some crunch for maximum flavor and texture. Chunks of zucchini may be used instead if you are not a green pepper lover.*

| | | |
|---|---|---|
| 750 g | lean round steak, cut into 5 mm (¼ in) strips | 1½ **lbs** |
| 25 mL | all purpose flour | 2 **tbsp** |
| 2 mL | salt | ½ **tsp** |
| 1 mL | freshly ground pepper | ¼ **tsp** |
| 15 mL | vegetable oil | 1 **tbsp** |
| 450 mL | beef broth | 1¾ **cups** |
| 250 mL | canned tomatoes with juice | 1 **cup** |
| 1 | medium onion, sliced | 1 |
| 1 | clove garlic, finely chopped | 1 |
| 1 | large green pepper, seeded and cut into strips | 1 |
| 7 mL | Worcestershire sauce | 1½ **tsp** |

Coat strips of meat with flour mixed with salt and pepper. Heat oil in a large frypan; brown meat on all sides. Drain off any fat. Add broth, tomato juice (reserving the tomato pieces for later), onion and garlic to the meat. Cover and simmer 1.5 h until meat is tender. Add tomato pieces, green pepper strips and Worcestershire sauce. Stir-cook 4 to 5 min longer.

Makes 6 servings.

### Each serving: 1/6 recipe

| | |
|---|---|
| 3 ⊘ Protein Choices | 6 g carbohydrate |
| ½ ◨ Fruits & Vegetables Choice | 23 g protein |
| ½ ▲ Fats & Oils Choice | 11 g fat |
| | 900 kilojoules (215 Calories) |

The kilojoule (Calorie) is not a nutrient but a measure of energy which is provided by the carbohydrate, protein and fat in our food. (4.2 kilojoules = 1 Calorie)
  1 g carbohydrate yields 17 kilojoules (4 Calories)
  1 g protein yields 17 kilojoules (4 Calories)
  1 g fat yields 37 kilojoules (9 Calories)
  1 g pure alcohol yields 29 kilojoules (7 Calories)

## MEATBALLS

*You'll find many uses for these meatballs; keep some in your freezer to use in sauces or to make emergency snacks or meals. Simply heat as they are or in a savory or spicy sauce. Vary the flavor by using other herbs or by adding 25 mL (2 tbsp) finely chopped onion. Lean ground pork or lamb may be substituted for the beef.*

| | | | |
|---|---|---|---|
| 1 | egg | 1 | |
| 175 mL | water | 2/3 | cup |
| 50 mL | dry bread crumbs | ¼ | cup |
| 15 mL | dried parsley | 1 | tbsp |
| 5 mL | oregano or Italian seasoning | 1 | tsp |
| 2 mL | salt | ½ | tsp |
| 1 mL | freshly ground pepper | ¼ | tsp |
| 500 g | lean ground beef or pork | 1 | lb |

Beat together egg and water in a mixing bowl; stir in bread crumbs, parsley, oregano, salt and pepper; add ground beef and mix thoroughly; let stand 3 min. Form into meatballs using about 25 mL (2 tbsp) meat mixture per meatball. (Wet hands with cold water to make the job easy.) Place meatballs on a rack in a shallow baking pan. Bake in a 160°C (325°F) oven 35 min until meat is no longer pink.

Makes 6 servings, 24 meatballs.

**Each serving: four, 4 cm (1½ in) meatballs**

2 🟢 Protein Choices

3 g carbohydrate
15 g protein
7 g fat

570 kilojoules
(135 Calories)

## SPICY LUNCHEON ROLL

Spicy Luncheon Roll *is a homemade deli-meat perfect for picnics, brown bag lunches and cold buffets.*

| | | |
|---|---|---|
| 250 g | lean ground beef | ½ lb |
| 250 g | lean ground pork | ½ lb |
| 1 | strip bacon, finely chopped and lightly cooked | 1 |
| 50 mL | fresh, whole wheat bread crumbs | ¼ cup |
| 2 | beef bouillon cubes | 2 |
| 50 mL | boiling water | ¼ cup |
| 1 | egg, beaten | 1 |
| 2 mL | salt | ½ tsp |
| 1 mL | each of nutmeg and freshly ground pepper | ¼ tsp |
| 2 drops | hot pepper sauce | 2 drops |
| 1 | bay leaf | 1 |

Combine ground beef and pork in a mixing bowl. Blot fat from bacon with a paper towel; add to meat mixture; stir in bread crumbs. Crush and dissolve bouillon cubes in boiling water; add to meat mixture. Stir in egg, salt, nutmeg, pepper and hot pepper sauce; mix thoroughly. Form into a firm, 20 x 6 cm (8 x 2½ in) sausage roll. Wrap roll in cheesecloth or all-purpose cloth. Tie ends securely. Place on a rack in large saucepan or Dutch oven. Add hot water just to cover; add bay leaf; cover and bring to a boil; simmer 1.5 h. Lift roll from water and allow to drain. Remove cloth. Serve hot as a meat loaf or chill and serve as deli luncheon meat.

Makes 6 servings.

**Each serving: about 50 g (2 oz)**

| 2 ▨ Protein Choices | 3 g carbohydrate |
|---|---|
| ½ ▲ Fats & Oils Choice | 16 g protein |
| | 8 g fat |
| | 620 kilojoules (148 Calories) |

## LIVER, TOMATOES AND GREEN ONIONS

*The secret of success in cooking liver is to not overcook it. For an economical meal use beef, pork or lamb liver for this dinner-in-a-dish.*

| | | |
|---|---|---|
| 250 g | beef, pork or calves liver | ½ lb |
| 15 mL | all purpose flour | 1 tbsp |
| 1 mL | each of salt and freshly ground pepper | ¼ tsp |
| 10 mL | vegetable oil | 2 tsp |
| 5 mL | butter or margarine | 1 tsp |
| 1 | medium tomato, cut into pieces | 1 |
| 2 | medium green onions, chopped | 2 |
| 15 mL | fresh lemon juice | 1 tbsp |

Slice liver into 2.5 cm (1 in) strips. Coat lightly with a mixture of flour, salt and pepper. Heat 5 mL (1 tsp) oil and butter in a medium frypan; sauté liver over medium heat until just cooked and tender. *Do not overcook.* Remove to a serving dish and keep warm. Wipe out frypan. Heat remaining oil in frypan; add tomato pieces and green onions; stir-cook until piping hot. Add to cooked liver and sprinkle with lemon juice.

Makes 2 servings.

**Each serving: ½ recipe**

| | | |
|---|---|---|
| 3½ ⬭ | Protein Choices | 12 g carbohydrate |
| 1   ◢ | Fruits & Vegetables Choice | 25 g protein |
| 1   ▲ | Fats & Oils Choice | 17 g fat |

1260 kilojoules
(301 Calories)

> **Iron combines with protein to form hemoglobin, a part of the red blood cells which is essential in the transport of oxygen and carbon dioxide in the body. Sources of iron include liver, kidney, lean meats, egg yolk, dark green leafy vegetables, dried peas and beans, enriched or whole grain breads and cereals.**

## BROWN 'N' SERVE SAUSAGE

*Your butcher will probably be happy to trim and grind pork shoulder, loin or leg for top-notch pork which makes these sausages so good. The two-step cooking procedure ensures the removal of most of the fat.*

| | | | |
|---|---|---|---|
| **500 g** | lean ground pork | **1 lb** | |
| **50 mL** | cracker crumbs | **¼ cup** | |
| **50 mL** | water | **¼ cup** | |
| **5 mL** | each of sage and salt | **1 tsp** | |
| **2 mL** | each of thyme and oregano | **½ tsp** | |
| **1 mL** | freshly ground pepper | **¼ tsp** | |
| **pinch** | ground cloves | **pinch** | |

Combine ground pork and cracker crumbs. Stir in water, sage, salt, thyme, oregano, pepper and cloves. Mix until thoroughly combined. Divide into 12 portions; form each into a sausage-shaped roll or flat patty. (Wet hands with cold water to make the job easy.) Place in a cold, lightly oiled frypan. Cook over medium heat, turning often, about 4 min each side until just beginning to brown and pieces are no longer pink. Remove to paper towels and blot to absorb any fat. Wrap; store in refrigerator up to 5 days or in the freezer up to 2 months. Or cook a second time and serve immediately.

*To serve:* Return sausages or patties to a *clean*, cold frypan. Cook over medium heat, turning once or twice, about 4 min until sausages are brown and crisp. (Cook frozen sausages in the same manner, allowing about 2 min longer for cooking.)

Makes 12 sausages or patties.

**Each serving: 1 sausage or patty**

1 🖉 Protein Choice

1 g carbohydrate
7 g protein
3 g fat

250 kilojoules
(59 Calories)

> **Always crush or rub dried herbs before using. This releases more of the aroma and adds to the flavor.**

## STUFFED BUTTERFLY CHOPS

*Pork adapts beautifully to a variety of flavor combinations. Low-energy, vegetable-herb stuffing transforms butterfly chops into a deliciously different meat course.*

| | | |
|---|---|---|
| 1 | medium zucchini, shredded, 250 mL (1 cup) | 1 |
| 1 | medium carrot, shredded, 75 mL (1/3 cup) | 1 |
| 10 mL | vegetable oil | 2 tsp |
| 15 mL | finely chopped onion | 1 tbsp |
| 50 mL | fresh, whole wheat bread crumbs | ¼ cup |
| 1 mL | each of sage and rosemary | ¼ tsp |
| 2 | butterfly pork chops, 1 cm (½ in) thick | 2 |
| 1 mL | dry mustard | ¼ tsp |

Toss zucchini and carrot together in a small bowl; reserve 250 mL (1 cup) and sprinkle remainder in a greased, shallow baking dish. Heat oil in a small frypan; add onion and stir-cook 3 min. Add bread crumbs, sage and rosemary; continue cooking until crispy; stir into reserved zucchini mixture. Spoon onto pork chops; fold over and secure each with 2 or 3 toothpicks. Trim any fat off chops and rub with dry mustard; place on vegetables in baking dish. Cover and bake in a 160°C (325°F) oven 30 min. Uncover and bake 10 min longer.

Makes 2 servings.

**Each serving: 1 stuffed chop**

| | | |
|---|---|---|
| 4 | ⊘ | Protein Choices |
| 1 | ☐ | Starchy Choice |
| 1 | ▲ | Fats & Oils Choice |

14 g carbohydrate
31 g protein
17 g fat

1390 kilojoules
(333 Calories)

## GOURMET LAMB WITH PORK

*Guests will be intrigued and wonder what the mysterious ingredients are in this luxurious roast. Serve with* Velouté Sauce *flavored with mint.*

| | | | |
|---|---|---|---|
| 3 kg | leg of lamb | 7 | lbs |
| 750 g | pork tenderloin | 1½ | lbs |
| 5 mL | mixed herbs (basil, marjoram, oregano) | 1 | tsp |
| 2 mL | freshly ground pepper | ½ | tsp |
| 1 mL | garlic powder | ¼ | tsp |
| 250 mL | Velouté Sauce (recipe, p.48) | 1 | cup |

Ask your butcher to bone a leg of lamb and replace the bone with pork tenderloin. Have the roast rolled and tied securely. Crush the herbs in the palm of your hand and rub into the surface of the roast. Sprinkle with pepper and garlic powder. Insert a meat thermometer into the center of the roast. Place on a rack in a roasting pan. Cook in a 160°C (325°F) oven 2.5 to 3 h until meat thermometer registers 80°C (170°F) or until meat juices are no longer pink. Remove from oven, cover and let stand 10 min before carving.

Makes 16 servings.

**Each serving: 100 g (4 oz)**

4  ⊘  Protein Choices

28 g protein
12 g fat

920 kilojoules
(220 Calories)

## CARIBBEAN STEWED CHICKEN

*Serve this beautifully-seasoned stew with* Fluffy Dumplings *(recipe, p.52) for a praise-winning dinner.*

| | | |
|---|---|---|
| 1.5 kg | chicken pieces | 3 lb |
| 1 | large onion, chopped | 1 |
| 1 | large tomato, coarsely chopped | 1 |
| 25 mL | fresh lime or lemon juice | 2 tbsp |
| 15 mL | chopped fresh parsley | 1 tbsp |
| 2 mL | each of thyme and rosemary | ½ tsp |
| 1 mL | each of ground ginger and cinnamon | ¼ tsp |
| 750 mL | water | 3 cups |
| 2 mL | salt | ½ tsp |
| 1 mL | freshly ground pepper | ¼ tsp |
| 15 mL | margarine or butter | 1 tbsp |
| 25 mL | all purpose flour | 2 tbsp |
| 1 mL | nutmeg | ¼ tsp |

Remove skin and all visible fat from chicken pieces. Place chicken, onion, tomato, lime juice, parsley, thyme, rosemary, ginger and cinnamon in a glass bowl; cover and let stand in refrigerator 2 h to marinate. Transfer to a Dutch oven or stewing pot; add water, salt and pepper. Cover, bring to a boil; reduce heat and simmer 1.5 h until chicken is tender. Melt margarine in a small saucepan; stir in flour and nutmeg until blended. Remove and strain 375 mL (1½ cups) liquid from stew and add to flour mixture; stir-cook about 2 min until thickened. Place chicken pieces on a warm platter; serve with sauce. (Strain remaining liquid from stew for later use.)

Makes 6 servings.

**Each serving: 1/6 recipe**

3 🖉 Protein Choices

½ ▲ Fats & Oils Choice

2 g carbohydrate
21 g protein
11 g fat

800 kilojoules
(191 Calories)

## CHICKEN ITALIANO

*Young people rate* Chicken Italiano *tops. Discarding the skin removes most of the fat, making each portion energy-wise.*

| | | |
|---|---|---|
| 1 can | 398 mL (14 oz) tomatoes | 1 can |
| 2 mL | each of dried basil, tarragon and salt | ½ tsp |
| 1 mL | freshly ground pepper | ¼ tsp |
| 10 mL | margarine, oil or butter | 2 tsp |
| 1 | clove garlic, finely chopped | 1 |
| 4 | chicken breasts, 1 kg (2 lb), skinned | 4 |
| 25 mL | chopped fresh parsley or 10 mL (2 tsp) dried parsley | 2 tbsp |
| 125 mL | shredded Mozzarella cheese | ½ cup |

Pour tomatoes into container of a blender or food processor. Add basil, tarragon, salt and pepper. Purée until smooth. Melt margarine in a large frypan. Sauté garlic over medium heat 1 min. Add chicken breasts; sauté, turning once or twice until golden on both sides. Turn chicken fleshy side down and cover with tomato mixture. Bring to a boil, reduce heat and simmer 15 min until tender. Remove chicken and place fleshy side up, in a warm oven-proof dish. Stir parsley into sauce and spoon over chicken breasts. Sprinkle with Mozzarella. Place under heated broiler 1 min just until cheese melts.

Makes 4 servings.

**Each serving: 1 chicken breast with sauce**

3 **⊘** Protein Choices

½ **◪** Fruits & Vegetables Choice

1 **▲** Fats & Oils Choice

5 g carbohydrate

25 g protein

15 g fat

1070 kilojoules
(255 Calories)

## CHICKEN PAPRIKA

*This is a slimmed-down version of an old Hungarian favorite. It has all the flavor of the traditional dish but less fat.*

| | | | |
|---|---|---|---|
| 5 mL | margarine or butter | 1 | tsp |
| 5 mL | vegetable oil | 1 | tsp |
| 250 mL | chopped onion | 1 | cup |
| 10 mL | paprika | 2 | tsp |
| 2 mL | salt | ½ | tsp |
| pinch | freshly ground pepper | | pinch |
| 1 kg | chicken breasts or legs | 2 | lbs |
| 200 mL | water | ¾ | cup |
| 1 | small green pepper, seeded and cut into chunks | 1 | |
| 15 mL | all purpose flour | 1 | tbsp |
| 125 mL | 2% milk | ½ | cup |
| 75 mL | commercial sour cream | 1/3 | cup |

Melt margarine with oil in a heavy frypan. Sauté onion 5 min. Stir in paprika, salt and pepper. Remove skin from chicken parts, wash and pat dry. Add chicken to frypan and cook over medium heat until lightly browned on both sides. Do not allow onion to burn. Add water, cover and simmer 1 h until chicken is tender. Add green pepper and cook 5 min longer. Place flour and milk in a covered, screw-top jar. Shake well until thoroughly mixed. Stir into liquid around chicken. Stir-cook 2 to 3 min until thickened. Stir in sour cream and heat but *do not boil.*

Makes 4 servings.

**Each serving: ¼ recipe**

3 ☑ Protein Choices
½ ☑ Fruits & Vegetables Choice
1 ▲ Fats & Oils Choice

6 g carbohydrate
23 g protein
14 g fat

1010 kilojoules
(242 Calories)

## BAKED CHICKEN WITH WINE SAUCE

*Chicken never lacks loyal supporters. A wine-flavored sauce adds a flavor variation that makes it fit for a gourmet. The salt hasn't been forgotten—the consommé or broth contains plenty for most tastes.*

| | | |
|---|---|---|
| 1 **kg** | chicken thighs or chicken breasts | 2 **lbs** |
| 50 **mL** | *Seasoned Bread Crumbs* (recipe, p.53) | ¼ **cup** |
| 10 **mL** | vegetable oil | 2 **tsp** |
| 15 **mL** | cornstarch | 1 **tbsp** |
| 1 **can** | 284 mL (10 oz) consommé or beef broth, undiluted | 1 **can** |
| 75 **mL** | port wine or dry sherry | 1/3 **cup** |

Remove skin and all visible fat from chicken pieces. (If chicken breasts are used, remove bones; roll up chicken and fasten with a toothpick.) Rinse under cold water and shake off excess. Coat with seasoned crumbs. Spread oil in a shallow baking pan; arrange chicken pieces in the pan. Bake in a 220°C (425°F) oven 25 min. Turn chicken over and bake an additional 20 min until golden. Mix together cornstarch with 25 mL (2 tbsp) consommé; set aside. Combine remaining consommé and wine in a saucepan; bring to a boil. Boil about 10 min until sauce is reduced to 250 mL (1 cup). Stir in cornstarch mixture; stir-cook until sauce is clear and slightly thickened. Serve over hot chicken.

Makes 4 servings.

**Each serving: ¼ recipe**

3 ⊘ Protein Choices
½ ☐ Starchy Choice

8 g carbohydrate
25 g protein
6 g fat

780 kilojoules
(186 Calories)

## HERBED CHICKEN

*Serve this versatile and tasty chicken over toast, or in crêpes, tortillas or popovers. Make it ahead of time to reheat just before serving. It's handy to have in the freezer for emergencies.*

| | | |
|---|---|---|
| 2 | chicken breasts, 500 g (1 lb) | 2 |
| 500 mL | water | 2 cups |
| 5 mL | marjoram | 1 tsp |
| 2 mL | salt | ½ tsp |
| 1 | stalk celery, chopped | 1 |
| 1 | small onion, chopped | 1 |
| 15 mL | instant skim milk powder | 1 tbsp |
| 5 mL | cornstarch | 1 tsp |
| pinch | freshly ground pepper | pinch |

Place chicken, water, marjoram and salt in a saucepan. Bring to a boil; reduce heat and simmer about 25 min until chicken is tender. Remove chicken; chill broth until fat sets on top; remove fat. Remove and discard bones and skin from cooked chicken. Cut chicken into bite-sized pieces. Heat 50 mL (¼ cup) skimmed chicken broth to a boil in a heavy saucepan. Add celery and onion. Stir-cook about 4 min until tender. Mix together remaining cool broth, milk powder, cornstarch and pepper until smooth; stir into celery mixture. Stir-cook over medium heat about 3 min until mixture thickens slightly. Add chicken; continue cooking until thoroughly heated.

Makes 2 servings.

**Each serving: 200 mL (¾ cup)**

| | |
|---|---|
| 3 ▨ Protein Choices | 5 g carbohydrate |
| ½ ▨ Fruits & Vegetables Choice | 22 g protein |
| | 9 g fat |
| | 790 kilojoules |
| | (189 Calories) |

**Foods with high protein value and relatively low cost include eggs, beef or pork liver, organ meats, poultry, milk powder and many vegetarian combinations such as soybeans and rice. When buying meats it is important to consider the cost per edible serving rather than the cost per kilogram or pound.**

## PACIFIC SALMON PIE

*Salmon and Swiss cheese are baked together in this rice-crusted pie that is as good cold as it is hot.*

| | | |
|---|---|---|
| 375 mL | water | 1½ **cups** |
| 5 mL | salt | 1 **tsp** |
| 125 mL | long grain rice | ½ **cup** |
| 15 mL | margarine or butter | 1 **tbsp** |
| 250 mL | finely chopped celery | 1 **cup** |
| 50 mL | finely chopped onion | ¼ **cup** |
| 2 | eggs | 2 |
| pinch | freshly ground pepper | **pinch** |
| 125 mL | shredded Swiss cheese | ½ **cup** |
| 1 can | 220 g (7¾ oz) salmon, undrained and flaked | 1 **can** |
| 125 mL | skim milk | ½ **cup** |
| pinch | each of nutmeg, curry powder and cinnamon | **pinch** |

Bring water and salt to a boil; add rice; bring to boil again, cover, reduce heat and simmer about 15 min until all water is absorbed and rice is tender. Grease a 1 L (9 in) pie plate with 5 mL (1 tsp) margarine. Melt remaining margarine in a frypan. Sauté celery and onion about 4 min until tender. Beat 1 egg with pepper and mix into rice. Press rice onto bottom and sides of prepared pie plate to form crust. Sprinkle half the cheese over rice, spread with half the celery mixture and salmon. Top with remaining celery mixture and cheese. Beat together remaining egg, milk, nutmeg, curry powder and cinnamon. Pour over ingredients in pie plate. Bake in 190°C (375°F) oven 30 to 35 min until a tester inserted in the center comes out clean. Cool 5 min. Cut into 6 wedges.

Makes 6 servings.

**Each serving: 1 wedge**

2 ⊘ Protein Choices
1 ☐ Starchy Choice
1 ▲ Fats & Oils Choice

15 g carbohydrate
15 g protein
10 g fat

880 kilojoules
(210 Calories)

## BROILED FILLETS ALMONDINE

*Always popular as restaurant fare, this is a distinctive way to serve fish fillets, and one of the best. It is a fish dinner to make you proud and it is unbelievably quick and easy to prepare.*

| | | | |
|---|---|---|---|
| 500 g | fish fillets | 1 | lb |
| 25 mL | melted margarine or butter | 2 | tbsp |
| 50 mL | almond slices | ¼ | cup |
| | Juice of ½ lemon | | |
| 2 mL | salt | ½ | tsp |
| 1 mL | white pepper | ¼ | tsp |

Place fish fillets on broiler pan or oven-proof, shallow baking dish. Broil 15 cm (6 in) from heat about 6 min. Turn each piece. Mix together margarine, almond slices, lemon juice, salt and pepper. Spoon evenly over fish fillets. Return to broiler and broil about 3 min until fish is done and almonds are toasted.

Makes 4 servings.

**Each serving: about 90 g (3½ oz)**

| | | |
|---|---|---|
| 3 ⊘ | Protein Choices | 2 g carbohydrate |
| 2 ▲ | Fats & Oils Choices | 22 g protein |
| | | 18 g fat |
| | | 1070 kilojoules |
| | | (258 Calories) |

## CRISPY BAKED FISH

*Crispy Baked Fish has all the flavor and texture of fried fish, without the fat and oil necessary for the frying. It is an excellent way to cook both fresh and frozen fillets.*

| | | | |
|---|---|---|---|
| 500 g | fish fillets, haddock or sole (fresh or frozen, thawed) | 1 | lb |
| 25 mL | *Tangy Boiled Dressing* (recipe, p.89) | 2 | tbsp |
| 125 mL | *Seasoned Bread Crumbs* (recipe, p.53) | ½ | cup |

Pat fillets with paper towel to remove excess liquid. Brush with dressing. Coat with crumb mixture, pressing crumbs into fish. Place on a lightly greased baking sheet. Bake in a 230°C (450°F) oven 15 to 20 min until fish flakes and crumbs are crisp.

Makes 4 servings.

**Each serving: about 90 g (3½ oz)**

| | | |
|---|---|---|
| 3 | ☑ | Protein Choices |
| ½ | ☐ | Starchy Choice |

6 g carbohydrate
23 g protein
10 g fat

860 kilojoules
(206 Calories)

## TUNA IMPROMPTU

*Canned tuna and salmon are time-savers. Either one makes a great foundation for incredibly quick and easy dishes like Tuna Impromptu.*

| 10 | mL | margarine or butter | 2 | tsp |
|---|---|---|---|---|
| 4 | | eggs, lightly beaten | 4 | |
| 2 | | stalks celery, chopped | 2 | |
| 2 | | green onions, chopped | 2 | |
| 1 | can | 198 g (7 oz) chunk tuna, rinsed and drained | 1 | can |
| 2 | mL | tarragon | ½ | tsp |
| 1 | | large tomato, peeled and chopped | 1 | |
| | | Salt and freshly ground pepper | | |

Heat 5 mL (1 tsp) margarine in a heavy frypan. Add eggs; cook over medium heat until set (do not stir). Flip eggs, cook 30 seconds; remove from pan; chop; set aside. Add remaining 5 mL (1 tsp) margarine to frypan. Sauté celery and onions about 3 min until tender-crisp. Add tuna and tarragon; stir-fry 2 min. Stir in tomato and eggs; continue cooking until heated through. Season with salt and pepper. Serve immediately.

Makes 4 servings.

**Each serving: ¼ recipe**

| | | |
|---|---|---|
| 3 | ☑ | Protein Choices |
| ½ | ▲ | Fats & Oils Choice |

3 g carbohydrate
19 g protein
12 g fat

820 kilojoules
(196 Calories)

## SALMON BROCCOLI LOAF

*The flavor and color contributed by canned salmon and vitamin C-rich broccoli account for the popularity of this loaf with people of all ages.*

| | | |
|---|---|---|
| 2 | eggs, beaten | 2 |
| 1 can | 220 g (7¾ oz) salmon, undrained | 1 can |
| 375 mL | finely chopped fresh or frozen broccoli, blanched; well drained | 1½ cups |
| 250 mL | 2% cottage cheese | 1 cup |
| 50 mL | chopped onion | ¼ cup |
| 25 mL | dry bread crumbs | 2 tbsp |
| 2 mL | salt | ½ tsp |
| 1 | small tomato | 1 |
| 50 mL | grated Parmesan cheese | ¼ cup |

Combine eggs, salmon, broccoli, cottage cheese, onion, bread crumbs and salt in a bowl; mix well. Cut tomato into 5 slices; place overlapping in the bottom of a well greased 1.5 L (8 x 4 in) loaf pan. Sprinkle with Parmesan cheese. Spoon salmon mixture over tomatoes. Bake in a 180°C (350°F) oven 1 h until tester inserted in center comes out clean. Let cool 5 min; turn out onto serving platter. Cut into 6 slices.

Makes 6 servings.

**Each serving: 1 slice**

| | | |
|---|---|---|
| 3 **⊘** | Protein Choices | 6 g carbohydrate |
| ½ **◑** | Fruits & Vegetables Choice | 20 g protein |
| | | 7 g fat |
| | | 700 kilojoules (167 Calories) |

## CREOLE FISH BAKE

*Only minutes are required to prepare this fish-based meal-in-a-dish. Select the fish best suited to your family's taste preferences and budget.*

| | | |
|---|---|---|
| 1 can | 398 mL (14 oz) tomatoes | 1 can |
| 250 mL | frozen mixed vegetables | 1 cup |
| 125 mL | broth or water | ½ cup |
| 1 | small onion, finely chopped | 1 |
| 75 mL | chopped fresh parsley | 1/3 cup |
| 2 mL | each of thyme, salt and freshly ground pepper | ½ tsp |

| 500 g | frozen fish fillets, partially thawed | 1 lb |
|---|---|---|
| 4 | lemon wedges | 4 |

Combine tomatoes, mixed vegetables, broth, onion, parsley, thyme, salt and pepper in a 2 L (8 cup) casserole. Cut fish into 2.5 cm (1 in) chunks and arrange in vegetable mixture. Bake in a 200°C (400°F) oven 25 to 30 min, until fish flakes. Serve in shallow soup bowls garnished with lemon wedges.

Makes 4 servings.

**Each serving: 425 mL (1-2/3 cups)**

3 ☑ Protein Choices
1 ☑ Fruits & Vegetables Choice

12 g carbohydrate
23 g protein
9 g fat

930 kilojoules
(221 Calories)

### POACHED FISH

*Onion, lemon and bay leaf flavor low-energy white fish for an appealing entrée that is as easy on the cook as it is on the figure.*

| 375 mL | water | 1½ cups |
|---|---|---|
| 1 | medium onion, chopped | 1 |
| 4 | slices lemon | 4 |
| 3 | sprigs parsley | 3 |
| 6 | peppercorns | 6 |
| 1 | bay leaf | 1 |
| 5 mL | salt | 1 tsp |
| 500 g | fish fillets | 1 lb |

Combine water, onion, lemon slices, parsley, peppercorns, bay leaf and salt in a large frypan. Bring to a boil. Arrange fish fillets in a single layer in pan, cover and simmer 10 to 12 min until fish flakes. Lift fish from pan with slotted spoon. Lift onions and lemon from pan to serve with fish, if desired.

Makes 4 servings.

**Each serving: about 90 g (3½ oz)**

3 ☑ Protein Choices

1 g carbohydrate
21 g protein
9 g fat

710 kilojoules
(169 Calories)

## STUFFED BAKED FILLETS

*For a finishing touch, serve these quick and easy stuffed fillets with Mushroom or Velouté Sauce. For a more special presentation, spread one quarter of the filling on each of four, long, thin fillets; roll up, secure with a toothpick; cover and bake as directed.*

| | | |
|---|---|---|
| 125 mL | finely chopped celery | ½ cup |
| 75 mL | finely chopped sweet red or green pepper | 1/3 cup |
| 3 | green onions, finely chopped | 3 |
| 175 mL | chicken broth | 2/3 cup |
| 45 mL | dry bread crumbs | 3 tbsp |
| 25 mL | chopped fresh parsley | 2 tbsp |
| 25 mL | chopped walnuts or almonds | 2 tbsp |
| 15 mL | fresh lemon juice | 1 tbsp |
| 2 mL | grated lemon peel | ½ tsp |
| 2 mL | salt | ½ tsp |
| 500 g | fish fillets | 1 lb |
| | Paprika, optional | |

Combine celery, red pepper, onions and 75 mL (1/3 cup) broth in a small frypan. Cover and steam over medium heat about 7 min until vegetables are tender. Stir in bread crumbs, parsley, walnuts, lemon juice, lemon peel and salt. Place half of fillets in a greased, shallow baking dish. Top with vegetable mixture; then remaining fillets. Pour remaining broth over fish. Sprinkle with paprika, if desired. Cover loosely. Bake in a 220°C (425°F) oven 20 min until fish flakes.

Makes 4 servings.

**Each serving: ¼ recipe**

| | | |
|---|---|---|
| 3 | Protein Choices | 5 g carbohydrate |
| ½ | Fruits & Vegetables Choice | 22 g protein |
| ½ | Fats & Oils Choice | 12 g fat |
| | | 900 kilojoules (216 Calories) |

# One-Dish Meals

Meals in one dish range from the elaborate to the simple, and are always easy to serve.

Convenience is what makes them special. Many can be prepared ahead of time when schedules are hectic, so that all the fuss and muss is long gone at meal time.

In these dishes the nourishment and ingredients of a whole meal are cooked in one pan or dish. Flavors, colors and textures marry as combinations bake or simmer in a creamy or piquant sauce, or mix with a subtle blending of herbs and spices.

Casseroles allow you the opportunity to create combinations that cook virtually unattended.

And stir-frying cooks pre-cut meats and vegetables so quickly that it produces some of the best fast and fresh meals possible.

The addition of a crisp green salad, crunchy pickles or snappy vegetable sticks offers just the right amount of contrast in taste and texture for our dinners-in-a-dish.

For a finishing touch, fruit is ideal, or a small serving of a sweet-tasting treat.

Appetizing and appealing one-dish meals are perfect for the family and equally good for entertaining.

129

## CHICKEN AND SNOW PEA ORIENTAL

*This quick-to-prepare, stir-fry combination makes a complete and colorful meal. French-cut green beans or chopped broccoli can be substituted for the snow peas.*

| | | |
|---|---|---|
| 500 g | boneless chicken, skinned | 1 lb |
| 10 mL | cornstarch | 2 tsp |
| 25 mL | vegetable oil | 2 tbsp |
| 2 | stalks celery, diagonally sliced | 2 |
| 1 | small onion, thinly sliced | 1 |
| 125 mL | chicken broth | ½ cup |
| 2 mL | ground ginger | ½ tsp |
| 100 g | snow peas | 4 oz |
| 15 mL | soy sauce | 1 tbsp |
| 25 mL | slivered almonds or sliced water chestnuts | 2 tbsp |
| | Salt and freshly ground pepper | |
| 500 mL | hot, cooked long grain rice | 2 cups |

Cut chicken into bite-sized pieces. Coat with cornstarch. Heat 15 mL (1 tbsp) oil in a frypan or wok until hot. Stir-fry chicken pieces 5 to 7 min until golden; remove to a warm plate. Wipe out frypan. Heat remaining oil in frypan; add celery and onion; stir-fry about 4 min. Stir in chicken broth and ginger; simmer about 4 min. Add snow peas, soy sauce, almonds and chicken. Cover and simmer about 2 min. Season with salt and pepper, to taste. Serve immediately over hot rice.

Makes 4 servings.

**Each serving: 500 mL (2 cups)**

| | | |
|---|---|---|
| 3 ⊘ | Protein Choices | 33 g carbohydrate |
| 2 ☐ | Starchy Choices | 26 g protein |
| 2 ▲ | Fats & Oils Choices | 19 g fat |

1710 kilojoules
(407 Calories)

### FRUITED CHICKEN CRÊPES

*When both the crêpes and filling are prepared ahead, a rather special, quick-and-easy meal can be put together in no time at all. Reheat the filling and spoon it into warm crêpes. If you are a microwave cook, the service will be faster. Simply fill crêpes and reheat in the microwave oven.*

| | | | |
|---|---|---|---|
| **300 mL** | chicken broth | **1¼** | **cups** |
| **15 mL** | raisins | **1** | **tbsp** |
| **6** | apricot halves, coarsely chopped | **6** | |
| **2 mL** | each of cinnamon and chili powder | **½** | **tsp** |
| **300 mL** | chopped cooked chicken | **1¼** | **cups** |
| **2** | *Crêpes* (recipe, p.52) | **2** | |
| **15 mL** | slivered almonds, toasted | **1** | **tbsp** |

Combine broth, raisins, apricots, cinnamon and chili powder in a saucepan. Bring to a boil; reduce heat and simmer uncovered, stirring occasionally, about 15 min until liquid is reduced by about half and is slightly thickened. Stir in chicken, simmer 5 min. Place warm crêpes on warm serving plates. Divide filling between crêpes, reserving a small amount for the top. Roll up crêpes; spoon reserved filling on top. Garnish with almonds. Serve immediately.

Makes 2 servings.

**Each serving: 175 mL (2/3 cup) sauce with 1 crêpe**

3  ☑   Protein Choices
1  ☐   Starchy Choice
½  ◧   Fruits & Vegetables Choice
1  ▲   Fats & Oils Choice

20 g carbohydrate
23 g protein
13 g fat

1210 kilojoules
(289 Calories)

## QUICK QUICHE

*Crustless quiche is a trim version of the usual quiche with its rich pastry. The mixture forms its own crust.*

| | | |
|---|---|---|
| 15 **mL** | margarine or butter | 1 **tbsp** |
| 250 **mL** | chopped, blanched broccoli | 1 **cup** |
| 375 **mL** | shredded Swiss cheese | 1½ **cups** |
| 50 **mL** | chopped onion | ¼ **cup** |
| 3 | slices lean luncheon meat, chopped | 3 |
| 500 **mL** | 2% milk | 2 **cups** |
| 2 | eggs | 2 |
| 2 | egg whites | 2 |
| 125 **mL** | all purpose flour | ½ **cup** |
| 5 **mL** | baking powder | 1 **tsp** |
| 2 **mL** | salt | ½ **tsp** |
| **pinch** | each of freshly ground pepper and nutmeg | **pinch** |

Grease a 1 L (9 in) pie plate with margarine. Combine broccoli, cheese, onion and luncheon meat; spread in prepared pie plate. Place milk, eggs, egg whites, flour, baking powder, salt, pepper and nutmeg in a blender or food processor. Blend at high speed 1 min or whisk vigorously in a bowl. Pour over vegetable mixture in pie plate. Bake in a 160°C (325°F) oven 45 min or until knife inserted near center comes out clean. Let stand 5 min before serving.

Makes 6 servings.

**Each serving: 1/6 pie**

| | | |
|---|---|---|
| 2 **◪** | Protein Choices | 13 g carbohydrate |
| 1 **☐** | Starchy Choice | 18 g protein |
| 2 **▲** | Fats & Oils Choices | 17 g fat |

1160 kilojoules
(277 Calories)

## BURGER PIZZA

*Favorite meat loaf ingredients are combined, then shaped, as a pizza crust and topped with an assortment of toppings. A tasty, hearty pizza results, good enough for a meal. Just add tossed greens and a few carrot sticks.*

| | | | |
|---|---|---|---|
| **500 g** | lean ground beef | **1 lb** | |
| 5 | soda crackers, crushed | 5 | |
| 50 mL | finely chopped onion | ¼ cup | |
| 50 mL | finely chopped celery | ¼ cup | |
| 1 | egg | 1 | |
| 5 mL | prepared mustard | 1 tsp | |
| 5 mL | Worcestershire sauce | 1 tsp | |
| 2 mL | oregano | ½ tsp | |
| 6 | mushrooms, sliced | 6 | |
| 2 | slices lean luncheon meat or 25 g (1 oz) salami, cut into strips | 2 | |
| 1 | medium tomato, sliced | 1 | |
| ½ | green pepper, slivered | ½ | |
| | Freshly ground pepper | | |
| **250 mL** | shredded Mozzarella | **1 cup** | |
| **15 mL** | grated Parmesan cheese | **1 tbsp** | |

Combine ground beef, cracker crumbs, onion, celery, egg, mustard, Worcestershire sauce and oregano; mix well. Line a jelly roll or pizza pan with foil. Pat beef mixture into a 25 cm (10 in) flat patty on foil. Form a ridge around the edge. Scatter mushrooms, luncheon meat, tomato and green pepper over top. Sprinkle with pepper. Top with Mozzarella and Parmesan cheeses. Bake in a 180°C (350°F) oven 15 to 20 min until meat is no longer pink. Cut into 8 wedges.

Makes 8 servings.

**Each serving: 1/8 pizza**

2 **⊘** Protein Choices
½ **▲** Fats & Oils Choice

3 g carbohydrate
16 g protein
9 g fat

660 kilojoules
(157 Calories)

## PIZZA LOVERS' PIZZA

*This is a hearty pizza—not for dieters—with a juicy and delicious topping which lives up to the wonderful aroma it produces as it cooks. It's for pizza lovers of all ages.*

| | | | |
|---|---|---|---|
| 5 mL | sugar | 1 | tsp |
| 125 mL | warm water | ½ | cup |
| 7 mL | active dry yeast (½ packet) | 1½ | tsp |
| 275 mL | all purpose flour | 1 | cup and 2 tbsp |
| 7 mL | baking powder | 1½ | tsp |
| 2 mL | salt | ½ | tsp |
| 15 mL | margarine | 1 | tbsp |

**Topping:**

| | | | |
|---|---|---|---|
| 250 mL | *Spaghetti Sauce* (recipe, p.46) | 1 | cup |
| 4 | green onions, chopped | 4 | |
| 1 | small green pepper, coarsely chopped | 1 | |
| 500 mL | sliced mushrooms | 2 | cups |
| 75 g | pepperoni, sliced | 3 | oz |
| 250 g | Mozzarella cheese, shredded | 8 | oz |
| 25 mL | grated Parmesan cheese | 2 | tbsp |

Dissolve sugar in warm water. Sprinkle yeast over water; let stand 5 min; stir well. Combine 125 mL (½ cup) flour, baking powder and salt. Cut in margarine. Add yeast mixture; beat vigorously to make a sticky dough. Gradually stir in another 125 mL (½ cup) flour to make a stiff dough. Knead remaining flour into dough on a board; continue kneading about 20 times until dough is smooth. Cover and let stand at least 10 min. Stretch and pat out dough onto a greased, 30 cm (12 in) pizza pan, forming a rim around the edge. Bake in a 190°C (375°F) oven 10 min. Remove and top with spaghetti sauce, green onions, green pepper, mushrooms, pepperoni, Mozzarella and Parmesan cheeses. (Place aluminum foil around edge of pan to catch drippings, if desired.) Bake in a 190°C (375°F) oven 20 to 25 min until crust is done in center. Cut into wedges.

Makes 4 servings.

**Each serving: 1/4 pizza**

| | | |
|---|---|---|
| 3 ▨ | Protein Choices | 33 g carbohydrate |
| 2 ☐ | Starchy Choices | 24 g protein |
| 3 ▲ | Fats & Oils Choices | 23 g fat |

1820 kilojoules
(435 Calories)

## CHILI CON CARNE

*Taste* Chili Con Carne *after it has cooked an hour or so to see if more chili powder is required.*

| | | | |
|---|---|---|---|
| 5 mL | vegetable oil | 1 | tsp |
| 750 g | lean ground beef | 1½ | lbs |
| 250 mL | chopped onion | 1 | cup |
| 1 | large green pepper, chopped | 1 | |
| 1 | clove garlic, finely chopped | 1 | |
| 2 cans | each 540 mL (19 oz) tomatoes | 2 | cans |
| 1 can | 398 mL (14 oz) tomato sauce | 1 | can |
| 5 to 7 mL | chili powder | 1 to 1½ | tsp |
| 5 mL | salt | 1 | tsp |
| 2 mL | oregano | ½ | tsp |
| pinch | each of ground cloves and freshly ground pepper | pinch | |
| 1 | bay leaf | 1 | |
| 1 can | 540 mL (19 oz) kidney beans | 1 | can |

Rub a large, heavy pot with vegetable oil. Stir-cook beef, onion and green pepper until meat loses its pink color. Spoon off any fat. Add garlic, tomatoes, tomato sauce, chili powder, salt, oregano, cloves, pepper and bay leaf. Cover loosely and simmer about 1 h. Stir in kidney beans and cook 20 min longer. Remove bay leaf and serve.

Makes 6 servings.

**Each serving: about 300 mL (1¼ cups)**

3½ 🖉 Protein Choices

2 ◻ Starchy Choices

31 g carbohydrate

29 g protein

10 g fat

1390 kilojoules
(330 Calories)

## LASAGNA

*This version of a favorite meal-in-a-dish is excellent with a green salad. It rates low enough in starch and carbohydrate to be included in most meal plans.*

| 125 mL | grated Parmesan cheese | ½ cup |
| 250 mL | Basic White Sauce (recipe, p.45) | 1 cup |
| 9 | lasagna noodles | 9 |
| 500 g | lean ground beef | 1 lb |
| 1 pkg | 340 g (12 oz) frozen chopped spinach, thawed | 1 pkg |
| 250 g | Mozzarella cheese, shredded | 8 oz |
| 750 mL | Spaghetti Sauce (recipe, p.46) | 3 cups |

Reserve 15 mL (1 tbsp) Parmesan cheese for topping. Stir remainder into the *Basic White Sauce;* set aside. Cook noodles according to package directions just until tender; drain and separate. Brown ground beef in a frypan over medium heat until no longer pink; spoon off fat. Place spinach in sieve; press out excess water. Spread about 200 mL (¾ cup) *Spaghetti Sauce* in the bottom of a greased, 3.5 L (13 x 9 in) baking dish. Top with 3 lasagna noodles, half the spinach and half the beef, a third of the Parmesan sauce and another 200 mL (¾ cup) *Spaghetti Sauce.* Repeat with same quantities of noodles, spinach, meat, Parmesan and spaghetti sauces. Top with last 3 noodles and remainder of Parmesan sauce, Mozzarella cheese, *Spaghetti Sauce* and reserved Parmesan cheese. Cover with aluminum foil. Bake in a 180°C (350°F) oven 35 min. Remove cover and bake 10 min longer until lightly browned. Let stand 5 min before serving.

Makes 9 servings.

**Each serving: one 7.5 x 10 cm (3 x 4 in) piece**

| | | |
|---|---|---|
| 3 | ⊘ | Protein Choices |
| 1 | ☐ | Starchy Choice |
| 1 | ▲ | Fats & Oils Choice |

15 g carbohydrate
21 g protein
13 g fat

1100 kilojoules
(261 Calories)

## CURRIED PORK AND FRUIT

*Prepare curry early in the day or the day before, and refrigerate. For the best flavor, add the peach or orange during the last 10 minutes of the reheating time.*

| | | |
|---|---|---|
| 500 g | lean pork shoulder, leg or loin | 1 lb |
| 25 mL | vinegar | 5 tsp |
| 2 mL | salt | ½ tsp |
| 1 mL | freshly ground pepper | ¼ tsp |
| 10 mL | vegetable oil | 2 tsp |
| 5 mL | curry powder | 1 tsp |
| 5 mL | finely chopped ginger root | 1 tsp |
| 1 mL | each of cinnamon and ground cloves | ¼ tsp |
| 1 | small clove garlic, finely chopped | 1 |
| 250 mL | water | 1 cup |
| 1 | medium onion, chopped | 1 |
| 25 mL | all purpose flour | 2 tbsp |
| 45 mL | raisins | 3 tbsp |
| 1 | peach or orange, peeled and cut into chunks | 1 |

Cut pork into bite-sized pieces. Combine vinegar, salt and pepper in a glass bowl; add meat and toss together. Combine oil, curry powder, ginger root, cinnamon, cloves and garlic in a heavy frypan. Stir-cook over medium heat just until mixture bubbles. Add 75 mL (1/3 cup) water and onion; stir-cook over medium heat 4 min. Sprinkle flour over meat mixture; toss together and add to onions; continue stir-cooking about 4 min until meat loses its pink color. Stir in remaining water and raisins. Heat to a boil; cover and reduce heat; simmer slowly 35 min but *do not boil*. Add peach chunks and continue cooking 10 min. Serve immediately.

Makes 4 servings.

**Each serving: 175 mL (2/3 cup)**

| | | |
|---|---|---|
| 3 | ⊘ Protein Choices | 11 g carbohydrate |
| 1 | ▱ Fruits & Vegetables Choice | 22 g protein |
| ½ | ▲ Fats & Oils Choice | 12 g fat |

1010 kilojoules
(240 Calories)

## POLYNESIAN PORK

*Pork is one of the most versatile meats. Here it goes well with pineapple and green pepper in a quick, stir-fry dish which is colorful and has terrific taste appeal.*

| | | | |
|---|---|---|---|
| 750 g | lean pork shoulder, loin or leg | 1½ | lb |
| 15 mL | vegetable oil | 1 | tbsp |
| 1 can | 398 mL (14 oz) unsweetened pineapple chunks | 1 | can |
| 15 mL | soy sauce | 1 | tbsp |
| 5 mL | ground ginger | 1 | tsp |
| 1 mL | freshly ground pepper | ¼ | tsp |
| 10 mL | cornstarch | 2 | tsp |
| 15 mL | water | 1 | tbsp |
| 1 | small green pepper, seeded, cut into chunks | 1 | |
| 10 mL | unsweetened shredded coconut | 2 | tsp |

Cut pork into bite-sized cubes. Heat oil in frypan. Stir-fry pork until lightly brown. Drain pineapple; set chunks aside. Combine pineapple liquid, soy sauce, ginger and pepper. Pour over pork. Cover and simmer 20 min. Blend together cornstarch and water. Stir into pan juices. Bring to a boil, stir and cook about 3 min until sauce thickens. Stir in pineapple chunks and green pepper. Cook 2 to 3 min longer, stirring, until mixture coats and glazes pork cubes. Serve garnished with coconut.

Makes 6 servings.

**Each serving: about 200 mL (¾ cup)**

3 ⊘ Protein Choices
1 ⊘ Fruits & Vegetables Choice
½ ▲ Fats & Oils Choice

10 g carbohydrate
21 g protein
12 g fat

970 kilojoules
(232 Calories)

## SAUCY HAM STUFFED POTATOES

*Ham and potatoes go well together, stuffed back into baked potato shells. The presentation is nice enough for company.*

| | | |
|---|---|---|
| 4 | small baking potatoes | 4 |
| 250 g | cooked ham, coarsely chopped; about 500 mL (2 cups) | 8 oz |
| 50 mL | dry white wine | ¼ cup |
| 125 mL | water | ½ cup |
| 10 mL | margarine or butter | 2 tsp |
| 1 mL | tarragon | ¼ tsp |
| 750 mL | sliced fresh mushrooms | 3 cups |
| 25 mL | tomato paste | 2 tbsp |
| 2 | green onions, finely chopped | 2 |
| 75 mL | evaporated 2% milk | 1/3 cup |

Wash potatoes; prick skins with fork. Bake in a 200°C (400°F) oven 45 min until tender. Place ham in casserole, cover and heat in oven with potatoes 10 min. Combine wine, 25 mL (2 tbsp) water, margarine and tarragon in a frypan. Add mushrooms, cover; bring quickly to a foaming boil, cook 2 min; remove mushrooms with slotted spoon to a warm plate. Add remaining water, tomato paste and green onions; stir-cook 2 min. Cut baked potatoes in half. Scoop out most of potato, leaving just enough so skin retains shell shape; keep warm. Mash potato, stir into mixture in frypan. Heat to a boil; stir-cook 1 min. Stir in ham, mushrooms and evaporated milk. Stir-cook until heated through, but *do not boil*. Spoon into reserved potato shells. Serve immediately.

Makes 4 servings.

**Each serving: 1 stuffed potato**

| | | |
|---|---|---|
| 2 ✪ | Protein Choices | 21 g carbohydrate |
| 1 ☐ | Starchy Choice | 19 g protein |
| 1 ◆ | Milk Choice (2%) | 9 g fat |
| | | 1010 kilojoules (241 Calories) |

## ENCHILADAS

*The herbs and peppers make this south-of-the-border favorite a flavorful but not spicy meal-in-a-dish for the whole family.*

| 12 | 15 cm (6 in) *Whole Wheat Flour Tortillas* (recipe, p.54) | 12 |
|---|---|---|
| 500 g | lean ground beef | 1 lb |
| 1 | clove garlic, finely chopped | 1 |
| 2 | sweet green peppers, seeded and chopped | 2 |
| 1 | small onion, chopped | 1 |
| 50 mL | chopped fresh cilantro or parsley | ¼ cup |
| 500 mL | water | 2 cups |
| 25 mL | fresh lime or lemon juice | 2 tbsp |
| 5 mL | salt | 1 tsp |
| 1 mL | each freshly ground pepper and chili powder | ¼ tsp |
| 375 mL | 2% cottage cheese | 1½ cups |
| 25 mL | grated Parmesan cheese | 2 tbsp |
| 125 mL | shredded Mozzarella cheese | ½ cup |

**Fresh Tomato Sauce:**

| 2 | firm tomatoes, seeded and chopped | 2 |
|---|---|---|
| 1 | sweet green pepper, seeded and chopped | 1 |
| 25 mL | chopped onion | 2 tbsp |
| 15 mL | chopped fresh cilantro or parsley | 1 tbsp |
| 50 mL | water | ¼ cup |

Cook tortillas until very lightly browned but still pliable. Brown ground beef and garlic in a frypan until meat is no longer pink. Add green pepper, onion, cilantro, water, lime juice, salt, pepper and chili powder. Simmer about 15 min or until liquid is reduced by half. Stir in cottage and Parmesan cheeses. Continue simmering 5 min. Spoon about 25 mL (2 tbsp) meat mixture into each tortilla; roll tortilla around filling to make enchiladas and place in a single layer seamside down in a 2 L (8 cup) lightly greased shallow baking dish. Pour remaining meat mixture over filled enchiladas. Bake in a 180°C (350°F) oven 15 min. Combine tomatoes, chopped pepper, onion, cilantro and water in a small saucepan. Stir-cook over medium heat about 7 min until vegetables are tender. Remove enchiladas from oven, sprinkle Mozzarella cheese over enchiladas, and top with *Tomato Sauce*. Return to oven for 5 min until cheese is melted.

Makes 6 servings.

**Each serving: 2 enchiladas and sauce**

| | | | |
|---|---|---|---|
| 4 | ◻ | Protein Choices | 21 g carbohydrate |
| 1 | ◻ | Starchy Choice | 29 g protein |
| ½ | ◻ | Fruits & Vegetables Choice | 13 g fat |

1330 kilojoules
(317 Calories)

## HAM AND ASPARAGUS ROLL-UPS

*Tucked inside each ham roll are sprightly green asparagus spears. In early spring, when fresh tender asparagus comes to produce bins, this creation becomes an outstanding specialty.*

| | | | |
|---|---|---|---|
| **12 slices** | each 25 g (1 oz) cooked ham | **12 slices** | |
| **200 mL** | shredded Cheddar, Edam or Gouda cheese | **¾ cup** | |
| **24** | fresh or frozen asparagus spears, partially cooked | **24** | |
| **275 mL** | *Cheese Sauce* (recipe, p.48) | **1 cup, 2 tbsp** | |
| **1 mL** | paprika | **¼ tsp** | |

Sprinkle approximately 15 mL cheese over each ham slice. Roll up 2 asparagus spears inside each; arrange in a shallow baking dish. Pour sauce over roll-ups. Sprinkle with paprika. Bake in a 180°C (350°F) oven 15 to 20 min until sauce bubbles.

Makes 6 servings.

**Each serving: 2 roll-ups and sauce**

| | | | |
|---|---|---|---|
| 3 | ◻ | Protein Choices | 5 g carbohydrate |
| ½ | ◻ | Fruits & Vegetables Choice | 22 g protein |
| 1 | ▲ | Fats & Oils Choice | 15 g fat |

1010 kilojoules
(243 Calories)

## TACOS

Tacos *come to us from our neighbors to the south. Their uniqueness is derived from the contrasting flavors and textures of crisp, fresh vegetables, a tasty meat and bean filling and the bland tortillas.*

**Filling:**

| | | |
|---|---|---|
| 5 mL | vegetable oil | 1 tsp |
| 25 mL | finely chopped onion | 2 tbsp |
| 25 mL | finely chopped green pepper | 2 tbsp |
| 250 g | lean ground beef | ½ lb |
| 5 mL | chili powder | 1 tsp |
| 2 mL | salt | ½ tsp |
| 1 mL | freshly ground pepper | ¼ tsp |
| 1 mL | Worcestershire sauce, optional | ¼ tsp |
| 2 drops | hot pepper sauce | 2 drops |
| 1 can | 156 mL (5½ oz) tomato paste | 1 can |
| 50 mL | water | ¼ cup |
| 1 can | 398 mL (14 oz) red kidney beans | 1 can |
| 12 | *Whole Wheat Flour Tortillas,* each 15 cm (6 in) (recipe, p.54) | 12 |

**Topping:**

| | | |
|---|---|---|
| 750 mL | assorted chopped vegetables (lettuce, tomatoes, cucumber, celery) | 3 cups |
| 125 mL | shredded Cheddar cheese | ½ cup |

Heat oil in saucepan. Sauté onion and green pepper 2 min. Add ground meat. Stir-cook until brown; drain off fat. Season with chili powder, salt, pepper, Worcestershire sauce, if desired, and hot pepper sauce. Stir in tomato paste, water and kidney beans. Simmer, stirring occasionally, 20 min. (Mixture should be very thick.) Prepare tortillas while sauce cooks. Fold each in half once it is removed from frypan. Fill each tortilla shell with 50 mL (¼ cup) sauce. Top each with 50 mL (¼ cup) chopped vegetables and sprinkle with 10 mL (2 tsp) shredded cheese.

Makes 12 tacos.

**Each serving: 1 taco**

| | | |
|---|---|---|
| 1 | ⊘ Protein Choice | 16 g carbohydrate |
| 1 | ☐ Starchy Choice | 9 g protein |
| ½ | ▲ Fats & Oils Choice | 5 g fat |
| | | 610 kilojoules |
| | | (145 Calories) |

## SHEPHERD'S PIE

*Use ground beef, pork or lamb to make this quick-to-prepare family favorite. If desired, substitute 375 g (¾ lb) cooked meat such as leftover roast, for the fresh. Chop the leftover meat into small pieces and omit the meat browning step.*

| | | | |
|---|---|---|---|
| 500 mL | peeled potatoes, cut into pieces | 2 | cups |
| 25 mL | grated Parmesan cheese | 2 | tbsp |
| 500 g | lean ground meat | 1 | lb |
| 500 mL | water | 2 | cups |
| 15 mL | all purpose flour | 1 | tbsp |
| 10 mL | Worcestershire sauce | 2 | tsp |
| 1 | bouillon cube, crushed | 1 | |
| 2 mL | celery salt | ½ | tsp |
| 25 mL | chopped onion | 2 | tbsp |
| 375 mL | frozen mixed vegetables | 1½ | cups |
| 250 mL | sliced fresh mushrooms | 1 | cup |

Cook potatoes in lightly salted water just until tender. Drain, reserving 45 mL (3 tbsp) cooking liquid. Mash potatoes with reserved cooking liquid until fluffy; fold in Parmesan cheese. Set aside. Stir-cook meat in a frypan until pinkness disappears; remove to a plate. Remove any fat from frypan. Combine water, flour, Worcestershire sauce, bouillon cube and celery salt in a screw top jar; shake until thoroughly mixed; pour into frypan. Add onion and stir-cook over medium heat 3 min; add vegetables, return to a boil, and stir-cook 2 min. Stir in mushrooms and browned meat. Continue cooking until heated through. Spoon into a 1.5 L (6 cup) casserole; top with potato mixture. Bake in a 190°C (375°F) oven 30 min until potatoes are lightly browned and mixture is bubbly.

Makes 4 servings.

**Each serving: 325 mL (1-1/3 cups)**

| | | |
|---|---|---|
| 3 ⊘ | Protein Choices | 25 g carbohydrate |
| 1 ☐ | Starchy Choice | 26 g protein |
| 1 ⬗ | Fruits & Vegetables Choice | 10 g fat |

1240 kilojoules
(294 Calories)

## EASY OVEN STEW

*Call this one "stay-away stew" if you wish. Let it cook in the oven while you are busy or out for the afternoon. Reduce broth to 125 mL (½ cup) if you prefer making this stew in a slow-cooker or crock pot.*

| | | |
|---|---|---|
| **500 g** | lean stewing beef, cut into bite-sized pieces | **1 lb** |
| **1 can** | 284 mL (10 oz) tomato soup, undiluted | **1 can** |
| **250 mL** | beef broth or water | **1 cup** |
| **2** | medium onions, cut into wedges | **2** |
| **250 mL** | carrot slices | **1 cup** |
| **1** | bay leaf | **1** |
| **2 mL** | salt | **½ tsp** |
| **pinch** | freshly ground pepper | **pinch** |
| **200 mL** | frozen peas | **¾ cup** |

Place beef, tomato soup, broth, onions, carrot slices, bay leaf, salt and pepper in a medium casserole; stir well. Cover. Bake in a 140°C (275°F) oven about 4 h until meat is tender. (Stir once or twice during cooking period.) Add peas about 20 min before stew is done.

Makes 4 servings.

**Each serving: 200 mL (about ¾ cup)**

3 ⊘ Protein Choices
2 ◨ Fruits & Vegetables Choices
½ ▲ Fats & Oils Choice

22 g carbohydrate
25 g protein
11 g fat

1210 kilojoules
(287 Calories)

## COUNTRY SUPPER CABBAGE ROLLS

*Make these cabbage rolls with either sauerkraut or tomato juice. Freezing the head of cabbage is an easy way to wilt the leaves, which helps to remove them from the core.*

| | | |
|---|---|---|
| 24 | medium cabbage leaves (1 medium head) | 24 |
| 500 g | lean ground pork | 1 lb |
| 250 g | lean ground beef | ½ lb |
| 125 mL | uncooked rice | ½ cup |
| 250 mL | water | 1 cup |
| 75 mL | chopped onion | 1/3 cup |
| 1 | clove garlic, finely chopped, optional | 1 |
| 7 mL | salt | 1½ tsp |
| 1 mL | freshly ground pepper | ¼ tsp |
| 250 mL | sauerkraut with juice or tomato juice | 1 cup |

Place head of cabbage in freezer overnight to wilt leaves. (If necessary, hold frozen head under warm water to help remove leaves.) Carefully remove 24 leaves, one at a time, cutting each from the core with a sharp knife. (Use remaining cabbage as a vegetable for other meals.) Trim center rib on individual leaves to make leaf same thickness throughout, but do not remove rib. Combine pork, beef, rice, 125 mL (½ cup) water, onion, garlic, if desired, salt and pepper. Work together with hands until well blended. Place about 25 mL (a heaping tablespoon) of meat mixture on the rib end of each cabbage leaf. Roll up and tuck in sides. Pack cabbage rolls tightly into a 2 L (8 cup) casserole, layering with either sauerkraut or tomato juice. Pour remaining 125 mL (½ cup) water over cabbage rolls. Cover tightly. Bake in a 150°C (300°F) oven 2 h. Reduce heat to 120°C (250°F) and bake an additional 1 h or until meat and rice are cooked.

Makes 8 servings, 24 cabbage rolls.

**Each serving: 3 cabbage rolls**

2 ⊘ Protein Choices
1 ☐ Starchy Choice

14 g carbohydrate
18 g protein
7 g fat

800 kilojoules
(191 Calories)

### SAVORY LUNCHEON BUNS

*These filled buns can help supply the protein for soup or salad meals. One batch makes 36 buns, so freeze extras to thaw later for quick snacks.*

| | | |
|---|---|---|
| 10 mL | sugar | 2 tsp |
| 250 mL | warm water | 1 cup |
| 2 pkgs | each 8 g active dry yeast | 2 pkgs |
| 250 mL | water | 1 cup |
| 125 mL | margarine | ½ cup |
| 75 mL | sugar | 1/3 cup |
| 5 mL | salt | 1 tsp |
| 2 | eggs, beaten | 2 |
| 1.5 L | all purpose flour | 6 cups |

**Filling:**

| | | |
|---|---|---|
| 500 g | finely chopped ham, about 750 mL (3 cups) | 1 lb |
| 1 can | 113 g (4 oz) shrimp, rinsed, drained and chopped | 1 can |
| 50 mL | finely chopped fresh parsley | ¼ cup |
| 50 mL | finely chopped chives or green onion | ¼ cup |
| | Sesame or poppy seeds, optional | |

Dissolve 10 mL (2 tsp) sugar in 250 mL (1 cup) warm water. Add yeast; let stand 10 min; stir well. Combine remaining water, margarine, sugar and salt in a saucepan. Heat just until margarine is melted. Cool to *lukewarm*. Stir margarine mixture into dissolved yeast. Beat in eggs and 750 mL (3 cups) flour until smooth. Gradually stir in enough of the remaining flour to make a soft dough. Turn out on a lightly floured board. Knead 8 to 10 min until smooth and elastic. Place in a greased bowl; turn to grease top. Cover and let rise in a draft-free place about 1 h until doubled in bulk. Prepare filling: Mix together ham, shrimp, parsley and chives until well combined. Set aside. Punch down dough and roll into a 45 cm (18 in) square about 5 mm (¼ in) thick. Cut into 36 circles using a 9 cm (3½ in) round cutter. (A clean food can with both ends removed may be used.) Place about 25 mL (2 tbsp) filling in center of each round. Pinch edges together tightly and roll between palms to form a bun. Place seam-side down about 5 cm (2 in) apart on greased baking sheets. If desired, lightly brush tops with water, sprinkle with sesame or poppy seeds, pressing seeds lightly into dough. Cover and let rise about 30 min until light. Bake in a 200°C (400°F) oven 12 to 14 min until golden brown. Serve warm. Refrigerate any leftovers.

Makes 36 filled buns.

**Each serving: 1 bun**

| | | | |
|---|---|---|---|
| 1 | ⊘ | Protein Choice | 16 g carbohydrate |
| 1 | ▢ | Starchy Choice | 7 g protein |

4 g fat

540 kilojoules
(128 Calories)

## LAMB CURRY

*Leftover lamb is best served warm. A curry presents a totally new flavor and appeal when the lamb "roast" makes its encore. Cooked pork or beef may be substituted.*

| | | |
|---|---|---|
| 375 **g** | cooked lean lamb | ¾ **lb** |
| 20 **mL** | vegetable oil | 4 **tsp** |
| 250 **mL** | chopped onion | 1 **cup** |
| 5 to 10 **mL** | curry powder | 1 to 2 **tsp** |
| 500 **mL** | beef broth | 2 **cups** |
| 25 **mL** | all purpose flour | 2 **tbsp** |
| 2 **mL** | salt | ½ **tsp** |
| **pinch** | freshly ground pepper | **pinch** |
| 1 **mL** | cinnamon | ¼ **tsp** |
| 1 | small apple, peeled, cored and chopped | 1 |

Cut meat into 2.5 cm (1 in) cubes and set aside. Heat 15 mL (1 tbsp) oil in a medium frypan; add chopped onion; sauté over low heat 5 min. Add remaining oil and stir in curry powder; cook 1 min. Pour broth and flour into a screw-top jar; shake well until thoroughly mixed. Pour over onion mixture in frypan and stir-cook over medium heat until thickened. Add meat, salt, pepper and cinnamon. Cover pan and simmer 20 min. Add apple and continue cooking 5 min longer.

Makes 4 servings.

**Each serving: 250 mL (1 cup)**

| | | | |
|---|---|---|---|
| 3 | ⊘ | Protein Choices | 9 g carbohydrate |
| 1 | ▨ | Fruits & Vegetables Choice | 25 g protein |
| 1 | ▲ | Fats & Oils Choice | 14 g fat |

1100 kilojoules
(262 Calories)

## TURKEY TETRAZZINI

*When there are no turkey leftovers on hand, economical turkey parts can be simmered to provide the cooked turkey for Tetrazzini. This is a popular dish for family meals and for entertaining.*

| | | | |
|---|---|---|---|
| 25 mL | margarine or butter | 2 | tbsp |
| 250 g | fresh mushrooms, sliced | ½ | lb |
| 15 mL | lemon juice | 1 | tbsp |
| 100 mL | all purpose flour | 6 | tbsp |
| 625 mL | turkey or chicken broth | 2½ | cups |
| 250 mL | 2% milk | 1 | cup |
| 50 mL | dry sherry | ¼ | cup |
| 25 mL | chopped fresh parsley or 10 mL (2 tsp) dried parsley | 2 | tbsp |
| 5 mL | salt | 1 | tsp |
| 2 mL | each of nutmeg and onion powder | ½ | tsp |
| pinch | each of paprika and white pepper | | pinch |
| 250 g | spaghetti or thin noodles | ½ | lb |
| 1 L | chopped, cooked turkey | 4 | cups |
| 50 mL | grated Parmesan cheese | ¼ | cup |

Heat 10 mL (2 tsp) margarine in a frypan; sauté mushrooms 5 min; sprinkle with lemon juice. Melt remaining margarine in a medium saucepan. Blend in flour until smooth. Add broth and milk, stirring briskly to remove any lumps. Bring to a boil; add sherry, parsley, salt, nutmeg, onion powder, paprika and pepper; continue cooking 2 to 3 min until thickened. Cook spaghetti according to package directions. Drain. Pour enough sauce into a lightly greased, 2.5 L (10 cup) casserole to coat the bottom. Layer mushrooms, spaghetti and turkey over sauce. Pour remainder of sauce over turkey. Sprinkle with Parmesan cheese. Bake in a 180°C (350°F) oven 30 to 40 min or until mixture bubbles.

Makes 8 servings.

**Each serving: 250 mL (1 cup)**

3 ⊘ Protein Choices
2 ☐ Starchy Choices

30 g carbohydrate
23 g protein
11 g fat

1310 kilojoules
(311 Calories)

# Meatless Dishes

It is possible to have a nutritionally well-balanced diet without the inclusion of meat, fish or poultry as the source of protein. For vegetarians who do not eat meat, there is a choice of alternatives—milk and milk products, eggs, dried peas, beans and lentils, nuts, seeds, breads and cereals.

The *quality of the protein* we eat is as important as the amount. Generally, protein obtained from animal sources is superior to that obtained from plants. Protein is composed of many smaller units called amino acids. The protein obtained from an animal source (meat, fish, eggs, milk and cheese) provides all of the essential amino acids required by the human body and is called a *complete protein*. Most protein obtained from plants is missing or low in one or more of the essential amino acids and is therefore called an *incomplete protein*.

The quality of a plant protein can be improved by combining it with another protein which will supply the missing amino acid. For instance, the addition of a small amount of an animal protein—milk, to a cereal protein such as rolled oats—will yield a combination of amino acids similar to that of a *complete protein*. Plant proteins from different sources also can be teamed up to improve their value, for example, rice and lentils. Other combinations that work are: corn and beans; macaroni and cheese; rice and peas; sesame seeds and yogurt; tortillas and kidney beans; and so on.

A meatless meal gives the budget a break, provides dietary fiber and is a flavorful change from traditional meat dishes. Meals based on combinations of plant proteins can provide protein that is equal in value to meats without the cholesterol or fat.

Our meatless dishes are relatively inexpensive, attractive and tasty—well worth trying.

## MOCK EGG SALAD

*Real egg salad contains quite a bit of fat from the egg yolk. This version, made with chick peas, provides the egg salad taste and protein with almost no fat. Serve it stuffed in a tomato on a lettuce leaf, or open-faced on whole wheat toast, garnished with cucumber slices.*

| | | |
|---|---|---|
| **1 can** | 540 mL (19 oz) chick peas, drained | **1 can** |
| **50 mL** | *Tangy Boiled Dressing* (recipe, p.89) | **¼ cup** |
| **50 mL** | chopped celery | **¼ cup** |
| **2 mL** | basil | **½ tsp** |
| **1 mL** | each of curry powder and garlic salt | **¼ tsp** |

Coarsely mash chick peas. Combine with *Tangy Boiled Dressing*, celery, basil, curry powder and garlic salt; mix until well blended. Note: mixture may be made in food processor or blender; *do not over-process*. A coarse texture is more like a real egg salad.

Makes 6 servings.

**Each serving: 75 mL (1/3 cup)**

½ 🖉 Protein Choice
1 ◻ Starchy Choice

15 g carbohydrate
5 g protein
2 g fat

410 kilojoules
(98 Calories)

**Vitamins are essential to life since they act as "spark plugs" or catalysts in many of the chemical processes which occur in the body. A well-balanced diet should provide adequate amounts, and vitamin supplements should not be necessary.**

## LENTIL BURGERS

Lentil Burgers *are a tasty, timely and inexpensive substitute for meat patties. You'll be surprised at how similar they are in taste. The addition of bread crumbs and cheese makes them a complete protein.*

| | | |
|---|---|---|
| **1 can** | 540 mL (19 oz) brown lentils | **1 can** |
| **175 mL** | bread crumbs | **2/3 cup** |
| **50 mL** | finely chopped onion | **¼ cup** |
| **50 mL** | finely chopped celery | **¼ cup** |
| **75 mL** | water | **1/3 cup** |
| **5 mL** | Worcestershire sauce | **1 tsp** |
| **2 mL** | each of salt and freshly ground pepper | **½ tsp** |
| **15 mL** | vegetable oil | **1 tbsp** |
| **2** | process cheese slices | **2** |

Rinse, drain and mash lentils in a large bowl; add bread crumbs, onion, celery, water, Worcestershire sauce, salt and pepper. Mix well and form into 4 burgers each about 1.5 cm (5/8 in) thick. Heat oil in frypan; brown burgers on both sides over medium heat, about 5 min per side. Top each with half a cheese slice.

Makes 4 servings.

**Each serving: 1 burger**

1 **⊘** Protein Choice
2 **▢** Starchy Choices
1 **▲** Fats & Oils Choice

28 g carbohydrate
12 g protein
9 g fat

1010 kilojoules
(241 Calories)

---

**Minerals have a variety of functions in the body including playing a role in bone formation, muscle contractions and activities of the cardiovascular system. A well-balanced diet should provide adequate amounts of minerals.**

### TOFU CHOP SUEY

*Tofu supplies the protein, and tastes similar to chicken breasts, in this quick-to-prepare, colorful vegetarian main dish.*

| | | |
|---|---|---|
| **250 g** | tofu | **8 oz** |
| **10 mL** | vegetable oil | **2 tsp** |
| **50 mL** | chicken or vegetable broth | **¼ cup** |
| **1 mL** | ground ginger | **¼ tsp** |
| **250 mL** | sliced celery | **1 cup** |
| **1** | small onion, coarsely chopped | **1** |
| **¼** | sweet red pepper, slivered | **¼** |
| **375 mL** | fresh bean sprouts, washed and well drained | **1½ cups** |
| **15 mL** | soy sauce | **1 tbsp** |
| | Freshly ground pepper and salt | |

Drain tofu; cut into 2 cm (¾ in) pieces, place between layers of paper towel and weight down with a dinner plate; let stand 10 min to compress and remove excess water. Heat oil, 25 mL (2 tbsp) broth and ginger in a frypan. Add celery, onion and red pepper; stir-cook over medium heat 3 min. Add bean sprouts; continue stir-cooking 1 min. Stir in remaining broth, soy sauce and tofu; cook and stir gently over medium heat until vegetables are tender-crisp, and liquid is evaporated. Season to taste with pepper and salt.

Makes 2 servings.

**Each serving: about 450 mL (1¾ cups)**

| | | |
|---|---|---|
| 2 | **⊘** Protein Choices | 13 g carbohydrate |
| 1 | **⊘** Fruits & Vegetables Choice | 13 g protein |
| 1 | **▲** Fats & Oils Choice | 10 g fat |

810 kilojoules
(194 Calories)

## BEAN-STUFFED CABBAGE ROLLS

*Black-eyed peas and barley go into the savory filling which steams inside green cabbage leaves.*

| 16 | medium cabbage leaves<br>(1 small head) | 16 |
|---|---|---|
| 500 mL | cooked black-eyed peas,<br>mashed | 2 cups |
| 250 mL | cooked barley | 1 cup |
| 250 mL | finely chopped celery | 1 cup |
| 125 mL | finely chopped onion | ½ cup |
| 5 mL | salt | 1 tsp |
| 2 mL | basil | ½ tsp |
| pinch | each of oregano and thyme | pinch |
| 2 drops | hot pepper sauce | 2 drops |
| 500 mL | tomato juice | 2 cups |

Place head of cabbage in freezer overnight to wilt leaves. (Hold frozen head under warm water to help remove leaves.) Carefully remove leaves one at a time, cutting each from the core with a sharp knife. (Use remaining cabbage as vegetable for other meals.) Trim center rib on individual leaves to make leaf same thickness throughout, but do not remove rib. Mash black-eyed peas and barley together in a mixing bowl. Add celery, onion, salt, basil, oregano, thyme and hot pepper sauce. Mix until well blended. Place about 50 mL (¼ cup) of pea mixture on rib end of each cabbage leaf. Roll up, tuck in sides. Pack cabbage rolls tightly into a 2 L (8 cup) casserole. Pour tomato juice over cabbage rolls; cover. Bake in a 180°C (350°F) oven 1 h.

Makes 16 cabbage rolls.

**Each serving: 1 cabbage roll**

1 ◪ Fruits & Vegetables Choice

10 g carbohydrate
3 g protein

220 kilojoules
(52 Calories)

**The B complex vitamins are obtained from a variety of foods such as whole grain and enriched breads and cereals, liver and other organ meats, lean meat, fish, milk products and dried peas and beans.**

## SPANISH BULGUR

*Bulgur, garbanzos and soy nuts combine to provide complete protein in Spanish Bulgur, which tastes as good or even better than Spanish rice.*

| | | |
|---|---|---|
| 25 mL | vegetable oil | 2 tbsp |
| 250 mL | thinly sliced carrot | 1 cup |
| 125 mL | coarsely chopped onion | ½ cup |
| 1 | clove garlic, finely chopped | 1 |
| 300 mL | bulgur | 1¼ cups |
| 750 mL | hot chicken or beef broth | 3 cups |
| 1 can | 540 mL (19 oz) tomatoes | 1 can |
| 10 mL | paprika | 2 tsp |
| 5 mL | each of tarragon and salt | 1 tsp |
| pinch | freshly ground pepper | pinch |
| 250 mL | coarsely chopped celery | 1 cup |
| 250 mL | coarsely chopped green pepper | 1 cup |
| 250 mL | cooked garbanzo beans (chick peas), drained | 1 cup |
| 125 mL | coarsely chopped soy nuts | ½ cup |

Heat oil in a frypan; add carrot, onion and garlic; stir-cook over medium heat 5 min. Add bulgur. Continue to stir-cook about 3 min until bulgur is coated with pan juices. Add broth, tomatoes, paprika, tarragon, salt and pepper. Heat to a boil; reduce heat, cover and simmer 30 min. Stir in celery, green pepper, chick peas and soy nuts; cover and simmer 15 min longer until bulgur is tender and juices are absorbed. Turn off heat, let stand, covered, 10 min. Fluff with a fork.

Makes 8 servings.

**Each serving: 250 mL (1 cup)**

| | |
|---|---|
| 1 ☑ Protein Choice | 32 g carbohydrate |
| 2 ☐ Starchy Choices | 7 g protein |
| | 5 g fat |
| | 850 kilojoules |
| | (201 Calories) |

## SCALLOPED SOYBEANS

*The soybeans pick up the flavor of the accompanying vegetables. They can be served in a vegetarian meal that might be low in protein.*

| | | |
|---|---|---|
| 250 mL | soybeans, soaked overnight, drained | 1 cup |
| 750 mL | water | 3 cups |
| 1 | onion, chopped | 1 |
| 250 mL | chopped celery | 1 cup |
| 125 mL | sweet red or green pepper | ½ cup |
| 125 mL | tomato sauce | ½ cup |
| 50 mL | boiling water | ¼ cup |
| 2 mL | salt | ½ tsp |
| 50 mL | fresh bread crumbs | ¼ cup |
| 10 mL | margarine or butter, softened | 2 tsp |

Place soybeans in saucepan with 750 mL (3 cups) water; boil 10 min. Cover and simmer 1.5 to 2 h, until beans soften. Pour into 1.5 L (6 cup) casserole. Stir in onion, celery, red pepper, tomato sauce, boiling water and salt. Combine bread crumbs and margarine; sprinkle over soybean mixture. Bake in a 180°C (350°F) oven 1.5 to 2 h until beans are tender.

Makes 6 servings.

**Each serving: 175 mL (2/3 cup)**

½ ∅ Protein Choice
½ ☐ Starchy Choice

7 g carbohydrate
3 g protein
3 g fat

280 kilojoules
(67 Calories)

The soybean is one of the oldest crops grown by man and is native to China. It has been one of the most important sources of protein there for many centuries. It contains a good quality protein and is rich in calcium, phosphorous and iron. As well as being eaten in its natural bean form, there are many other soybean products including commercial meat substitutes, soybean oil, soy flour, soy milk, Tofu (bean curd), Tempeh (a fermented soybean product) and soy nuts (cooked, roasted soybeans).

## MUSHROOM OMELET

*The secrets to making a good omelet are to beat the eggs just until frothy, and to cook over medium heat. Mushroom omelets are perfect for a breakfast party, brunch or a quick-to-fix light supper.*

| | | | |
|---|---|---|---|
| 5 mL | vegetable oil | 1 | tsp |
| 1 | small onion, chopped | 1 | |
| 250 g | sliced fresh mushrooms | ½ | lb |
| 4 | eggs, beaten lightly | 4 | |
| 50 mL | shredded Swiss cheese | ¼ | cup |
| 15 mL | chopped fresh basil or parsley or 5 mL (1 tsp) dried parsley | 1 | tbsp |
| 2 mL | salt | ½ | tsp |
| 1 mL | white pepper | ¼ | tsp |

Heat oil in omelet pan or frypan. Sauté onion about 2 min. Add mushrooms; sauté 3 min. Beat eggs with cheese, basil, salt and pepper. Pour over mushroom mixture. Lift edges of omelet with a spatula as soon as mixture starts to cook, and tilt pan to allow uncooked egg mixture to run underneath. Cook over low to medium heat 3 to 4 min or until mixture is set on top and golden on bottom. Run spatula around inside of frypan to loosen omelet. Fold omelet in half and turn it out onto a warm serving platter.

Makes 2 servings.

**Each serving: ½ omelet**

3 🖉 Protein Choices

1 🖉 Fruits & Vegetables Choice

2 ▲ Fats & Oils Choices

9 g carbohydrate

20 g protein

18 g fat

1160 kilojoules
(278 Calories)

To make perfect hard-cooked eggs, place eggs in a saucepan and cover with cold water. Bring to a boil. As soon as the water comes to a full boil, turn off the heat; cover tightly; let stand 20 min. After 20 min, pour off the hot water and immediately cool eggs in cold water to prevent a dark ring from forming around the yolks.

## VEGETABLE FRITTATA

*Choose green vegetables that are in season for* Vegetable Frittata. *That is when they are at their prime, and the best price.*

| | | |
|---|---|---|
| 10 mL | margarine or butter | 2 tsp |
| 125 mL | chopped broccoli or asparagus or green beans | ½ cup |
| 125 mL | chopped celery | ½ cup |
| 2 | green onions, chopped | 2 |
| 4 | eggs | 4 |
| 15 mL | water | 1 tbsp |
| 15 mL | chopped fresh parsley or 5 mL (1 tsp) dried parsley | 1 tbsp |
| 2 mL | oregano | ½ tsp |
| 1 mL | garlic salt, optional | ¼ tsp |
| pinch | freshly ground pepper | pinch |

Melt margarine in heavy frypan over medium heat. Add broccoli, celery and onion; stir-cook 4 to 5 min until tender-crisp. Beat together eggs, water, parsley, oregano, garlic salt, if desired, and pepper. Pour over vegetables in frypan; cook about 30 seconds. Cover pan and continue cooking 2 to 3 min or until set. Cut in half; slide out of frypan onto warmed plates.

Makes 2 servings.

**Each serving: ½ recipe**

| | | |
|---|---|---|
| 2 ▨ Protein Choices | | 5 g carbohydrate |
| ½ ▨ Fruits & Vegetables Choice | | 13 g protein |
| 2 ▲ Fats & Oils Choices | | 16 g fat |
| | | 900 kilojoules |
| | | (216 Calories) |

**Citrus fruits are not the only food source of Vitamin C. Other sources include broccoli, Brussels sprouts, cauliflower, green peppers, melons, strawberries and tomatoes.**

## NOODLES ROMANOFF

*Serve these noodles in place of potatoes or when you need to increase the protein in a meal. Whole wheat noodles used in this recipe will provide extra flavor and fiber as well. Chopped fresh parsley may be substituted for the dill weed.*

| | | |
|---|---|---|
| 250 mL | 2% cottage cheese | 1 cup |
| 125 mL | 2% milk | ½ cup |
| 50 mL | grated Parmesan cheese | ¼ cup |
| 2 | green onions, chopped | 2 |
| 15 mL | chopped fresh dill or 5 mL (1 tsp) dried dillweed | 1 tbsp |
| pinch | freshly ground pepper | pinch |
| 150 g | wide or narrow egg noodles, about 1 L (4 cups) | 6 oz |

Blend cottage cheese and milk together by hand, in food processor or blender until very smooth. Add Parmesan cheese, green onions, dill and pepper; mix well. Cook noodles in lightly salted boiling water just until tender; drain; return to saucepan. Fold in cheese mixture. Stir gently over heat just until mixture bubbles. Serve immediately, sprinkled with a little additional grated Parmesan cheese, if desired.

Makes 8 servings.

**Each serving: 125 mL (½ cup)**

1 ∅ Protein Choice
1 ☐ Starchy Choice

17 g carbohydrate
9 g protein
3 g fat

550 kilojoules
(131 Calories)

---

**Adults as well as children need a regular supply of calcium for maintaining strong bones, as well as for other body functions. Good sources of calcium include milk, yogurt and cheese.**

## MACARONI, CHEESE AND TOMATOES

*Tomatoes add a bright note to popular macaroni and cheese. It is an easy-to-make luncheon or supper dish loved by all ages.*

| 250 mL | elbow macaroni | 1 cup |
|---|---|---|
| 1 can | 540 mL (19 oz) tomatoes | 1 can |
| 2 mL | basil or dillweed | ½ tsp |
| 2 mL | prepared mustard | ½ tsp |
| pinch | freshly ground pepper | pinch |
| 250 mL | shredded Cheddar cheese | 1 cup |
| 25 mL | cornflakes, crushed | 2 tbsp |

Cook macaroni in lightly salted boiling water according to package directions. Drain. Break up tomatoes in their juice. Stir in basil, mustard and pepper; add macaroni and cheese; mix lightly. Spoon into a 1.5 L (6 cup) casserole. Sprinkle with cornflake crumbs. Bake in a 180°C (350°F) oven 30 min until crumbs brown and mixture is bubbly.

Makes 4 servings.

**Each serving: 300 mL (1¼ cups)**

1 ▨ Protein Choice
1 ☐ Starchy Choice
1 ▨ Fruits & Vegetables Choice
1 ▲ Fats & Oils Choice

24 g carbohydrate
11 g protein
10 g fat

970 kilojoules
(230 Calories)

### CREAMY MACARONI AND CHEESE

*Old-fashioned* Creamy Macaroni and Cheese *can be made as highly seasoned or as bland as you wish. The age or ripeness of the cheese will determine the strength of the flavor.*

| | | | |
|---|---|---|---|
| 300 mL | elbow macaroni | 1¼ | cups |
| 10 mL | margarine or butter | 2 | tsp |
| 25 mL | all purpose flour | 2 | tbsp |
| 500 mL | 2% milk | 2 | cups |
| 2 mL | salt | ½ | tsp |
| pinch | freshly ground pepper | | pinch |
| 1 mL | onion powder, optional | ¼ | tsp |
| 2 drops | hot pepper sauce | 2 | drops |
| 375 mL | shredded, aged Cheddar cheese | 1½ | cups |
| 25 mL | dry bread crumbs | 2 | tbsp |

Cook macaroni in lightly salted boiling water according to package directions. Drain. Melt margarine in a medium saucepan; whisk in flour, milk, salt, pepper, onion powder, if desired, and hot pepper sauce; cook over medium heat until mixture bubbles. Reserve 25 mL (2 tbsp) cheese for top. Layer the macaroni, cheese and sauce two times in a lightly greased, 1.5 L (6 cup) casserole. Combine bread crumbs with reserved cheese and sprinkle over top. Bake in a 180°C (350°F) oven 30 min until lightly browned and mixture is bubbly.

Makes 4 servings.

**Each serving: 250 mL (1 cup)**

| | | |
|---|---|---|
| 2 ⊘ | Protein Choices | 33 g carbohydrate |
| 2 ◻ | Starchy Choices | 19 g protein |
| 2 ▲ | Fats & Oils Choices | 18 g fat |
| | | 1550 kilojoules |
| | | (370 Calories) |

**For 375 mL (1½ cups) shredded cheese, purchase 150 g (6 oz).**

*On facing page, from lower right:* Turkey Tetrazzini, Enchiladas, Chicken and Snow Pea Oriental, Saucy Ham Stuffed Potatoes.

# Breads, Muffins and Cookies

Who can resist the fragrant lure of freshly baked bread or cookies? Even a simple muffin, hot from the oven, gives a warm feeling to a meal.

This collection of recipes offers a variety of quick breads which use baking powder, soda or steam for leavening. As well, there are some great breads using slower acting yeast as the leavener. All of the recipes are surprisingly easy to make. The cookies are sure to become favorites for kids of all ages.

Most breads, muffins and cookies can be baked ahead and stored in the freezer. They reheat beautifully, so it is a great idea to have rolls or popovers on hand which can be warmed up to round out a meal.

*On facing page, from lower right*: Scotch Scones, Popovers, Orange Nut Bread, Harvest Rolls, Peanut Butter Cookies, Cream Bread.

## SCOTCH SCONES

*Scotch Scones are so rich and tasty you won't want to add butter. Nutty flavored, they go well with soups or as an afternoon snack served with a little fruit spread.*

| | | | |
|---|---|---|---|
| 450 mL | quick rolled oats | 1¾ | cups |
| 375 mL | all purpose flour | 1½ | cups |
| 50 mL | sugar | ¼ | cup |
| 15 mL | baking powder | 1 | tbsp |
| 2 mL | salt | ½ | tsp |
| 125 mL | margarine or butter, melted | ½ | cup |
| 75 mL | 2% or skim milk | 1/3 | cup |
| 1 | egg | 1 | |

Combine rolled oats, flour, sugar, baking powder and salt in a large bowl. Beat together margarine, milk and egg. Stir liquid ingredients into flour just until combined. *Do not overmix.* Turn mixture onto a lightly floured surface and pat out or roll into a rectangle about 23 x 90 cm (9 x 12 in). Cut into 9 rectangles, then cut each again diagonally to form 18 triangles. Place on a lightly greased baking sheet. Bake in a 220°C (425°F) oven 12 to 14 min until golden brown. Serve warm.

Makes 18 scones.

**Each serving: 1 scone**

| | | |
|---|---|---|
| 1 ▢ | Starchy Choice | 16 g carbohydrate |
| 1 ▲ | Fats & Oils Choice | 3 g protein |
| | | 6 g fat |
| | | 550 kilojoules |
| | | (130 Calories) |

**The secret of a good muffin is in the mixing. Overmixing creates a tough texture and tunnels. Stir the wet and dry ingredients together until the dryness of the flour *just* disappears. The batter will be lumpy as it should be.**

## WHOLE WHEAT BISCUITS

*Biscuits really should be served warm to accentuate their delicate texture.*

| | | |
|---|---|---|
| 375 mL | whole wheat flour | 1½ cups |
| 125 mL | all purpose flour | ½ cup |
| 15 mL | baking powder | 1 tbsp |
| 2 mL | salt | ½ tsp |
| 25 mL | margarine or butter | 2 tbsp |
| 250 mL | skim milk | 1 cup |

Combine flours, baking powder and salt in a bowl. Cut in margarine with a pastry blender or 2 knives. Add milk; mix quickly. Turn out onto a floured board. Knead 6 to 8 strokes. Roll 1.5 cm (¾ in) thick. Cut into twelve 5-cm (2-in) round biscuits or into wedges or squares. Place on a lightly greased baking sheet. Bake in a 220°C (425°F) oven 12 to 15 min until lightly browned.

Makes 12 biscuits.

### VARIATIONS:

**HERB BISCUITS:** Add 1 mL (¼ tsp) each of basil and thyme and 5 mL (1 tsp) dried parsley to dry mixture. (These make great dumplings.)

Makes 12 biscuits or dumplings.

Whole Wheat and Herb Biscuits:
**Each serving: 1 biscuit**

| | |
|---|---|
| 1 ▢ Starchy Choice | 16 g carbohydrate |
| ½ ▲ Fats & Oils Choice | 4 g protein |
| | 2 g fat |
| | 410 kilojoules |
| | (98 Calories) |

**CHEESE BISCUITS:** Add 125 mL (½ cup) shredded Cheddar cheese and 50 mL (¼ cup) grated Parmesan cheese to dry ingredients.

Makes 12 biscuits.

Cheese Biscuits:
**Each serving: 1 biscuit**

| | |
|---|---|
| ½ ⊘ Protein Choice | 16 g carbohydrate |
| 1 ▢ Starchy Choice | 6 g protein |
| ½ ▲ Fats & Oils Choice | 4 g fat |
| | 520 kilojoules |
| | (124 Calories) |

## CORNMEAL MUFFINS

*Serve these hot for breakfast or as an accompaniment to bean or chili dinners.*

| | | | |
|---|---|---|---|
| 250 mL | skim milk | 1 | cup |
| 250 mL | cornmeal | 1 | cup |
| 300 mL | all purpose flour | 1¼ | cups |
| 50 mL | lightly packed brown sugar | ¼ | cup |
| 20 mL | baking powder | 4 | tsp |
| 5 mL | salt | 1 | tsp |
| 2 | eggs, beaten | 2 | |
| 45 mL | vegetable oil | 3 | tbsp |

Lightly grease 12 medium muffin cups. Stir milk into cornmeal in a mixing bowl; let stand 10 min. Combine flour, sugar, baking powder and salt. Add eggs and oil to cornmeal mixture; stir in flour mixture just until all dry ingredients are dampened. Fill muffin cups 2/3 full. Bake in a 200°C (400°F) oven 18 to 20 min until golden brown. Serve warm.

Makes 12 servings.

**Each serving: 1 muffin**

| | |
|---|---|
| 1½ ☐ Starchy Choices | 23 g carbohydrate |
| 1  ▲ Fats & Oils Choice | 4 g protein |
| | 5 g fat |
| | 640 kilojoules |
| | (153 Calories) |

## POPOVERS

*Use these traditional popovers as a quick bread at meal time, as a shell for meaty mixtures or as a cup for salads.*

| | | | |
|---|---|---|---|
| 5 mL | shortening | 1 | tsp |
| 250 mL | skim milk | 1 | cup |
| 2 | eggs | 2 | |
| 200 mL | all purpose flour | ¾ | cup |
| 1 mL | salt | ¼ | tsp |

Grease 12 custard cups or medium muffin cups using 5 mL (1 tsp) shortening, or use non-stick muffin cups. Beat together milk and eggs in a mixing bowl. Sprinkle flour and salt over milk mixture. Beat with a rotary beater or electric mixer until batter is smooth and free of lumps. Fill cups no more than half full of the thin batter. Place in a cold oven. Turn oven to 200°C (400°F). Bake 30 to 35 min until firm and browned. Pierce popovers to allow steam to escape. For drier popovers, turn off heat and allow them to dry 15 min with oven door ajar. Loosen popovers carefully with a knife. Serve warm. Popovers may be frozen and rewarmed in a hot oven.

Makes 12 popovers.

**Each serving: 1 popover**

½ ☐ Starchy Choice

6 g carbohydrate
2 g protein
1 g fat

170 kilojoules
(41 Calories)

### BANANA HEALTH LOAF

*When you make this loaf, let it cool, wrap it and allow it to stand overnight to allow the flavors to blend. If you keep the loaf longer than 2 days, store it in the refrigerator.*

| 375 mL | whole wheat flour | 1½ cups |
| 125 mL | unsweetened shredded coconut | ½ cup |
| 10 mL | baking powder | 2 tsp |
| 2 mL | baking soda | ½ tsp |
| 2 mL | salt | ½ tsp |
| 250 mL | mashed banana | 1 cup |
| 45 mL | vegetable oil | 3 tbsp |
| 25 mL | liquid honey | 2 tbsp |

Mix together flour, coconut, baking powder, baking soda and salt in a bowl. Combine banana, oil and honey. Stir into flour mixture quickly but gently until just combined. *Do not overmix.* (Batter will be rough or lumpy and stiff.) Spread batter evenly in a lightly greased 1.5 L (8 x 4 in) loaf pan. Bake in 180°C (350°F) oven 45 to 50 min until tester inserted in center comes out clean. Cool in pan 10 min; turn out of pan and cool completely on rack. Wrap in waxed paper and store overnight before slicing.

Makes 14 servings.

**Each serving: 1 slice, about 1.5 cm (½ in) thick**

1 ☐ Starchy Choice
1 ▲ Fats & Oils Choice

16 g carbohydrate
2 g protein
4 g fat

450 kilojoules
(108 Calories)

## BEST BRAN MUFFINS

Best Bran Muffins *are great for breakfast. The night before, combine the dry ingredients and prepare the muffin cups. In the morning you can mix the muffins in about 5 minutes, then let them bake while you get yourself ready for the day.*

| | | | |
|---|---|---|---|
| 250 mL | all purpose flour | 1 | cup |
| 250 mL | natural bran | 1 | cup |
| 75 mL | lightly packed brown sugar | 1/3 | cup |
| 12 mL | baking powder | 2½ | tsp |
| 5 mL | cinnamon | 1 | tsp |
| 2 mL | salt | ½ | tsp |
| 250 mL | 2% milk | 1 | cup |
| 50 mL | vegetable oil | ¼ | cup |
| 1 | egg | 1 | |

Lightly grease 12 medium muffin cups. Combine flour, bran, brown sugar, baking powder, cinnamon and salt in a mixing bowl. Mix together milk, oil and egg; beat lightly. Stir milk mixture quickly into flour mixture until lightly mixed. *Do not overmix or beat.* Batter should be rough or lumpy. Fill each muffin cup 2/3 full. Bake in a 200°C (400°F) oven 20 to 22 min until light golden brown. Serve warm.

Makes 12 muffins.

**Each serving: 1 muffin**

| | | |
|---|---|---|
| 1 ☐ | Starchy Choice | 14 g carbohydrate |
| 1 ▲ | Fats & Oils Choice | 3 g protein |
| | | 6 g fat |

510 kilojoules
(122 Calories)

**VARIATIONS:**

**NUTTY BRAN MUFFINS:** Add 50 mL (¼ cup) chopped walnuts to the flour mixture in *Best Bran Muffins* recipe. (This will increase the fat value slightly but will not change the Choices.)

**FRUIT AND NUT BRAN MUFFINS:** Add 25 mL (about 2 tbsp) each of chopped raisins and chopped nuts to the flour mixture in *Best Bran Muffins* recipe. (This will increase the carbohydrate and fat values slightly but will not change the Choices.)

## ORANGE NUT BREAD

*Try* Orange Nut Bread *for a delightful afternoon or evening snack. It's as attractive as it is flavorful.*

| | | | |
|---|---|---|---|
| **375 mL** | all purpose flour | **1½** | **cups** |
| **50 mL** | sugar | **¼** | **cup** |
| **10 mL** | baking powder | **2** | **tsp** |
| **2 mL** | salt | **½** | **tsp** |
| **75 mL** | chopped almonds or walnuts | **1/3** | **cup** |
| **50 mL** | raisins, chopped | **¼** | **cup** |
| **25 mL** | grated orange peel | **2** | **tbsp** |
| **1** | egg, beaten | **1** | |
| **125 mL** | orange juice | **½** | **cup** |
| **10 mL** | vegetable oil | **2** | **tsp** |

Combine flour, sugar, baking powder and salt in a mixing bowl. Stir in nuts, raisins and orange peel. Combine beaten egg, orange juice and oil. Pour into flour mixture. Mix only until flour is dampened and fruits and nuts are well distributed. Turn into a greased 1.5 L (8 x 4 in) loaf pan. Bake in 180°C (350°F) oven 40 min until cake tester comes out clean. Let cool in pan 10 min; turn out of pan and cool completely on rack. Wrap in waxed paper and store overnight before slicing.

Makes 15 servings.

**Each serving: 1 slice, about 1.5 cm (½ in) thick**

1 ☐ Starchy Choice
½ ▲ Fats & Oils Choice

14 g carbohydrate
2 g protein
3 g fat

380 kilojoules
(91 Calories)

## CREAM BREAD OR ROLLS

*This recipe makes a good bread to slice and use for sandwiches, or excellent dinner rolls. The cottage cheese adds flavor and increases the protein value of the bread.*

| | | |
|---|---|---|
| 10 mL | honey | 2 tsp |
| 125 mL | warm water | ½ cup |
| 2 pkg | active dry yeast | 2 pkg |
| 250 mL | 2% cottage cheese | 1 cup |
| 50 mL | orange juice | ¼ cup |
| 1 | egg, beaten | 1 |
| 875 mL to 1 L | all purpose flour | 3½ to 4 cups |
| 10 mL | salt | 2 tsp |
| 2 mL | aniseed, caraway seed or dillweed, optional | ½ tsp |

Dissolve honey in warm water. Sprinkle yeast over water mixture. Let stand 10 min; stir well. Combine cottage cheese, orange juice and egg in a small saucepan. Mix well; heat very gently just to warm ingredients. Set aside. Combine 625 mL (2½ cups) flour, salt and aniseed, if desired, in a mixing bowl. Stir together yeast and cottage cheese mixtures; add to flour mixture; beat well. Stir in enough remaining flour to make a soft dough which leaves sides of the bowl. Place remaining flour on a board. Turn out dough onto floured board and knead 5 to 10 min until dough is smooth, elastic and no longer sticky. Place in a lightly greased bowl and turn to grease all sides. Cover with plastic wrap. Allow to rise in a warm, draft-free place about 1 to 1.5 h until doubled in volume. Punch down. Shape into a loaf, braid, or make 24 rolls. Place loaf in a lightly greased 2 L (9 x 5 in) loaf pan. Place braid or rolls on a lightly greased baking sheet. Cover loosely with plastic wrap. Let rise in a warm, draft-free place 45 to 60 min until doubled in volume. Bake loaf or braid in a 190°C (375°F) oven 40 to 45 min until bread is nicely browned and sounds hollow when tapped. (Bake rolls 20 to 25 min until golden brown.) Remove from oven. Remove from pans immediately. Cool on wire racks.

Makes 1 loaf (24 slices) or 24 rolls.

**Each serving: 1 slice or 1 roll**

1 ☐ Starchy Choice

15 g carbohydrate
4 g protein
1 g fat

360 kilojoules
(85 Calories)

## HARVEST ROLLS

*Whole wheat rolls are popular for the extra flavor they give to sandwiches, and for fall suppers.*

| | | | |
|---:|---|---:|---|
| 5 mL | sugar | 1 | tsp |
| 125 mL | warm water | ½ | cup |
| 1 pkg | active dry yeast | 1 | pkg |
| 250 mL | skim milk | 1 | cup |
| 5 mL | molasses | 1 | tsp |
| 2 mL | salt | ½ | tsp |
| 750 mL | whole wheat flour | 3 | cups |
| 125 to 200 mL | all purpose flour | ½ to ¾ | cup |

Dissolve sugar in water. Sprinkle yeast over water mixture. Let stand 10 min; stir well. Combine milk, molasses and salt in a large bowl. Stir in yeast mixture. Add whole wheat flour; mix well. Place 50 mL (¼ cup) all purpose flour on a board. Turn out dough onto floured board; knead 5 to 8 min adding remaining all purpose flour if necessary. Continue kneading until dough is smooth, elastic and no longer sticky. Place in a lightly greased bowl and turn to grease all sides. Cover with plastic wrap. Allow to rise in a warm, draft-free place 1 to 1.5 h until doubled in volume. Punch down. Divide into 24 portions; form into rolls. Place 5 cm (2 in) apart on a lightly greased baking sheet. Cover loosely. Let rise in a warm, draft-free place 1 h, until doubled in volume. Bake in a 200°C (400°F) oven 12 to 15 min until brown. Remove from pan. Cool on wire rack.

Makes 24 servings.

**Each serving: 1 roll**

1 ▢ Starchy Choice

14 g carbohydrate
3 g protein

290 kilojoules
(68 Calories)

> **To activate yeast, always use sugar or honey, according to package directions. Artificial sweetener does not work.**

### GERMAN RYE BREAD

*Caraway seeds enhance the flavor of this easy-to-make rye bread.*

| | | |
|---:|:---|---:|
| 5 **mL** | sugar | 1 **tsp** |
| 125 **mL** | warm water | ½ **cup** |
| 1 **pkg** | active dry yeast | 1 **pkg** |
| 200 **mL** | water | ¾ **cup** |
| 15 **mL** | butter | 1 **tbsp** |
| 5 **mL** | honey | 1 **tsp** |
| 15 **mL** | caraway seeds, optional | 1 **tbsp** |
| 10 **mL** | salt | 2 **tsp** |
| 250 **mL** | rye flour | 1 **cup** |
| 625 to 750 **mL** | all purpose flour | 2½ **to** 3 **cups** |

Dissolve sugar in 125 mL (½ cup) warm water. Sprinkle yeast over water mixture; let stand 10 min; stir well. Combine 200 mL (¾ cup) water, butter, honey, caraway seeds, if desired, salt, rye flour and 250 mL (1 cup) all purpose flour. Beat 2 to 3 min until smooth. Work in remaining all purpose flour; knead 5 to 8 min until dough is smooth, elastic and no longer sticky. Place in a lightly greased bowl and turn to grease all sides. Cover with plastic wrap and let rise in a warm, draft-free place about 45 min until doubled in volume. Punch down. Form into a loaf about 23 cm (9 in) long; place on a lightly greased baking sheet or in a 2 L (9 x 5 in) greased loaf pan. Let rise in a warm place, about 45 min, until doubled in volume. Bake in a 190°C (375°F) oven 30 to 35 min until loaf is lightly browned and sounds hollow when tapped. Remove from pan; cool on rack.

Makes 1 loaf, 20 slices.

**Each serving: 1 slice**

1 ☐ Starchy Choice

14 g carbohydrate
2 g protein
1 g fat

310 kilojoules
(73 Calories)

## COTTAGE CASSEROLE BREAD

Cottage Casserole Bread *is simple and easy to prepare; no kneading is required. It gives a special touch to an everyday meal, or a meal for guests. Since this bread provides protein, it is a good choice to supplement the protein in a salad or vegetarian meal.*

| | | | |
|---|---|---|---|
| 5 mL | sugar | 1 | tsp |
| 50 mL | warm water | ¼ | cup |
| 1 pkg | active dry yeast | 1 | pkg |
| 300 mL | 2% cottage cheese | 1¼ | cups |
| 500 to 625 mL | all purpose flour | 2 to 2½ | cups |
| 15 mL | sugar | 1 | tbsp |
| 15 mL | poppy seeds | 1 | tbsp |
| 2 mL | each of salt and baking soda | ½ | tsp |
| 1 | egg, well beaten | 1 | |

Dissolve sugar in water. Sprinkle yeast over water mixture. Let stand 10 min; stir well. Heat cottage cheese in a saucepan, very gently, just until warm. Combine 250 mL (1 cup) flour, sugar, poppy seeds, salt and baking soda in a mixing bowl. Stir in warmed cottage cheese, egg and yeast mixture. Beat about 3 min until mixture becomes elastic. Stir in remaining flour to form a stiff dough. Cover with plastic wrap. Let rise in a warm, draft-free place about 1 h until doubled in volume. Stir down dough. Turn into a well greased 1.5 L (6 cup) casserole. Cover. Let rise in a warm place 30 to 45 min until light. Bake in a 180°C (350°F) oven 30 to 35 min until golden brown. Remove from oven. Immediately turn out of casserole. Cool. Cut into wedges.

Makes 12 servings.

**Each serving: 1 wedge**

½ ⊘ Protein Choice
1 ▢ Starchy Choice

16 g carbohydrate
7 g protein
1 g fat

430 kilojoules
(101 Calories)

**Did you know that margarine provides the same amount of energy as butter?**

## PINA COLADA SQUARES

*These scrumptious squares are delectable for tea time or dessert. Three layers—light pastry, fruity pineapple and flaky coconut—bake together to make a refreshing concoction that's moist, chewy and crunchy.*

| 250 | mL | all purpose flour | 1 | cup |
|---|---|---|---|---|
| 5 | mL | baking powder | 1 | tsp |
| 1 | mL | salt | ¼ | tsp |
| 50 | mL | margarine or butter | ¼ | cup |
| 1 | | egg, separated | 1 | |
| 50 | mL | 2% milk | ¼ | cup |
| 1 | can | 398 mL (14 oz) unsweetened crushed pineapple | 1 | can |
| 25 | mL | cornstarch | 2 | tbsp |
| 10 | mL | rum extract | 2 | tsp |
| 5 | mL | vanilla | 1 | tsp |
| 1 | mL | cream of tartar | ¼ | tsp |
| 15 | mL | sugar | 1 | tbsp |
| 250 | mL | unsweetened shredded coconut | 1 | cup |

**Bottom Layer:**
Combine flour, baking powder and salt. Cut in margarine until mixture is crumbly. Beat egg yolk and milk together with a fork. Stir into crumbs. Press evenly onto bottom of a lightly greased 23 cm (8 in) square cake pan.

**Middle Layer:**
Combine crushed pineapple and its juice and cornstarch in a saucepan; mix well. Stir-cook over medium heat until mixture boils and thickens. Stir in rum extract and vanilla. Pour over first layer.

**Top Layer:**
Beat egg white and cream of tartar until frothy. Add sugar and beat until soft peaks form. Fold in coconut. Spread evenly and carefully over pineapple layer. Press down lightly with a fork. Bake in a 180°C (350°F) oven 30 min until top is golden brown. Cool and cut into squares.

Makes 30 squares, 3 x 4 cm (1¼ x 1½ in)

**Each serving: 2 squares**

| | | |
|---|---|---|
| 1 ▨ | Fruits & Vegetables Choice | 11 g carbohydrate |
| 1 ▲ | Fats & Oils Choice | 2 g protein |
| | | 5 g fat |

410 kilojoules
(97 Calories)

## LEMON FINGERS

*These lemon-flavored sponge bars are like lady fingers. Their crispness provides a nice contrast to the smoothness of custards, puddings and gelatin desserts.*

| | | |
|---|---|---|
| 3 | egg whites | 3 |
| pinch | salt | pinch |
| 2 mL | baking powder | ½ tsp |
| 50 mL | sugar | ¼ cup |
| 2 | egg yolks | 2 |
| 15 mL | grated lemon peel | 1 tbsp |
| 5 mL | lemon juice | 1 tsp |
| 125 mL | all purpose flour | ½ cup |

Line a 23 cm (9 in) square cake pan with heavy waxed paper. Brush lightly with oil. Place egg whites and salt in a mixing bowl. Beat until frothy. Add baking powder and continue beating until soft peaks form. Add sugar; continue beating until stiff peaks form. Beat in egg yolks, lemon peel and lemon juice until well combined. Fold in flour. Spread in prepared pan. (Smooth with a knife dipped in water.) Bake in a 190°C (375°F) oven 20 min until light brown. Remove from oven. Immediately loosen edges with knife; turn out; remove paper. Cut baked dough into 60 oblong strips, each 2 x 5 cm (¾ x 2 in). Set strips on their sides on a baking sheet. Return to oven and bake 5 min longer. Turn off heat; allow to dry 15 min in oven. Cool. Store in a covered container.

### VARIATIONS:

**ORANGE FINGERS:** Use 15 mL (1 tbsp) grated orange peel and 5 mL (1 tsp) orange juice in place of lemon peel and juice.

**ANISE FINGERS:** Use 7 mL (1½ tsp) aniseed and 5 mL (1 tsp) vanilla in place of lemon peel and juice.

Makes 60 fingers.

**Each serving: 1 finger**

| | | |
|---|---|---|
| 1 ++ Extra | | 2 g carbohydrate |
| | | 30 kilojoules (8 Calories) |

**Honey and molasses are forms of sugar and provide about the same number of kilojoules (Calories) as table sugar.**

## PEANUT BUTTER NUGGETS

*These crispy nuggets are a tasty addition to a cookie tray for parties and desserts.*

| | | |
|---|---|---|
| 175 mL | crushed corn flakes | 2/3 **cup** |
| 125 mL | unsweetened shredded coconut | ½ **cup** |
| 125 mL | plain or crunchy peanut butter | ½ **cup** |
| 25 mL | liquid honey or corn syrup | 2 **tbsp** |

Combine 125 mL (½ cup) corn flake crumbs, coconut, peanut butter and honey; mix thoroughly. Measure out 10 mL (2 tsp) portions; shape into balls. Roll in remaining corn flake crumbs. Place on a plate. Chill until firm. Store in a covered container in refrigerator.

Makes 18 nuggets.

**Each serving: 1 nugget**

| | | |
|---|---|---|
| ½ ▱ Fruits & Vegetables Choice | | 5 g carbohydrate |
| 1 ▲ Fats & Oils Choice | | 2 g protein |
| | | 4 g fat |
| | | 270 kilojoules (64 Calories) |

## PEANUT BUTTER COOKIES

*These cookies are very easy to handle, and the low sugar content enhances the peanut flavor. Use crunchy peanut butter for added texture.*

| | | |
|---|---|---|
| 125 mL | shortening | ½ **cup** |
| 125 mL | lightly packed brown sugar | ½ **cup** |
| 250 mL | peanut butter | 1 **cup** |
| 2 | eggs | 2 |
| | Liquid artificial sweetener equivalent to 40 mL (8 tsp) sugar | |
| 5 mL | vanilla | 1 **tsp** |
| 375 mL | all purpose flour | 1½ **cups** |
| 5 mL | each of baking powder and baking soda | 1 **tsp** |
| 2 mL | salt | ½ **tsp** |

Cream together shortening and sugar until light and fluffy; beat in peanut butter, eggs, artificial sweetener and vanilla. Combine flour, baking powder, baking soda and salt. Stir into creamed mixture; mix well. Roll dough into balls using about 10 mL (2 tsp) per ball; place on a lightly greased baking sheet. Flatten with a wet fork, forming a criss-cross design on each cookie. Bake in a 180°C (350°F) oven 8 to 10 min until very light golden brown. Remove. Cool. Store in a covered container.

Makes 48 cookies.

**Each serving: 1 cookie**

½ ☐ Starchy Choice
1 ▲ Fats & Oils Choice

6 g carbohydrate
2 g protein
5 g fat

320 kilojoules
(77 Calories)

## CHOCOLATE CHIP COOKIES

*Although the sugar and chocolate have been reduced in this recipe, it will still be a favorite with cookie lovers of all ages.*

| 125 | mL | butter | ½ | cup |
|-----|-----|--------|-----|-----|
| 125 | mL | lightly packed brown sugar | ½ | cup |
| 1 | | egg | 1 | |
| 10 | mL | vanilla | 2 | tsp |
| 250 | mL | all purpose flour | 1 | cup |
| 2 | mL | baking soda | ½ | tsp |
| 2 | mL | salt | ½ | tsp |
| 125 | mL | quick rolled oats | ½ | cup |
| 125 | mL | semi-sweet chocolate chips | ½ | cup |

Cream butter and sugar together until light and fluffy. Beat in egg and vanilla. Combine flour, baking soda and salt. Stir into creamed mixture. Fold in rolled oats and chocolate chips. Using 10 mL (2 tsp) for each cookie, drop onto ungreased cookie sheets. Flatten with a fork. Bake in a 190°C (375°F) oven 10 min until cookies begin to brown around the edges. Remove from pan. Cool. Store in a covered container.

Makes 48 cookies.

**Each serving: 2 cookies**

1 ◨ Fruits & Vegetables Choice
1 ▲ Fats & Oils Choice

10 g carbohydrate
1 g protein
6 g fat

410 kilojoules
(98 Calories)

## RICE KRISPIE SQUARES

*Children love these squares, but don't forget that adults like them too—they often bring back fond childhood memories. This is not the place to use up marshmallows which have hardened. They must be fresh.*

| | | |
|---|---|---|
| 50 mL | margarine or butter | ¼ **cup** |
| 25 | large marshmallows or 750 mL (3 cups) mini marshmallows | 25 |
| 5 mL | vanilla | 1 **tsp** |
| 1.25 L | Rice Krispies | 5 **cups** |

Melt margarine in a medium heavy saucepan. Add marshmallows and stir-cook over low heat until marshmallows are melted. Remove from heat and quickly stir in vanilla and Rice Krispies; mix well. Moisten hands or spoon with water and press mixture into a greased 23 cm (9 in) square pan. Let set for at least 30 min; cut into 24 pieces, 5 x 3 cm (2 x 1½ in).

Makes 24 squares.

**Each serving: 1 square**

| | | |
|---|---|---|
| 1 ◪ Fruits & Vegetables Choice | | 9 g carbohydrate |
| ½ ▲ Fats & Oils Choice | | 2 g fat |
| | | 230 kilojoules (54 Calories) |

### VARIATION:

**RICE KRISPIE SNOWBALLS:** Using moistened hands, form 50 mL (¼ cup) portions of warm mixture into snowballs or other shapes. Mixture may be tinted to desired color by adding to the marshmallow mixture a few drops of liquid food coloring with the vanilla. (Each 50 mL [¼ cup] portion is equivalent to one square.)

## SHORTBREAD

*Do not undercook; shortbread should have a light golden color for best flavor. It is great for tea time, and to pack in lunches.*

| | | |
|---|---|---|
| 250 g | butter at room temperature | ½ **lb** |
| 125 mL | granulated sugar | ½ **cup** |
| 125 mL | rice flour | ½ **cup** |
| 450 mL | all purpose flour | 1¾ **cups** |

Cream butter with sugar in a mixing bowl until soft and fluffy. Stir in rice flour and all purpose flour until well blended. Roll out on a lightly floured board 6 mm (¼ in) thick. Cut into 4 cm (1½ in) rounds. Place on ungreased cookie sheets. Prick with a fork to form a design. Bake in a 160°C (325°F) oven 22 to 25 min until golden.

Makes 60 shortbread.

**Each serving: 3 shortbread**

| 1 | ☐ Starchy Choice | 15 g carbohydrate |
| 2 | ◢ Fats & Oils Choices | 2 g protein |
| | | 10 g fat |
| | | 660 kilojoules |
| | | (158 Calories) |

### CRISPY OATMEAL COOKIES

*Do not undercook these cookies if you want them to be flavorful and crisp. They freeze well in a covered container, so it's a good idea to make double the batch while you are at it.*

| 75 mL | butter | 1/3 cup |
| 75 mL | lightly packed brown sugar | 1/3 cup |
| 50 mL | warm water | ¼ cup |
| 250 mL | all purpose flour | 1 cup |
| 250 mL | quick rolled oats | 1 cup |
| 5 mL | cinnamon | 1 tsp |
| 2 mL | baking soda | ½ tsp |

Cream butter and sugar together until light and fluffy. Beat in water. Combine flour, oats, cinnamon and baking soda. Stir into creamed mixture. Roll out 5 mm (1/8 in) thick on a lightly floured surface. Cut into 6 cm (2½ in) circles. Place on a lightly greased baking sheet. Bake in a 180°C (350°F) oven 10 to 12 min, until golden brown around edges. Remove from pan. Cool; store in a covered container.

Makes 36 cookies.

**Each serving: 3 cookies**

| 1 | ☐ Starchy Choice | 16 g carbohydrate |
| 1 | ◢ Fats & Oils Choice | 2 g protein |
| | | 6 g fat |
| | | 530 kilojoules |
| | | (126 Calories) |

## VANILLA CRISPS

Vanilla Crisps *are a lighter version of commercial vanilla wafers. They may be used in place of vanilla wafers in most recipes.*

| | | |
|---|---|---|
| 2 | eggs, separated | 2 |
| 2 mL | baking powder | ½ tsp |
| pinch | salt | pinch |
| 50 mL | sugar | ¼ cup |
| 10 mL | vanilla | 2 tsp |
| 75 mL | all purpose flour | 1/3 cup |

Line two cookie sheets with brown paper. Beat egg whites until frothy. Add baking powder and salt; continue beating until soft peaks form. Add sugar and continue beating until stiff peaks form. Beat together egg yolks and vanilla with a fork. Fold into beaten egg whites just until combined. Sift flour over egg mixture and fold in until batter is smooth and very light. Drop 10 mL (2 tsp) at a time on brown paper, 5 cm (2 in) apart. Bake in a 190°C (375°F) oven 15 to 18 min until golden brown. Cool 10 min and remove from paper. (If necessary, place cookies on a baking sheet; turn off oven heat and return cookies to oven 5 to 10 min to crisp.) Store in a covered container.

Makes 36 cookies.

### VARIATIONS:

**ORANGE CRISPS:** Substitute 10 mL (2 tsp) grated orange peel and 5 mL (1 tsp) orange juice for vanilla in *Vanilla Crisps* recipe.

**LEMON CRISPS:** Substitute 10 mL (2 tsp) grated lemon peel and 5 mL (1 tsp) lemon juice for vanilla in *Vanilla Crisps* recipe.

**ALMOND CRISPS:** Substitute 10 mL (2 tsp) almond extract for the vanilla and fold 15 mL (1 tbsp) ground almonds into batter with flour when preparing *Vanilla Crisps.*

**Each serving: 4 crisps**

1 ▢ Fruits & Vegetables Choice

9 g carbohydrate
2 g protein
1 g fat

220 kilojoules
(53 Calories)

# Desserts

A meal seems incomplete without the finishing touch of fruit or a sweet for dessert. Whatever your weakness, it is probably included in our after-dinner delights. You'll find treats for all seasons and all occasions, for family meals and special celebrations: cheesecake, creamy pies, puddings, crêpes and a different twist to an old-time favorite, blueberry pie.

Many of our desserts can be made well in advance if time is a factor, while others can be prepared in a hasty fashion. All provide a glamorous ending to a meal.

### Sweeteners

The most common sweeteners are sugars, including white and brown sugar, honey, molasses and syrups. Sugars require very little digestion, so they reach the blood stream quickly and may cause a rapid rise in the blood sugar level of a person with diabetes. Therefore, extra sugars should be avoided, where possible, in cooking. Some recipes in this collection do call for a small amount of sugar, but only where it is necessary to make an acceptable product.

Sugar does more than simply sweeten foods. It aids in the browning of baked products and, more importantly, it helps make them tender and light. We have tested the recipes containing sugar many times to ensure that the minimum amount was used without sacrificing good texture, taste and appearance. In recipes where sugar is required, its carbohydrate content is included in the nutrient values and food Choices listed below them.

The sweet taste needed by some foods can be achieved by using a sugar substitute or artificial sweetener rather than sugar. These sweeteners all have their advantages and disadvantages. Aspartame has a taste which is much like sugar, but it loses its sweetness in baking. The liquid artificial sweeteners available in Canada are stable to heat and can be used in baking, but they do not have the tenderizing or browning qualities of sugar. The granular sugar substitutes are a combination of an artificial sweetener such as sodium cyclamate, and a high proportion of natural sugar such as lactose or dextrin. The Canadian Diabetes Association recommends that these granular sugar substitutes be limited to 3 or 4 small packets per day. For the recipes in this collection which include an artificial sweetener or sugar substitute, we have specified the type of sweetener that gives the most satisfactory results. However, you may use another type as you prefer.

## SPONGE CAKE

*When fresh fruits (strawberries, blueberries, peaches, apricots) are in season, use this cake as a perfect base for shortcake.*

| | | |
|---|---|---|
| 4 | egg whites | 4 |
| 1 mL | cream of tartar | ¼ tsp |
| 1 mL | salt | ¼ tsp |
| 75 mL | sugar | 1/3 cup |
| 2 | egg yolks | 2 |
| 10 mL | almond extract | 2 tsp |
| 75 mL | all purpose flour | 1/3 cup |

Line the bottom of a 20 cm (8 in) square pan with waxed paper. Place egg whites, cream of tartar and salt in a mixer bowl. Beat with a rotary beater or electric mixer until foamy. Beat in sugar gradually; continue beating until stiff peaks form. Beat in egg yolks and almond extract. Fold flour lightly into egg mixture. Spread batter in prepared pan. Bake in a 200°C (400°F) oven 15 min until cake springs back when lightly touched. Loosen edges with a sharp knife; turn out immediately onto a paper towel-lined cake rack to cool.

Makes one 20 cm (8 in) square cake, 12 servings.

**Each serving: 1 piece, 5 x 6 cm (2 x 2½ in)**

1 ▨ Fruits & Vegetables Choice

9 g carbohydrate
2 g protein
1 g fat

220 kilojoules
(53 Calories)

**VARIATION:**

**SPONGE ROLL:** Bake the *Sponge Cake* batter in a waxed paper-lined 24 x 34-cm (9½ x 13-in) jelly roll pan. Cool and fill with *Cream Topping and Filling* (recipe, p.184); roll up jelly roll style.

Makes 8 servings.

**Each serving: 1 slice**

1 ◆ Milk Choice (whole)
1 ▮ Fruits & Vegetables Choice

16 g carbohydrate
5 g protein
3 g fat

470 kilojoules
(111 Calories)

## DOUBLE CHOCOLATE ROLL

*In this delicate sponge roll, chocolate appears twice; in the cake, and in the filling. It makes a lovely party.*

| 1 **batch** | Chocolate Sponge Cake batter (recipe, p.182) | 1 **batch** |
| 1 **batch** | Chocolate Cream Topping and Filling (recipe, p.184) | 1 **batch** |

Line bottom of a 24 x 34 cm (9½ x 13 in) jelly roll pan with heavy waxed paper. Spread *Chocolate Sponge Cake* batter in prepared pan. Bake in 200°C (400°F) oven 10 min or until cake springs back when touched lightly. Loosen edges with a sharp knife. Turn out immediately onto a clean cloth. Cut off edges, if too crisp. Roll up in cloth to shape roll. (This prevents cracking of roll.) Set aside, seam-side down, to cool. Unroll. Remove cloth. Spread with *Chocolate Cream Topping and Filling*. Reroll; place seam-side down on serving platter. Cut into 2.5 cm (1 in) slices to serve.

Makes 8 servings.

**Each serving: 1 slice**

1 ◆ Milk Choice (whole)
1 ▮ Fruits & Vegetables Choice

15 g carbohydrate
6 g protein
4 g fat

510 kilojoules
(120 Calories)

## VARIATION:

**PEPPERMINT CHOCOLATE ROLL:** Use peppermint flavored *Cream Topping and Filling* tinted pink or green, if desired, to fill *Chocolate Sponge Cake*.

Serving size and Choices, same as above.

Nutrient value approximately the same as above.

## CHOCOLATE SPONGE CAKE

*If you love chocolate, you'll love this version of sponge cake.*

| | | |
|---|---|---|
| 4 | egg whites | 4 |
| 1 mL | cream of tartar | ¼ tsp |
| 1 mL | salt | ¼ tsp |
| 75 mL | sugar | 1/3 cup |
| 2 | egg yolks | 2 |
| 5 mL | vanilla | 1 tsp |
| 50 mL | all purpose flour | ¼ cup |
| 50 mL | cocoa | ¼ cup |

Line a 20 cm (8 in) square or round cake pan with waxed paper. Place egg whites, cream of tartar and salt in a mixing bowl; beat with rotary beater or electric mixer until foamy. Beat in sugar gradually; continue beating until stiff peaks form. Beat in egg yolks and vanilla. Combine flour and cocoa and fold lightly into egg mixture. Spread batter in prepared pan. Bake in 200°C (400°F) oven 10 min or until cake springs back when lightly touched. Loosen sides with a sharp knife. Turn out immediately onto a paper towel-lined cake rack to cool.

Makes one 1 L (8 in) square or round cake; 12 servings.

**Each serving: 1 piece, 5 x 6 cm (2 x 2½ in)**

1 ◨ Fruits & Vegetables Choice

8 g carbohydrate
2 g protein
1 g fat

210 kilojoules
(49 Calories)

## RIBBON CREAM TORTE

Ribbon Cream Torte *is our choice for a birthday cake. You can vary the flavor and color of the filling to suit your taste.*

| | | |
|---|---|---|
| 1 | baked *Sponge Cake* (recipe, p.180) | 1 |
| 1 batch | *Cream Topping and Filling* (recipe, p.184) | 1 batch |

Cut cake in half. Split each half horizontally to make 4 thin layers. Spread 3 layers with about 250 mL (1 cup) *Cream Topping and Filling;* stack; top with remaining layer. Frost top and sides of cake with remaining *Cream Topping and Filling.* Cover loosely and refrigerate until serving time. Cut into 2.5 cm (1 in) slices to serve.

Makes 8 servings.

**Each serving: 1 slice**

| 1 ◆ Milk Choice (whole) | 16 g carbohydrate |
| 1 ▰ Fruits & Vegetables Choice | 5 g protein |
| | 3 g fat |
| | 470 kilojoules |
| | (111 Calories) |

## CREAM PUFF SHELLS

*If you want éclairs instead of puffs, shape the paste into little oblong shapes before baking. Whichever one you pick, this is one of the easiest pastries to make.*

| 250 | mL | water | 1 | cup |
| 75 | mL | vegetable oil | 5 | tbsp |
| | pinch | salt | | pinch |
| 250 | mL | all purpose flour | 1 | cup |
| 4 | | eggs | 4 | |
| 5 | mL | vanilla | 1 | tsp |

Pour water and oil into a saucepan; add salt. Bring to a rapid boil. Add flour all at once, beating vigorously with a wooden spoon to mix in all dry flour. Beat until mixture forms a ball and draws away from the sides of the pan. Remove from heat and cool 5 min. Beat in eggs one at a time, by hand or in a mixer or food processor. Add vanilla. Beat 1 or 2 min longer until dough is very smooth and glossy. Spoon about 15 mL (1 tbsp) for each shell, about 5 cm (2 in) apart, onto dampened, non-stick baking sheets. Bake in a 200°C (400°F) oven 10 min, then raise heat to 230°C (450°F) and bake 12 to 15 min longer until puffs are lightly browned, crisp and firm to the touch. Slit each puff with the tip of a sharp knife to release steam. Cool on wire rack before filling.

Makes 30 puffs.

**Each serving: 2 puffs**

| ½ ▢ Starchy Choice | 6 g carbohydrate |
| ▲ Fats & Oils Choice | 3 g protein |
| | 6 g fat |
| | 380 kilojoules |
| | (90 Calories) |

## CREAM TOPPING AND FILLING

*You can tint peppermint flavored filling with red or green food coloring, and use it to make the* Peppermint Chocolate Roll *as pictured. And maple flavored filling in the* Ribbon Cream Torte *is a wonderful idea.*

| | | | |
|---|---|---|---|
| **1 packet** | unflavored gelatin | **1 packet** | |
| **50 mL** | cold water | **¼ cup** | |
| **250 mL** | boiling water | **1 cup** | |
| **200 mL** | instant skim milk powder | **¾ cup** | |
| | Artificial sweetener equivalent to 60 mL (12 tsp) sugar (12 aspartame tablets, crushed) | | |
| **5 mL** | vanilla | **1 tsp** | |
| **10 mL** | maple or orange extract or 5 mL (1 tsp) peppermint extract | **2 tsp** | |
| **10 mL** | vegetable oil | **2 tsp** | |
| **1** | egg white, stiffly beaten | **1** | |

Sprinkle gelatin over cold water to soften; let stand 5 min. Stir in boiling water until gelatin dissolves. Cool 5 min. Stir in milk powder and sweetener until completely dissolved. Refrigerate until partially set. Chill beaters. Beat at high speed until stiff peaks form. Beat in vanilla, maple extract and vegetable oil. Fold in stiffly beaten egg white until thoroughly mixed.

Makes 1.25 L (5 cups), 10 servings.

**Each serving: a generous 125 mL (½ cup)**

½ ◆ Milk Choice (skim)

2 g carbohydrate
2 g protein
1 g fat

110 kilojoules
(25 Calories)

**VARIATION:**

**CHOCOLATE CREAM TOPPING AND FILLING:** Combine 25 mL (5 tsp) cocoa and 125 mL (½ cup) water in a saucepan until smooth. Stir in additional 125 mL (½ cup) water. Bring to a boil. Substitute for boiling water in recipe above.

**Each serving: 125 mL (½ cup)**

½ ◆ Milk Choice (skim)

3 g carbohydrate
3 g protein
1 g fat

140 kilojoules
(33 Calories)

## BAKED CINNAMON CUSTARD

*Count on baked custard to star as the finale for an everyday meal or an elegant company dinner. If you feel like being innovative, try our variations.*

| 2 | eggs | 2 | |
| 1 | egg yolk | 1 | |
| 15 mL | brown sugar | 1 | tbsp |
| pinch | salt | | pinch |
| 5 mL | vanilla | 1 | tsp |
| 300 mL | 2% milk | 1¼ | cups |
| | Cinnamon | | |

Beat eggs and egg yolk slightly; beat in sugar, salt and vanilla; stir in milk. Pour through a fine sieve into 4 individual custard cups or 1 small casserole. Sprinkle lightly with cinnamon. Set custard cups or casserole in a pan; place in oven. Pour boiling water in pan nearly to the top of the custard cups. Bake in a 180°C (350°F) oven 45 min until tester inserted in the center comes out clean. Serve warm, at room temperature or thoroughly chilled.

### VARIATIONS:

**SAUCY BAKED CUSTARD:** Place 5 mL (1 tsp) fruit spread or diet jam in each individual custard cup before pouring in custard, or place 20 mL (4 tsp) in a small casserole before pouring in custard. Omit cinnamon. Turn out custards into dessert dishes. Sauce forms over custard.

**BAKED COCONUT CUSTARD:** Place 5 mL (1 tsp) unsweetened shredded coconut in each individual custard cup before pouring in custard, or place 20 mL (4 tsp) coconut in a small casserole before pouring in custard.

Makes 4 servings.

**Each serving: 125 mL (½ cup)**

| ½ | ⊘ Protein Choice | 7 g carbohydrate |
| 1 | ◆ Milk Choice (2%) | 6 g protein |
| ½ | ▲ Fats & Oils Choice | 6 g fat |
| | | 440 kilojoules |
| | | (106 Calories) |

**Regular fruit-flavored gelatin desserts are high in sugar. Choose instead the kind that are unsweetened or those which are sweetened with aspartame or an artificial sweetener.**

## SOFT CUSTARD

*Serve this delightful treat as a dessert on its own, or as a velvety sauce over a small slice of angel food cake or a small dish of fruit.*

| | | | |
|---|---|---|---|
| 2 | eggs | 2 | |
| 25 mL | sugar | 2 tbsp | |
| pinch | salt | pinch | |
| 375 mL | 2% milk | 1½ cups | |
| 2 mL | vanilla | ½ tsp | |

Beat together eggs, sugar and salt in the top of a double boiler; stir in milk. Place over simmering water. Stir-cook until mixture forms a coating on a metal spoon. Pour immediately into a cool bowl or pitcher. Stir in vanilla. Use as a sauce or pour into serving dishes when cool.

Makes 4 servings.

**Each serving: 125 mL (½ cup)**

2 ◆ Milk Choices (2%)

11 g carbohydrate
6 g protein
5 g fat

470 kilojoules
(113 Calories)

## CHOCOLATE ALMOND CREAM PUFFS

*Since the airy filling is as light as the puffs themselves, these could be called "chocolate pillows."*

| | | | |
|---|---|---|---|
| 30 | *Cream Puff Shells* (recipe, p.183) | 30 | |
| 1 batch | *Chocolate Almond Filling* (recipe, p.187) | 1 batch | |

Place *Chocolate Almond Filling* in a pastry bag fitted with a small plain tube. Fill puffs with 15 mL (1 tbsp) cream through slit made in puff, or cut top off and spoon cream into puffs. Refrigerate until serving time.

Makes 15 servings.

**Each serving: 2 filled puffs**

½ ▢ Starchy Choice
1½ ▲ Fats & Oils Choices

8 g carbohydrate
3 g protein
8 g fat

480 kilojoules
(116 Calories)

## CHOCOLATE ALMOND FILLING

Chocolate Almond Filling *is superb in cream puffs, but also makes a beautiful frosting for our* Sponge Cake.

| | | |
|---|---|---|
| 1 **packet** | whipped topping mix (for 500 mL [2 cups] whipped topping) | 1 **packet** |
| 125 **mL** | cold 2% milk | ½ **cup** |
| 10 **mL** | cocoa | 2 **tsp** |
| 5 **mL** | almond extract | 1 **tsp** |
| 6 | almonds, toasted and chopped | 6 |

Combine whipped topping mix, milk, cocoa and almond extract in a small deep bowl. Beat with rotary beater or electric mixer at high speed until stiff peaks form. Continue to beat 2 min longer until fluffy. Fold in chopped almonds. Store in covered container in refrigerator.

**VARIATION:**

**MOCHA ALMOND CREAM FILLING:** Add 5 mL (1 tsp) instant coffee to topping mix and milk mixture before beating.

Makes 500 mL (2 cups).

**Each serving: 25 mL (2 tbsp)**

½ ▲ Fats & Oils Choice

2 g carbohydrate
2 g fat

110 kilojoules
(26 Calories)

## NOVA SCOTIA GINGERBREAD

*Molasses and a small amount of brown sugar sweeten this old-fashioned cake. It is mellow and soft when warm, with a lightly-spiced, heavenly taste.*

| | | |
|---|---|---|
| 50 mL | shortening | ¼ cup |
| 50 mL | lightly packed brown sugar | ¼ cup |
| 75 mL | molasses | 1/3 cup |
| 1 | egg | 1 |
| 375 mL | all purpose flour | 1½ cups |
| 5 mL | salt | 1 tsp |
| 5 mL | baking soda | 1 tsp |
| 5 mL | each of cinnamon and ground ginger | 1 tsp |
| 1 mL | ground cloves | ¼ tsp |
| 200 mL | boiling water | ¾ cup |

Cream shortening and sugar together until light and fluffy; beat in molasses and egg. Combine flour, salt, baking soda, cinnamon, ginger and cloves. Stir dry ingredients gently into creamed mixture alternately with boiling water until just mixed, beginning and ending with dry ingredients. *Do not overmix.* Spoon batter into a lightly greased 1.5 L (8 x 4 in) loaf pan. Bake in a 180°C (350°F) oven 40 to 45 min until tester inserted in center comes out clean. Cool in pan 10 min; remove and cool completely. Wrap tightly to store. Cut into slices to serve.

Makes 12 servings.

**Each serving: 2 cm (½ in) slice**

| | | |
|---|---|---|
| ½ ☐ Starchy Choice | 20 g carbohydrate |
| 1 ◪ Fruits & Vegetables Choice | 2 g protein |
| 1 ▲ Fats & Oils Choice | 5 g fat |
| | 560 kilojoules |
| | (133 Calories) |

## CRANBERRY PEAR KUCHEN

*Here is an old-fashioned baked dessert combining two fruits not often seen together, but the combination is perfectly pleasing in our kuchen.*

**Fruit Layer:**

| | | |
|---|---|---|
| 300 mL | water | 1¼ cups |
| 500 mL | cranberries, chopped | 2 cups |
| pinch | cinnamon | pinch |

| | | |
|---|---|---|
| **15 mL** | cornstarch | **1 tbsp** |
| | Liquid artificial sweetener equivalent to 40 mL (8 tsp) sugar | |
| ½ | peeled pear or apple, coarsely chopped | ½ |

**Kuchen Layer:**

| | | |
|---|---|---|
| **250 mL** | all purpose flour | **1 cup** |
| **7 mL** | baking powder | **1½ tsp** |
| **2 mL** | salt | **½ tsp** |
| **1 mL** | cinnamon | **¼ tsp** |
| **45 mL** | sugar | **3 tbsp** |
| **1** | egg | **1** |
| **75 mL** | water | **1/3 cup** |
| **10 mL** | vegetable oil | **2 tsp** |
| **2 mL** | vanilla | **½ tsp** |
| **125 mL** | *Crunchy Topping* (recipe, p.204) | **½ cup** |

Combine 250 mL (1 cup) water, cranberries and cinnamon in a saucepan. Bring to a boil; stir-cook 5 min. Mix together remaining water and cornstarch; stir into cranberry mixture. Continue to cook until mixture thickens. Remove from heat; stir in sweetener and pear. Set aside. To make kuchen layer, combine flour, baking powder, salt and cinnamon in a mixing bowl. Beat together sugar, egg, water, oil and vanilla until frothy. Add to flour mixture; stir *just* until combined. *Do not overmix.* Spread in a greased 23 cm (9 inch) round or square baking dish. Pour fruit mixture over kuchen layer. Sprinkle with *Crunchy Topping.* Bake in a 180°C (350°F) oven 45 min. Serve warm.

Makes 12 servings.

**Each serving: 1/12 recipe**

| | | |
|---|---|---|
| ½ ▢ | Starchy Choice | 16 g carbohydrate |
| 1 ◪ | Fruits & Vegetables Choice | 2 g protein |
| ½ ▲ | Fats & Oils Choice | 3 g fat |

420 kilojoules
(99 Calories)

### FRUIT FLAVOR JELLY

*For a succulent salad or dessert, add chopped vegetables or fruit to this jelly. Just remember to check whether or not the addition changes the nutrient value.*

| | | | |
|---|---|---|---|
| 2 | **packets** | unflavored gelatin | 2 **packets** |
| 500 | **mL** | cold water | 2 **cups** |
| 500 | **mL** | boiling water | 2 **cups** |
| | | Any flavor unsweetened Kool-Aid or Freshie powder to make 2 L (8 cups) | |
| | | Artificial sweetener equivalent to 60 mL (12 tsp) sugar (12 aspartame tablets, crushed) | |

Sprinkle gelatin over 125 mL (½ cup) cold water; let stand 5 min. Add boiling water, Kool-Aid and sweetener; stir until gelatin dissolves. Stir in remaining 375 mL (1½ cups) cold water. Pour into a rinsed 1 L (4 cup) mold. Chill about 4 h until set.

Makes 8 servings.

**Each serving: 125 mL (½ cup)**

1 **++** Extra

2 g protein

30 kilojoules
(8 Calories)

### ORANGE CUSTARD CLOUD

*The delicate flavor and texture of this light orange fluff complements almost any meal. For variety, substitute Peach Refresher for the orange juice. Serve either flavor with strawberry or raspberry Berry Sauce. It adds exciting flavor and color contrast.*

| | | | |
|---|---|---|---|
| 1 | **packet** | unflavored gelatin | 1 **packet** |
| 500 | **mL** | unsweetened orange juice | 2 **cups** |
| 5 | **mL** | grated orange peel, optional | 1 **tsp** |
| 2 | | eggs, separated | 2 |
| | | Artificial sweetener equivalent to 40 mL (8 tsp) sugar (8 aspartame tablets, crushed) | |
| 1 | | egg white | 1 |
| 1 | **mL** | cream of tartar | ¼ **tsp** |

Sprinkle gelatin over 125 mL (½ cup) orange juice to soften; set aside 5 min. Whisk together in a saucepan the remaining orange juice, orange peel, if desired, and egg yolks. Heat, stirring constantly, about 5 min, until mixture thickens slightly and coats a metal spoon. Remove from heat and stir in sweetener and gelatin until they dissolve. Refrigerate until partially set. Beat egg whites with cream of tartar until stiff. Fold into orange mixture. Spoon into a 1.5 L (6 cup) mold. Chill about 4 h until set.

Makes 8 servings.

**Each serving: 175 mL (2/3 cup)**

½ 🖉 Protein Choice

½ 🖾 Fruits & Vegetables Choice

5 g carbohydrate
3 g protein
2 g fat

210 kilojoules
(50 Calories)

## ORANGE BLOCKS

Orange Blocks *are a colorful, cool confection greatly enjoyed by young people.*

| 500 mL | orange juice | 2 cups |
| 4 packets | unflavored gelatin | 4 packets |
| 10 mL | vanilla | 2 tsp |

Pour 250 mL (1 cup) orange juice into a bowl. Sprinkle gelatin over top to soften; let stand 5 min. Heat remaining orange juice to boiling. Stir into gelatin mixture until it dissolves. Stir in vanilla. Pour into a rinsed 20 cm (8 in) square cake pan. Chill about 4 h until firm. Cut into 2.5 cm (1 in) squares to serve.

**VARIATION:**

**GRAPE BLOCKS:** Substitute 250 mL (1 cup) unsweetened grape juice and 250 mL (1 cup) water for the orange juice.

Makes 64 squares.

**Each serving: 2 squares**

1 ➕➕ Extra

2 g carbohydrate
1 g protein

50 kilojoules
(12 Calories)

## BAKED RICE PUDDING

*This rice pudding is wonderfully smooth and lightly spiced. The secret of its creamy perfection is the twice-cooked rice.*

| | | | |
|---|---|---|---|
| 125 mL | water | ½ | cup |
| 1 mL | salt | ¼ | tsp |
| 50 mL | rice | ¼ | cup |
| 1 | egg | 1 | |
| 300 mL | 2% milk | 1¼ | cups |
| 20 mL | brown sugar | 4 | tsp |
| 2 mL | vanilla | ½ | tsp |
| 1 mL | each of cinnamon and nutmeg | ¼ | tsp |
| 25 mL | raisins | 2 | tbsp |

Bring water and salt to a boil. Add rice, reduce heat, cover and cook slowly for 15 min. Beat together egg, milk, brown sugar, vanilla, cinnamon and nutmeg. When rice is cooked, stir it into the milk mixture. Add raisins and spoon into a lightly greased 1 L (4 cup) oven-proof baking dish. Place this in a large pan in oven. Pour boiling water in pan to half way up baking dish. Bake in a 180°C (350°F) oven 30 min. Stir. Continue to bake 30 min longer until lightly browned.

Makes 4 servings.

**Each serving: 75 mL (1/3 cup)**

| | | |
|---|---|---|
| 1 ☐ Starchy Choice | | 20 g carbohydrate |
| 1 ◆ Milk Choice (2%) | | 5 g protein |
| | | 3 g fat |
| | | 540 kilojoules |
| | | (127 Calories) |

> **Vanilla extract and other flavorings enhance sweet treats, baked goods and desserts. They perform wonders where sugar is eliminated or used in small amounts. Some of the quantities used in recipes in this book seem large, but the resultant dishes taste best with the measures used.**

*On facing page, from lower right*: Peppermint Chocolate Roll, Pina Colada Squares, Light and Lemony Cheesecake with Berry Sauce.

## PINEAPPLE DREAM

Pineapple Dream *is, as the Greeks say, "food fit for the gods." For a glorious party pie, pour filling into a graham crumb or oatmeal pie crust.*

| | | |
|---|---|---|
| 1 packet | unflavored gelatin | 1 packet |
| 125 mL | canned unsweetened pineapple juice | ½ cup |
| 5 mL | coconut or almond extract | 1 tsp |
| 125 mL | canned unsweetened pineapple chunks | ½ cup |
| 250 mL | 2% cottage cheese | 1 cup |
| | Artificial sweetener equivalent to 5 mL (1 tsp) sugar | |
| 1 packet | whipped topping mix | 1 packet |
| 125 mL | 2% milk | ½ cup |
| 10 mL | toasted unsweetened shredded coconut | 2 tsp |

Sprinkle gelatin over pineapple juice in a small saucepan; let stand 5 min to soften. Add coconut extract. Heat just until gelatin melts. Cool to room temperature. Place pineapple chunks, cottage cheese and sweetener in a blender or food processor. Process until puréed. Mix in gelatin mixture. Combine whipped topping mix and milk. Beat until stiff peaks form. Fold into gelatin mixture. Pour into a 1 L (4 cup) bowl or serving dish. Sprinkle with toasted coconut. Chill at least 2 hours before serving.

Makes 8 servings.

**Each serving: 125 mL (½ cup)**

½ 🖊 Protein Choice
1 🖊 Fruits & Vegetables Choice

8 g carbohydrate
5 g protein
3 g fat

330 kilojoules
(79 Calories)

---

*On facing page, bottom from right*: Hamburger Relish, White Grape Jelly, Pear Plum Spread, Pickled Onion Rings, Bread and Butter Pickles, Spicy Pickled Beets. *On shelf from left*: Spicy Pear Spread, Peppy Dill Wedges, Cinnamon Apple Jelly, Minted Apple Butter, Cranberry-Orange Relish, Peach Spread, Spicy Apple Chutney.

## BLUEBERRY CUPCAKES

Blueberry Cupcakes *make a delicious dessert when served with* Lemon
Pudding Sauce.

| | | | |
|---|---|---|---|
| 75 mL | butter or margarine | 1/3 | cup |
| 90 mL | lightly packed brown sugar | 6 | tbsp |
| 1 | egg | 1 | |
| 375 mL | all purpose flour | 1½ | cups |
| 5 mL | baking powder | 1 | tsp |
| 2 mL | each of baking soda and salt | ½ | tsp |
| 1 mL | each of cinnamon and nutmeg | ¼ | tsp |
| 175 mL | sour milk or buttermilk | 2/3 | cup |
| 250 mL | fresh or partially thawed frozen blueberries | 1 | cup |

Cream butter and sugar until light and fluffy. Beat in egg. Combine flour,
baking powder, baking soda, salt, cinnamon and nutmeg. Stir into creamed
mixture alternately with sour milk, just until mixed. *Do not overmix.* Fold in
blueberries. Fill 12 lightly greased muffin cups 2/3 full. Bake in a 190°C (375°F)
oven 20 min until golden. Serve warm.

Makes 12 medium cupcakes.

**Each serving: 1 cupcake**

| | | |
|---|---|---|
| ½ ▢ | Starchy Choice | 19 g carbohydrate |
| 1 ◪ | Fruits & Vegetables Choice | 3 g protein |
| 1 ▲ | Fats & Oils Choice | 6 g fat |
| | | 600 kilojoules |
| | | (142 Calories) |

> **To sour fresh milk for this recipe, pour 10 mL (2 tsp) vinegar into a
> measuring cup; fill with 2% milk to 175 mL (2/3 cup).**

## LEMON PUDDING SAUCE

*For a fabulous dessert, drizzle* Lemon Pudding Sauce *over oven-fresh, piping
hot,* Blueberry Cupcakes *or* Nova Scotia Gingerbread.

| | | | |
|---|---|---|---|
| 20 mL | cornstarch | 4 | tsp |
| 250 mL | water | 1 | cup |
| | Finely grated peel of 1 lemon | | |
| 50 mL | lemon juice | ¼ | cup |
| 1 | egg | 1 | |

| 10 mL | margarine or butter | 2 tsp |
|---|---|---|
|  | Artificial sweetener equivalent to 40 mL (8 tsp) sugar (8 aspartame tablets, crushed) |  |

Combine cornstarch, water, lemon peel and lemon juice in a small heavy saucepan; beat in egg. Cook over medium heat, stirring constantly, until thickened and clear. Stir in margarine and sweetener.

Makes 10 servings.

**Each serving: 25 mL (2 tbsp)**

1  **++**  Extra

2 g carbohydrate
1 g protein
1 g fat

90 kilojoules
(21 Calories)

## BERRY SAUCE

*This ruby red sauce is delicious served warm or cold on cheesecake, sponge cake or baked custard.*

| 250 mL | unsweetened raspberries or strawberries | 1 cup |
|---|---|---|
|  | Liquid artificial sweetener equivalent to 60 mL (12 tsp) sugar |  |
| 15 mL | fresh lemon juice | 1 tbsp |

Place fruit and sweetener in a blender; purée until free of lumps. Strain the sauce through a fine sieve to remove seeds. Press well with the back of a spoon to push through as much fruit as possible. Stir in lemon juice. Store in a tightly covered container in refrigerator. Serve warm or cold as a dessert sauce.

Makes about 200 mL (¾ cup).

**Each serving: 45 mL (3 tbsp)**

1  **++**  Extra

3 g carbohydrate

50 kilojoules
(12 Calories)

## LIGHT AND LEMONY CHEESECAKE

*Dessert lovers delight in the creamy smoothness and tangy taste of this "refrigerator baked" cheesecake. For a change, press the crust into a pie shell, then fill it. You will end up with a heavenly cheesepie.*

| | | | |
|---|---|---|---|
| 375 mL | 2% cottage cheese or drained tofu | 1½ | cups |
| 10 mL | grated lemon peel | 2 | tsp |
| 1 packet | unflavored gelatin | 1 | packet |
| 50 mL | fresh lemon juice | ¼ | cup |
| 3 | eggs, separated | 3 | |
| 125 mL | 2% milk | ½ | cup |
| | Artificial sweetener equivalent to 40 mL (8 tsp) sugar (8 aspartame tablets, crushed) | | |
| 5 mL | vanilla | 1 | tsp |
| 1 mL | cream of tartar | ¼ | tsp |
| 1 | *Graham Cracker Crust* (recipe, p.204) in a 23 cm (9 inch) spring form pan | 1 | |
| | *Berry Sauce* (recipe, p.195), optional | | |

Beat cottage cheese in a food processor or press through a sieve until very smooth. Stir in lemon peel. Sprinkle gelatin over lemon juice to soften; set aside 5 min. Combine the egg yolks and milk in the top of a double boiler. Cook over simmering water, stirring until mixture thickens slightly and coats a metal spoon. Remove from heat. Stir in gelatin mixture until it dissolves. Add sweetener, vanilla and cottage cheese. Chill, stirring occasionally, until mixture mounds when dropped from a spoon. Beat egg whites with cream of tartar until stiff peaks form. Fold into gelatin mixture; pour over *Graham Cracker Crust* in spring form pan. Chill about 4 h until firm. Serve with 25 mL (2 tbsp) *Berry Sauce* per serving, if desired.

Makes 8 servings.

**Each serving: 1/8 of cheesecake**

*Made with cottage cheese:*

| | |
|---|---|
| 1½ 🪧 Protein Choices | 11 g carbohydrate |
| 1 ▰ Fruits & Vegetables Choice | 11 g protein |
| 1 ▲ Fats & Oils Choice | 9 g fat |
| | 710 kilojoules (169 Calories) |

*Made with tofu:*
1 🖊 Protein Choice
1 🖊 Fruits & Vegetables Choice
1 ▲ Fats & Oils Choice

10 g carbohydrate
7 g protein
9 g fat

620 kilojoules
(149 Calories)

## MANDARIN PIE

*Serve this cool refreshing pie with a sprightly garnish of mint or a twist of lemon.*

| 1 packet | unflavored gelatin | 1 packet |
|---|---|---|
| 25 mL | cold water | 2 tbsp |
| 125 mL | boiling water | ½ cup |
| 50 mL | orange juice | ¼ cup |
| | Liquid artificial sweetener equivalent to 60 mL (12 tsp) sugar | |
| 5 mL | grated orange peel | 1 tsp |
| 250 mL | plain yogurt | 1 cup |
| 1 can | 284 mL (10 oz) unsweetened mandarin oranges, drained, or 250 mL (1 cup) orange sections | 1 can |
| 1 | *Graham Cracker Crust* (recipe, p. 204) in 1 L (9 in) pie plate Cinnamon | 1 |

Sprinkle gelatin over cold water in a medium mixing bowl; let stand 5 min. Add boiling water, stirring until gelatin dissolves. Stir in orange juice, sweetener and orange peel. Beat in yogurt until thoroughly mixed. Refrigerate about 45 min, until partially set. Fold in orange sections. Taste for sweetness, add more sweetener, if desired. Pour into pie shell. Sprinkle lightly with cinnamon. Refrigerate about 4 h until set.

Makes 6 servings.

**Each serving: 1/6 pie including crust**

½ ⬜ Starchy Choice
1 🖊 Fruits & Vegetables Choice
1½ ▲ Fats & Oils Choices

16 g carbohydrate
3 g protein
8 g fat

620 kilojoules
(148 Calories)

## CRÊPES ÉLÉGANTES

*Tender crêpes with a brilliant ruby glaze are the perfect dessert for a busy party giver to serve. Both can be made ahead, and the final combining of the crêpes and sauce can be done over a burner at the table for an elegant finale to a meal.*

| | | |
|---|---|---|
| **500 mL** | cranberries | **2 cups** |
| **500 mL** | water | **2 cups** |
| **10 mL** | grated orange peel | **2 tsp** |
| **10 mL** | cornstarch | **2 tsp** |
| **10 mL** | molasses | **2 tsp** |
| | Artificial sweetener equivalent to 60 mL (12 tsp) sugar (12 aspartame tablets, crushed) | |
| **25 mL** | brandy | **2 tbsp** |
| **8** | *Crêpes* (see recipe, p.52) | **8** |
| **375 mL** | strawberries, sliced | **1½ cups** |

Combine cranberries, 450 mL (1¾ cups) water and orange peel in a saucepan. Bring to a boil; reduce heat and simmer 5 min. Pour into a blender or food processor. Mix together remaining 50 mL (¼ cup) cold water, cornstarch and molasses. Add to cranberry mixture. Process 1 to 2 min to a smooth purée. Return mixture to saucepan. Stir-cook over medium heat about 4 min until mixture boils and thickens. Remove from heat, add sweetener, stirring until it dissolves. Store in refrigerator until ready to serve.

*To serve:* Mix sauce and brandy in a large frypan. Bring to a boil; reduce heat and simmer 1 min. Place crêpes one at a time in sauce; coat both sides; fold in half then in half again to form a triangle; move to side of frypan. Add strawberries to frypan; stir-cook 1 min until heated through. Spoon a crêpe, sauce and a few strawberries onto a warm dessert plate for each serving.

Makes 8 servings.

### Each serving: 1 crêpe with about 75 mL (1/3 cup) sauce and fruit

| | | |
|---|---|---|
| ½ ⬮ | Protein Choice | 12 g carbohydrate |
| 1 ⬛ | Fruits & Vegetables Choice | 3 g protein |
| | | 3 g fat |
| | | 370 kilojoules (87 Calories) |

(**Note:** If desired, substitute one of these fruits for the strawberries: 200 mL (¾ cup) raspberries, or 1½ peaches, or 1 small peeled apple or pear, thinly sliced.)

## PEACHY BLUEBERRY PIE

*The two-fruit filling baked in a nutty tasting* Oatmeal Pie Crust *makes an extra special pie that is bound to become a family favorite.*

| | | |
|---|---|---|
| 125 mL | water | ½ cup |
| 25 mL | cornstarch | 2 tbsp |
| 15 mL | lemon juice | 1 tbsp |
| 1 mL | nutmeg | ¼ tsp |
| pinch | salt | pinch |
| | Liquid artificial sweetener equivalent to 40 mL (8 tsp) sugar (8 aspartame tablets) | |
| 500 mL | sliced fresh or thawed frozen peaches | 2 cups |
| 125 mL | fresh or partially thawed frozen blueberries | ½ cup |
| 1 L | *Oatmeal Pie Crust* (recipe, p.203) | 9 in |
| 125 mL | *Crunchy Topping* (recipe, p.204) | ½ cup |

Combine water, cornstarch, lemon juice, nutmeg and salt in a saucepan; stir until well combined. Bring to a boil and stir-cook about 2 min until clear and thickened. Remove from heat, stir in sweetener. Fold in peaches then blueberries; spoon immediately into prepared pie shell. Sprinkle with *Crunchy Topping.* Cover pie filling loosely with a tent of aluminum foil to prevent over-browning. Bake in a 220°C (425°F) oven 30 min, remove foil tent and continue to bake 10 min or until fruit is tender.

Makes 8 servings.

**Each serving: 1/8 pie including crust**

| | | |
|---|---|---|
| 1 ▢ Starchy Choice | 24 g carbohydrate |
| 1 ▨ Fruits & Vegetables Choice | 3 g protein |
| 2 ▲ Fats & Oils Choices | 10 g fat |
| | 830 kilojoules (198 Calories) |

**Fresh fruits and unsweetened fruit juices are sources of sugar. For example, a large apple contains about 30 mL (6 tsp) natural sugar.**

## CHOCOLATE SAUCE

*This sauce is so good it disappears quickly. It is delectable as a dessert topping over ice cream, sponge cake or fresh pears, and is superb as the base for chocolate drinks.*

| | | |
|---|---|---|
| 10 mL | cornstarch | 2 tsp |
| 125 mL | cocoa | ½ cup |
| 500 mL | cold water | 2 cups |
| | Artificial sweetener equivalent to 40 mL (8 tsp) sugar (8 aspartame tablets) | |
| 10 mL | vanilla | 2 tsp |

Combine cornstarch and cocoa. Whisk into cold water in a saucepan until there are no dry bits. Cook, stirring frequently, until mixture comes to a boil. Stir 1 min until mixture thickens. Remove from heat, stir in sweetener and vanilla, cover and allow to cool. Store in clean jar in refrigerator up to 6 weeks.

Makes about 550 mL (2¼ cups) sauce, 12 servings.

**Each serving: 45 mL (3 tbsp)**

1 **++** Extra

2 g carbohydrate
1 g protein

50 kilojoules
(12 Calories)

**VARIATION:**

**MOCHA SAUCE:** Substitute 500 mL (2 cups) strong coffee for water in the above recipe.

## CHOCOLATE DREAM PIE

*The combination of a crunchy, crisp crust holding a velvety, smooth chocolate filling is a delectable dessert treat.*

| | | |
|---|---|---|
| 1 packet | unflavored gelatin | 1 packet |
| 375 mL | skim milk | 1½ cups |
| 50 mL | cocoa | ¼ cup |
| 15 mL | cornstarch | 1 tbsp |
| 1 | egg, separated | 1 |
| | Artificial sweetener equivalent to 80 mL (16 tsp) sugar (16 aspartame tablets, crushed) | |
| 5 mL | vanilla | 1 tsp |

| 50 mL | instant skim milk powder | ¼ cup |
|---|---|---|
| 50 mL | ice water | ¼ cup |
| 1 L | baked *Oatmeal Pie Crust* (recipe, p.203) | 9 in |

Sprinkle gelatin over 50 mL (¼ cup) milk to soften. Let stand 5 min. Whisk 250 mL (1 cup) milk and cocoa together until well blended. Heat to boiling in a heavy saucepan; reduce heat and simmer 5 min. Stir together cornstarch, egg yolk and remaining 50 mL (¼ cup) milk. Stir into cocoa mixture; continue cooking over low heat until mixture thickens. Mix in gelatin and sweetener until they dissolve. Remove from heat and stir in vanilla. Chill until partially set. Beat together egg white, skim milk powder and ice water until stiff peaks form. Fold into chocolate mixture. Spoon into pie shell. Chill about 4 h until set.

Makes 8 servings.

**Each serving: 1/8 pie including crust**

| | | |
|---|---|---|
| 1 ◆ | Milk Choice (whole) | 17 g carbohydrate |
| 1 ▨ | Fruits and Vegetables Choice | 6 g protein |
| 1 ▲ | Fats & Oils Choice | 9 g fat |

720 kilojoules
(173 Calories)

**VARIATION:**

**CHOCOLATE MOUSSE:** Prepare filling as in recipe above. Spoon into 6 individual molds or a rinsed 1 L (4 cup) mold. Chill about 4 h until set.

Makes 6 servings.

**Each serving: about 125 mL (½ cup)**

| | | |
|---|---|---|
| 1 ◆ | Milk Choice (2%) | 7 g carbohydrate |

5 g protein
2 g fat

280 kilojoules
(66 Calories)

## STRAWBERRY ANGEL PIE

*Fresh or frozen strawberries work equally well in this colorful, light-tasting pie.*

| | | |
|---|---|---|
| **750 mL** | frozen unsweetened or fresh strawberries | **3 cups** |
| **250 mL** | water | **1 cup** |
| **1 packet** | unflavored gelatin | **1 packet** |
| **15 mL** | cornstarch | **1 tbsp** |
| **1** | egg, separated | **1** |
| | Artificial sweetener equivalent to 70 mL (14 tsp) sugar (14 aspartame tablets, crushed) | |
| **5 mL** | vanilla | **1 tsp** |
| **2 mL** | almond extract | **½ tsp** |
| **50 mL** | instant skim milk powder | **¼ cup** |
| **50 mL** | ice water | **¼ cup** |
| **1 L** | *Graham Cracker Crust* (recipe, p.204) | **9 in** |

Slice strawberries. Pour water over strawberries; let stand 1 h at room temperature. Drain water from strawberries into a saucepan; reserve strawberries. Sprinkle gelatin over 25 mL (2 tbsp) of liquid drained from strawberries. Whisk cornstarch and egg yolk into remaining water. Cook and stir over medium heat until mixture boils and thickens slightly. Remove from heat. Add softened gelatin, sweetener, vanilla and almond extract, stirring until gelatin and sweetener dissolve. Stir in strawberries. Chill about 30 min or until mixture is partially set. Beat egg white, skim milk powder and ice water in a chilled bowl. Fold into thickened strawberry mixture. Spoon into *Graham Cracker Crust*. Chill, about 4 h, until completely set.

Makes 6 servings.

**Each serving: 1/6 pie including crust**

| | | |
|---|---|---|
| 1 ◆ Milk Choice (2%) | 17 g carbohydrate |
| 1 ▨ Fruits & Vegetables Choice | 4 g protein |
| 1 ▲ Fats & Oils Choice | 8 g fat |

650 kilojoules
(156 Calories)

**VARIATION:**

**STRAWBERRY ANGEL MOUSSE:** Prepare filling as in recipe above. Spoon into rinsed 1 L (4 cup) mold. Chill until set.

Makes 4 servings.

**Each serving: about 175 mL (2/3 cup)**

½ ▨ Protein Choice

1 ◪ Fruits & Vegetables Choice

11 g carbohydrate

5 g protein

2 g fat

350 kilojoules

(82 Calories)

## OATMEAL PIE CRUST

*Oatmeal contributes to the flaky texture and provides the nutty flavor for this deliciously different pie crust.*

| 200 mL | all purpose flour | ¾ cup |
| 125 mL | quick rolled oats | ½ cup |
| 2 mL | salt | ½ tsp |
| 60 mL | vegetable oil | 4 tbsp |
| 45 to 60 mL | ice water | 3 to 4 tbsp |

Combine flour, rolled oats and salt in a mixing bowl. Slowly drizzle in oil, mixing with a fork. Continue lightly mixing with fork and cutting through mixture until all dry ingredients are moistened and mixture resembles fine crumbs. Add 45 to 60 mL (3 to 4 tbsp) ice water, a few drops at a time, until mixture begins to form a ball. Pat into a 1 L (9 in) pie plate. (Or roll between two sheets of waxed paper. Remove top sheet and turn pastry into pie plate; remove second piece of waxed paper.) Form a rim and flute edges. Fill and bake according to pie recipe.

*For baked pastry shell:* Prick pastry with fork in several places. Bake in a 200°C (400°F) oven 10 min until light golden brown.

Makes 6 servings.

**Each serving: 1/6 pie crust excluding filling**

1 ▢ Starchy Choice

2 ▲ Fats & Oils Choices

15 g carbohydrate

3 g protein

10 g fat

680 kilojoules

(162 Calories)

## CRUNCHY TOPPING

*A sprinkling of toasted* Crunchy Topping *enhances simple puddings, baked custards and fruit cups.*

| | | |
|---|---|---|
| 50 mL | butter or margarine | ¼ **cup** |
| 375 mL | quick rolled oats | 1½ **cups** |
| 50 mL | lightly packed brown sugar | ¼ **cup** |
| 50 mL | chopped nuts | ¼ **cup** |
| 2 mL | cinnamon | ½ **tsp** |

Melt butter in a frypan. Add rolled oats, brown sugar, nuts and cinnamon. Stir-cook over medium heat about 3 min until golden brown. Remove from heat; spread on a large plate or cookie sheet to cool. Store in a tightly covered container in refrigerator for up to 2 months.

Makes 500 mL (2 cups).

**Each serving: 15 mL (1 tbsp)**

½ ▲ Fats & Oils Choice

3 g carbohydrate
2 g fat

130 kilojoules
(30 Calories)

## GRAHAM CRACKER CRUST

*A touch of cinnamon and nutmeg makes this popular pie crust tasty, and there is no need for the addition of sweetener.*

| | | |
|---|---|---|
| 200 mL | graham wafer crumbs | ¾ **cup** |
| 45 mL | melted butter or margarine | 3 **tbsp** |
| 1 mL | each of cinnamon and nutmeg | ¼ **tsp** |

Combine graham wafer crumbs, butter, cinnamon and nutmeg. Press into a 1 L (9 in) pie plate or 2 L (8 in) square cake pan or 23 cm (9 in) spring form pan. Chill in refrigerator 2 h before filling. If desired, reserve 25 mL (2 tbsp) of the crumb mixture to sprinkle on top of the filling.

Makes a 1 L (9 in) pie crust, 8 servings.

**Each serving: 1/8 pie crust excluding filling**

½ ☐ Starchy Choice
1 ▲ Fats & Oils Choice

7 g carbohydrate
1 g protein
5 g fat

320 kilojoules
(77 Calories)

# Preserves and Pickles

Home preserved spreads, jellies, pickles and relishes add variety to year-round menu planning. Try one of our jellies or spreads on hot biscuits or bread, drop a dollop of relish on hamburgers, or accompany your favorite sandwich with a crunchy dill or bread and butter pickles.

These preserves are easy to prepare, and many of them can be made at any time during the year. However, it is smart to stock the pantry or freezer when fruits and vegetables are in season, when it is penny-wise to do so.

The better the quality of fresh fruit, the better the preserves, so always select firm, ripe fruit at its prime.

These recipes are for small batches of jellies and spreads. Since sugar was not used, we found that we had best results cooking up small amounts at a time. Instead of doubling the recipes, make them up two or three times if you wish.

Any of the preserves make ideal personalized gifts for holidays or birthdays. Simply decorate the jar to suit the occasion and make the gift extra special. You might even add a copy of this book.

## STRAWBERRY OR RASPBERRY SPREAD

*The tastes of early summer are captured in this berry spread that freezes beautifully. It is succulent for a cake filling or ice cream sauce.*

| | | | |
|---|---|---|---|
| 7 mL | unflavored gelatin | 1½ tsp |
| 50 mL | water | ¼ cup |
| 500 mL | sliced fresh or frozen unsweetened strawberries or raspberries | 2 cups |
| | Artificial sweetener equivalent to 40 to 60 mL (8 to 12 tsp) sugar | |
| | Red food coloring | |

Sprinkle gelatin over water to soften. Let stand 5 min. Place berries in a medium saucepan; bring to a boil; cook, stirring occasionally for 5 min. Add softened gelatin, sweetener and food coloring; stir until gelatin dissolves. Skim foam from the surface. Ladle into hot sterilized jars leaving 1 cm (½ in) headspace. Wipe jar rims. Seal. Store in refrigerator or freezer.

Makes about 450 mL (1¾ cups).

**Each serving: 25 mL (2 tbsp)**

1 **++** Extra

2 g carbohydrate

30 kilojoules
(8 Calories)

## SPICY PEAR SPREAD

*This spread is so good it will make a splendid gift. It is thick and goes well with both meats and breads. For a tasty variation, use peaches instead of pears.*

| | | | |
|---|---|---|---|
| 500 mL | peeled, cored and crushed pears (about 4) | 2 cups |
| 5 mL | ascorbic acid color keeper | 1 tsp |
| 10 mL | fresh lemon juice | 2 tsp |
| 8 | whole cloves | 8 |
| 1 stick | cinnamon, 10 cm (4 in) long | 1 stick |
| 5 mL | unflavored gelatin | 1 tsp |
| 25 mL | water | 2 tbsp |
| | Artificial sweetener | |

Combine pears, ascorbic acid color keeper, lemon juice, cloves and cinnamon in a medium saucepan. Bring to a boil; reduce heat and simmer 10 min, stirring frequently. Sprinkle gelatin over water to soften, let stand 5 min. Stir into hot pear mixture until gelatin dissolves. Discard cloves and cinnamon stick. Stir in sweetener to taste. Ladle into hot sterilized jars, leaving 1 cm (½ in) headspace. Wipe jar rims. Seal. Store in refrigerator or freezer.

Makes about 450 mL (1¾ cups).

**Each serving: 15 mL (1 tbsp)**

1 **++** Extra

3 g carbohydrate

50 kilojoules
(12 Calories)

## CINNAMON APPLE JELLY

*This sparkling jelly for toast or muffins is tantalizing, and has a subtle spicy scent.*

| 5 | mL | unflavored gelatin | 1 | tsp |
|---|---|---|---|---|
| 425 | mL | unsweetened apple juice | 1-2/3 | cups |
| 10 | mL | fresh lemon juice | 2 | tsp |
| 1 | piece | cinnamon stick, 2.5 cm (1 in) long | 1 | piece |
| 1 | drop | each of yellow and red food coloring, optional | 1 | drop |
| | | Artificial sweetener equivalent to 20 mL (4 tsp) sugar | | |

Soften gelatin in 50 mL (¼ cup) apple juice. Combine remaining apple juice, lemon juice, cinnamon stick and food coloring, if desired, in a saucepan. Boil about 7 min to reduce by 1/3. Remove from heat. Stir in sweetener and softened gelatin until it dissolves. Discard cinnamon stick. Pour into a sterilized jar. Cover tightly. Store in refrigerator.

Makes about 250 mL (1 cup).

**Each serving: 15 mL (1 tbsp)**

1 **++** Extra

3 g carbohydrate

50 kilojoules
(12 Calories)

## WHITE GRAPE JELLY

*This grape jelly can be made any time of the year and requires no special equipment.*

| | | | |
|---|---|---|---|
| 5 mL | unflavored gelatin | 1 tsp | |
| 425 mL | unsweetened white grape juice | 1-2/3 cups | |
| 10 mL | fresh lemon juice | 2 tsp | |
| 3 | allspice berries or whole cloves | 3 | |
| | Artificial sweetener equivalent to 10 mL (2 tsp) sugar | | |

Sprinkle gelatin over 50 mL (¼ cup) grape juice. Combine remaining grape juice, lemon juice and allspice berries in a saucepan. Boil about 7 min to reduce by 1/3. Remove from heat. Stir in sweetener and softened gelatin until it dissolves. Discard allspice berries. Pour into a sterilized jar. Cover tightly. Store in refrigerator.

Makes about 250 mL (1 cup)

**Each serving: 10 mL (2 tsp)**

1 **++** Extra

3 g carbohydrate

50 kilojoules (12 Calories)

## CRANBERRY-ORANGE RELISH

*Try this rich, ruby relish with roast lamb or pork. It is a no-cook version of a popular combination.*

| | | | |
|---|---|---|---|
| 1 L | fresh cranberries | 4 cups | |
| 1 | medium orange, unpeeled | 1 | |
| 25 mL | chopped candied ginger | 2 tbsp | |
| 2 mL | cinnamon | ½ tsp | |
| | Artificial sweetener equivalent to 60 mL (12 tsp) sugar | | |

Wash cranberries. Place in container of blender or food processor. Wash orange, cut into eighths, seed and place in blender. Add ginger and cinnamon. Process at high speed with on/off motion, about 2 min, until coarsely chopped. Add sweetener; continue to purée about 30 sec longer or until desired consistency.

Makes about 375 mL (1½ cups).

**Each serving: 10 mL (2 tsp)**

1 ++ Extra                                                2 g carbohydrate

                                                          30 kilojoules
                                                          (8 Calories)

## PEAR-PLUM SPREAD

*Smooth pears and tart plums combine in a luscious purée, perfect on warm-from-the-oven muffins or biscuits.*

| | | |
|---|---|---|
| 4 | medium pears | 4 |
| 10 mL | ascorbic acid color keeper | 2 tsp |
| 5 | red plums | 5 |
| 5 mL | whole cloves | 1 tsp |
| 1 piece | fresh ginger, size of a penny, optional | 1 piece |
| 1 piece | cinnamon stick, 7.5 cm (3 in) long | 1 piece |
| 125 mL | water | ½ cup |
| | Artificial sweetener equivalent to 45 mL (9 tsp) sugar (9 aspartame tablets, crushed) | |

Peel and core pears; chop coarsely. Place in a large saucepan and sprinkle with ascorbic acid color keeper. Remove pits from plums and cut each plum into 8 pieces; stir plums into pears. Wrap plum pits, cloves and ginger, if desired, in a piece of cheesecloth and bury in fruit. Add cinnamon stick and water. Cover, bring to a boil and simmer 15 to 20 min or until fruit is tender. Discard spice bag and cinnamon stick. Purée fruit mixture in a blender or food processor or press through a sieve. Return to saucepan. Simmer, uncovered, 15 to 20 min or until mixture coats a metal spoon. Remove from heat. Stir in sweetener. Ladle into hot clean jars, leaving 1 cm (½ in) headspace. Wipe jar rims. Seal. Process 10 min in a boiling water bath. Store in a cool, dark, dry place.

Makes about 800 mL (3¼ cups).

**Each serving: 15 mL (1 tbsp)**

1 ++ Extra                                                3 g carbohydrate

                                                          50 kilojoules
                                                          (12 Calories)

## GRAPE SPREAD

*What a combination! Grapes and apples mingle to make the darkest, richest spread ever.*

| | | |
|---|---|---|
| **1.5 L** | blue grapes, about 1 kg (2 lbs) | **6 cups** |
| **4** | firm ripe apples, cut up (not peeled or cored) | **4** |
| **pinch** | ground cloves | **pinch** |

Simmer grapes and apples together 30 min. Push pulp through a sieve to yield 1.25 L (5 cups) purée. Return to a clean saucepan, add cloves, bring to a boil then simmer 20 min longer. Ladle into hot clean jars, leaving 1 cm (½ in) headspace. Wipe jar rims. Seal. Process 10 min in a boiling water bath. Store in a cool, dark, dry place.

Makes about 1 L (4 cups).

**Each serving: 15 mL (1 tbsp)**

1 ++ Extra

3 g carbohydrate

50 kilojoules
(12 Calories)

> If *Choice Cooking* **spreads are to be used within a short period of time, the boiling water process can be omitted. The spreads can be stored in the refrigerator up to 1 month, or in the freezer up to 3 months.**

## PEACH SPREAD

*This golden, fruity jam may be sweetened after cooking with aspartame or liquid artificial sweetener, if desired. However, we liked the taste best without the additional sweetener.*

| | | |
|---|---|---|
| **1 kg** | peaches, about 8 medium | **2 lbs** |
| **5 mL** | ascorbic acid color keeper | **1 tsp** |
| **500 mL** | water | **2 cups** |
| **7** | allspice berries | **7** |

Peel and pit peaches. Place peelings and pits in a saucepan. Cut up fruit into a mixing bowl; stir in ascorbic acid color keeper; set aside. Add water and allspice berries to peelings in saucepan. Bring to a boil; reduce heat and cook about 25 min or until liquid is reduced to about 125 mL (½ cup). Discard peel and pits. Stir in peaches. Bring to a boil; reduce heat and cook over medium heat 35 min, stirring and mashing occasionally. Remove from heat, mash well or purée, if desired. Ladle into hot clean jars, leaving 1 cm (½ in) headspace. Wipe jar rims. Seal. Process 10 min in a boiling water bath. Store in a cool, dark, dry place.

Makes about 425 mL (1-2/3 cups).

**Each serving: 15 mL (1 tbsp)**

1  ++  Extra

3 g carbohydrate

50 kilojoules
(12 Calories)

## MINTED APPLE BUTTER

*The hint of mint brings a change to an old-time smoothy. It is tasty with ham and lamb or on gingerbread or pancakes.*

| | | |
|---|---|---|
| 4 | cooking apples, unpeeled and coarsely chopped | 4 |
| 125 mL | water | ½ cup |
| 15 mL | dried mint or 45 mL (3 tbsp) chopped fresh mint | 1 tbsp |
| 5 mL | ascorbic acid color keeper | 1 tsp |

Combine apples (core included), water, mint and ascorbic acid color keeper in a saucepan. Bring to a boil; reduce heat and simmer about 15 min until apples are tender. Mash. Continue to simmer about 10 min, until thick. Press through a sieve. Discard peel and core. Ladle into hot clean jars, leaving 1 cm (½ in) headspace. Wipe jar rims. Process 10 min in a boiling water bath. Store in a cool, dark, dry place.

Makes about 425 mL (1-2/3 cups).

**Each serving: 15 mL (1 tbsp)**

1  ++  Extra

3 g carbohydrate

50 kilojoules
(12 Calories)

### SPICY APPLE CHUTNEY

Spicy Apple Chutney *is just right as an accompaniment for curries. It is also excellent as a spread and as a tangy condiment for chicken, pork and ham.*

| | | | |
|---|---|---|---|
| 4 | large apples | 4 | |
| 250 mL | water | 1 | cup |
| 10 mL | ascorbic acid color keeper | 2 | tsp |
| 125 mL | chopped sweet red pepper | ½ | cup |
| 125 mL | raisins | ½ | cup |
| 75 mL | chopped onion | 1/3 | cup |
| | Juice and grated peel from 1 lemon | | |
| 10 mL | ground ginger | 2 | tsp |
| 25 mL | molasses | 2 | tbsp |

Peel and core apples; place peelings and cores in a saucepan with water. Cover, bring to a boil; cook 10 min. Chop apples and toss with ascorbic acid color keeper into another saucepan. Drain liquid from peelings and add to apples; discard peelings. Add red pepper, raisins, onion, lemon peel, lemon juice and ginger to apples; mix well. Bring to a boil; reduce heat and cook about 35 min, stirring often to prevent sticking, until mixture thickens. Stir in molasses and remove from heat. Ladle into hot clean jars, leaving 1 cm (½ in) headspace. Wipe jar rims. Seal. Process 10 min in a boiling water bath. Store in a cool, dark, dry place.

Makes about 825 mL (3-1/3 cups).

**Each serving: 10 mL (2 tsp)**

1  **++**  Extra

3 g carbohydrate

50 kilojoules
(12 Calories)

## PEAR AND MELON CHUTNEY

*Peaches or nectarines can be used in place of pears in this colorful condiment. Its preparation fills the house with a rich, spicy aroma. Small jars of Pear and Melon Chutney make lovely hostess gifts.*

| | | | | |
|---|---|---|---|---|
| 500 | mL | cider vinegar | 2 | cups |
| 15 | mL | whole cloves | 1 | tbsp |
| 10 | mL | each of ground ginger and allspice | 2 | tsp |
| 7 | mL | nutmeg | 1½ | tsp |
| 1.25 | L | chopped onion | 5 | cups |
| 250 | mL | golden raisins | 1 | cup |
| 250 | mL | currants | 1 | cup |
| 50 | mL | thinly sliced crystallized ginger | ¼ | cup |
| 6 | | cloves garlic, finely chopped | 6 | |
| 10 | | medium pears, peeled, cored and chopped | 10 | |
| 1 | L | chopped cantaloupe | 4 | cups |
| 50 | mL | molasses | ¼ | cup |

Combine vinegar, cloves, ground ginger, allspice and nutmeg in a large saucepan. Heat to boiling. Cover tightly; reduce heat and simmer 30 min. Add onion, raisins, currants, crystallized ginger and garlic. Cook 15 min. Add pears and cantaloupe. Cook about 30 min, stirring often to prevent sticking, until mixture thickens. Stir in molasses and remove from heat. Ladle into hot clean jars, leaving 1 cm (½ in) headspace. Wipe jar rims. Seal. Process 10 min in a boiling water bath. Store in a cool, dark, dry place.

Makes about 2 L (8 cups).

**Each serving: 10 mL (2 tsp)**

1 **++** Extra

3 g carbohydrate

50 kilojoules
(12 Calories)

### HAMBURGER RELISH

*The prime time for relish making is early September. That is when assorted vegetables are plentiful and so inexpensive. Rely on a food processor to ease and speed up the chore of chopping.*

| | | |
|---|---|---|
| 1 L | finely chopped unpeeled cucumber | 4 cups |
| 750 mL | finely chopped onion | 3 cups |
| 750 mL | finely chopped celery | 3 cups |
| 500 mL | finely chopped green pepper | 2 cups |
| 250 mL | finely chopped sweet red pepper | 1 cup |
| 50 mL | pickling salt | ¼ cup |
| 1 L | white vinegar | 4 cups |
| 15 mL | each of celery seed and mustard seed | 1 tbsp |
| | Liquid artificial sweetener equivalent to 300 mL (1¼ cups) sugar | |
| 4 drops | green food coloring | 4 drops |

Combine cucumber, onion, celery, green pepper, red pepper and pickling salt in a bowl; cover and let stand overnight. Drain well. Mix vinegar, celery seed and mustard seed in a large saucepan. Add drained vegetables and bring to a boil. Reduce heat; cook 10 min. Add sweetener and food coloring; stir well. Ladle into hot sterilized jars. Seal. Store in a cool, dark, dry place.

Makes about 1.75 L (7 cups).

**Each serving: 25 mL (2 tbsp)**

1 ++ Extra

2 g carbohydrate

30 kilojoules
(8 Calories)

### PICKLED ONION RINGS

*A little sugar is absorbed by the rings as they stand in their pickle juice. Always drain well before serving.*

| | | |
|---|---|---|
| 1 | large Spanish onion | 1 |
| | Boiling water | |
| 250 mL | white vinegar | 1 cup |
| 250 mL | water | 1 cup |
| 75 mL | sugar | 1/3 cup |

| 2 mL | salt | ½ tsp |
|---|---|---|
| 4 drops | hot pepper sauce | 4 drops |

Cut onion into thin slices. Separate into rings; put into two 500 mL (2 cup) sterilized jars. Pour boiling water over to cover onions. Allow to cool, then drain. Mix together vinegar, water, sugar, salt and hot pepper sauce and bring to a boil. Pour over onion rings. Cover tightly and refrigerate. Use after 2 days. Store in refrigerator up to 2 months.

Makes about 1 L (4 cups).

**Each serving: 2 to 3 onion rings**

1 ++ Extra

approximately 3 g carbohydrate

50 kilojoules (12 Calories)

## SPICY PICKLED BEETS

*Start by cooking fresh beets for this pickle pantry classic. If fresh beets are unavailable, well-drained canned beets will work nearly as well.*

| 500 mL | sliced cooked small beets | 2 cups |
|---|---|---|
| 125 mL | white vinegar | ½ cup |
| 125 mL | water | ½ cup |
| 15 mL | brown sugar | 1 tbsp |
| 10 mL | whole cloves | 2 tsp |
| 2 mL | cinnamon | ½ tsp |
| 1 mL | salt | ¼ tsp |

Place beets in a sterilized jar. Combine vinegar, water, brown sugar, cloves, cinnamon and salt in a saucepan; bring to a boil. Pour over sliced beets; cover tightly; refrigerate for 8 h or longer until beets are pickled. (Remove cloves after 3 days.) Store in refrigerator up to 2 months.

Makes about 500 mL (2 cups).

**Each serving: about 3 slices**

1 ++ Extra

3 g carbohydrate

50 kilojoules (12 Calories)

## PEPPY DILL WEDGES

*Try to use garden fresh, crisp cucumbers for these perky dills. A variety that is not too seedy is best.*

| | | | |
|---|---|---|---|
| 1 L | cucumber wedges (1 large cucumber) quartered and cut into 2.5 cm (1 in) pieces | 4 | cups |
| 2 | cloves garlic, optional | 2 | |
| 25 mL | pickling salt | 2 | tbsp |
| 500 mL | ice cubes | 2 | cups |
| 250 mL | cider vinegar | 1 | cup |
| 250 mL | water | 1 | cup |
| 15 mL | dill seed | 1 | tbsp |
| 2 mL | crushed red pepper | ½ | tsp |

Combine cucumber, garlic, if desired, and salt in a glass bowl. Cover with ice cubes. Let stand in a cool place at least 6 h or overnight. Drain well. Combine vinegar, water, dill seed and crushed red pepper in a saucepan. Bring to a boil. Add drained cucumbers; return to a boil; cover and cook 2 min. Remove garlic cloves. Spoon into hot sterilized jars. Wipe jar rims. Seal. Store in a cool, dark, dry place.

Makes about 1 L (4 cups).

**Each serving: 50 mL (¼ cup)**

1 **++** Extra

2 g carbohydrate

30 kilojoules
(8 Calories)

## BREAD AND BUTTER PICKLES

*Crisp, crunchy* Bread and Butter Pickles *are good in or with sandwiches. With deli cuts or cold roast beef or pork, they're superb.*

| | | |
|---|---|---|
| 1 L | cucumber slices, 3 mm (1/8 in) thick | 4 cups |
| 250 mL | thin onion slices | 1 cup |
| 1 | clove garlic | 1 |
| 25 mL | pickling salt | 2 tbsp |
| 500 mL | ice cubes | 2 cups |
| 250 mL | cider vinegar | 1 cup |
| 250 mL | water | 1 cup |
| 7 mL | mustard seed | 1½ tsp |
| 5 mL | celery seed | 1 tsp |
| 2 mL | tumeric | ½ tsp |
| | Liquid artificial sweetener equivalent to 80 mL (16 tsp) sugar | |

Combine cucumber, onion and garlic in a glass bowl. Sprinkle with pickling salt. Cover with ice cubes. Let stand in a cool place, at least 6 h or overnight. Drain well. Combine vinegar, water, mustard seed, celery seed and tumeric in a large saucepan. Bring to a boil; add drained cucumber mixture; return to a boil and cook 2 min. Discard garlic clove. Stir in sweetener. Spoon into hot sterilized jars. Wipe jar rims. Seal. Store in a cool, dark, dry place.

Makes about 1 L (4 cups).

**Each serving: 50 mL (¼ cup)**

1 **++** Extra

2 g carbohydrate

30 kilojoules
(8 Calories)

> Table salt is the major source of dietary sodium and should be used in moderation by everyone. People with high blood pressure should use very small amounts of salt. Many processed and convenience foods are high in sodium, such as seasoned salts, dried and canned soups, pickles, olives, processed meats, soy sauce, ketchup, salted crackers and snack foods.

# Index

## FURTHER INFORMATION

The Canadian Diabetes Association (CDA) offers information on diabetes for all those interested in good health and good eating. Membership is open to everyone, whether diabetic or not.

Educational programs and literature are available through the Branches of CDA for people with diabetes and their families who wish to learn about nutrition and self-care. If you are unable to locate a CDA Branch in your telephone directory, write to the National office (see below).

"Hope for tomorrow; help for today" is our current theme. It reflects CDA's ongoing commitment to fund research into the causes and cures of diabetes and its treatment. This theme also reflects our concern for those who must live with diabetes until a cure is found.

Professional membership in CDA is encouraged for physicians in the Clinical and Scientific Section and for other qualified health professionals in the Professional Health Workers Section. Continuing professional education is provided through these two sections.

For information on the following:

⊙ Information about the Canadian Diabetes Association

⊙ Membership application (please specify)
    Senior (over 65 years)
    Regular
    Professional Health Workers Section
    Clinical and Scientific Section

⊙ Brochure on research being funded by CDA

⊙ Order forms listing the information available from the Canadian Diabetes Association

write to: National Office
    Canadian Diabetes Association
    123 Edward Street, Suite 601
    Toronto, Ontario
    M5G 1E2

**Canadian Diabetes Association**